Janice Lynn Ellerby

Laura Elizabeth Pinto

Victoria Esposito Brady

InsighTs:

Succeeding in the Information Age

IRWIN
PUBLISHING

Toronto/Vancouver, Canada

Copyright © 2001 by Irwin Publishing Ltd.

National Library of Canada Cataloguing in Publication Data

Ellerby, Janice L. (Janice Lynn)
  InsighTs : succeeding in the information age

For use in grades 9/10.
Includes index.
ISBN 0-7725-2873-X
1. Information storage and retrieval systems—Business.
2. Business—Data processing. 3. Information technology.
I. Pinto, Laura Elizabeth II. Brady, Victoria Esposito
III. Title.

HF5548.2.E43 2001   650'.0285   C2001-900843-0

Cover and Text Design:
FIZZZ Design Inc.

Page Layout: FIZZZ Design Inc.

Art: Kevin Jon Hall, David Hunter, Jock MacRae, Manijeh Mortazavi, and Jeff Nichol

Project Developer: Doug Panasis

Editor: Norma Pettit

Production Editor: Jennifer Howse

Photo Research: Mark Philpott

Proofreader: Shirley Tessier

Indexer: Liba Berry

Published by
Irwin Publishing Ltd.
325 Humber College Blvd
Toronto, ON M9W 7C3

French edition
Tremplin
Réussir à l'ère de l'information
ISBN 2-89310-876-8
available from Chenelière/McGraw-Hill

Printed and bound in Canada
1 2 3 4 5 05 04 03 02 01

Author Acknowledgements

I would like to thank my husband, and best friend, Rick, for his immeasurable support and encouragement to pursue this endeavour. To my family, your indulgence once again as I go off on another of my tangents is appreciated. My thanks also go to Teresa Lipsett for being a sounding board throughout the entire process. And to my fellow authors, Laura and Vicky—you are amazing!

Janice Ellerby
Toronto, April 2001

I was incredibly fortunate to have at my disposal the talents and vast knowledge of an extraordinary family, who volunteered their time and provided invaluable input to this project – heartfelt thanks to Brone, Bob, and Rob, Ačiū tau Močiute for her support and encouragement. I would also like to thank my friends – especially Anne-Marie, Justine, Wendy, and Adam – for their patience on countless occasions when I was unavailable. Last but certainly not least, I would like to acknowledge the undying support of Finnegan, who is a constant source inspiration to me and was at my side for countless hours throughout this project.

Laura Pinto
Toronto, April 2001

Several groups and individuals provided support and inspiration that made it possible for me to contribute to this book. Many thanks to the administration of Havergal College for their support over the last year. To my friends and colleagues at St. Joseph's College School and the TCDSB; you have inspired and encouraged me throughout my teaching career. To my husband, John, your support and understanding have been incredible; to my sons, Michael and Anthony, I can join you on those family outings now! Finally, to my dear mother, Camilla, thanks for providing delicious home-cooked meals when they were most needed.

Victoria Brady
Toronto, April 2001

The authors would like to thank Doug Panasis for championing this project and seeing it through to fruition. To Norma Pettit, our incredibly talented and supportive editor, our humble thanks for guiding us through the writing process, and for keeping us on track with your valuable input. We appreciate your tremendous patience, positive attitude, and sense of humour. Finally, we would like to acknowledge Scott Hughes for ensuring the content was correct from a Mac perspective.

The authors and publisher would like to thank the following reviewers for their valuable insights and suggestions:

Marcy Bell
Algoma District School Board

Helen McGregor
Hamilton Wentworth District School Board

Phyllis Dalgleish
Lakehead District School Board

Janice Pearson
Toronto District School Board

Fran Ditschun
Peel District School Board

Frank Piddisi
Toronto Catholic District School Board

Fran Fraser
York Region Catholic District School Board

Terry Whitmell
Peel District School Board

Bonnie Lewis-Watts
Thames Valley District School Board

Table of Contents

ROAD MAP TO
InsighTs: Succeeding in the

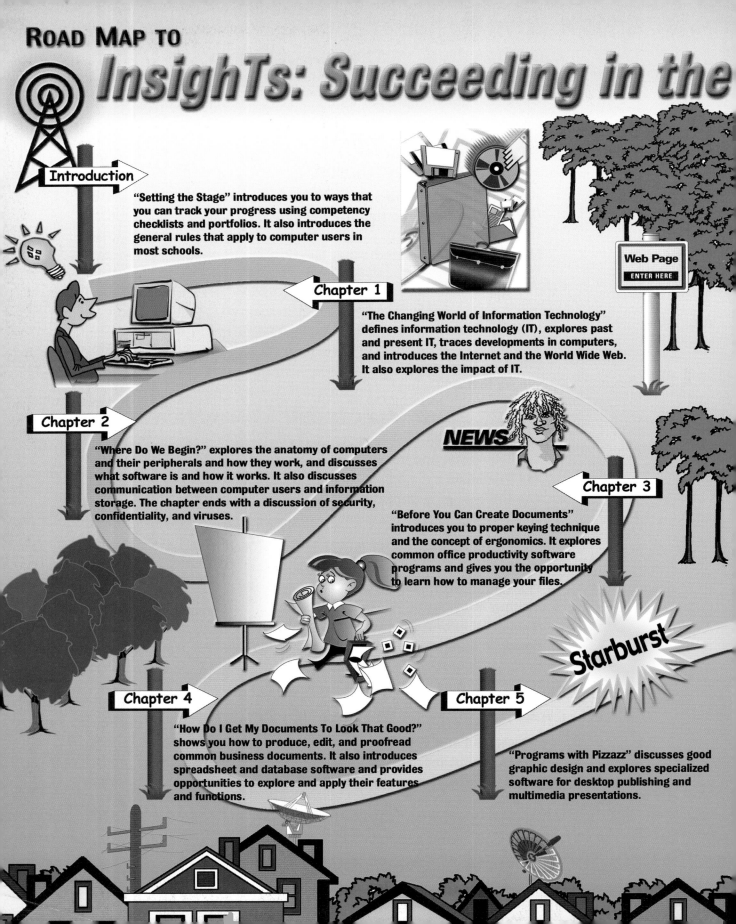

Introduction

"Setting the Stage" introduces you to ways that you can track your progress using competency checklists and portfolios. It also introduces the general rules that apply to computer users in most schools.

Web Page
ENTER HERE

Chapter 1

"The Changing World of Information Technology" defines information technology (IT), explores past and present IT, traces developments in computers, and introduces the Internet and the World Wide Web. It also explores the impact of IT.

Chapter 2

"Where Do We Begin?" explores the anatomy of computers and their peripherals and how they work, and discusses what software is and how it works. It also discusses communication between computer users and information storage. The chapter ends with a discussion of security, confidentiality, and viruses.

NEWS

Chapter 3

"Before You Can Create Documents" introduces you to proper keying technique and the concept of ergonomics. It explores common office productivity software programs and gives you the opportunity to learn how to manage your files.

Chapter 4

"How Do I Get My Documents To Look That Good?" shows you how to produce, edit, and proofread common business documents. It also introduces spreadsheet and database software and provides opportunities to explore and apply their features and functions.

Starburst

Chapter 5

"Programs with Pizzazz" discusses good graphic design and explores specialized software for desktop publishing and multimedia presentations.

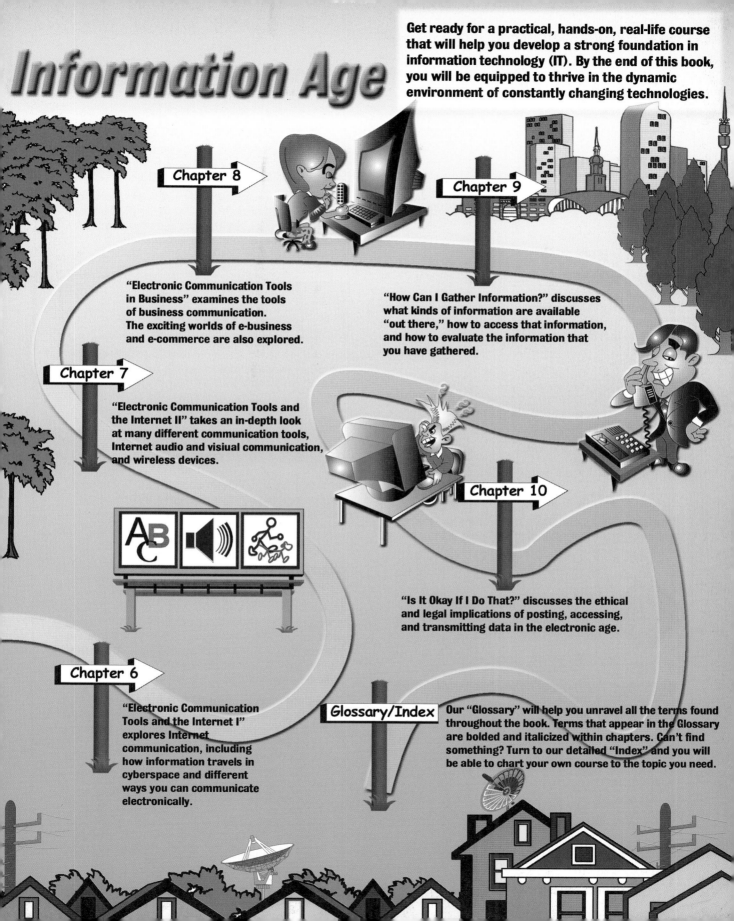

Information Age

Get ready for a practical, hands-on, real-life course that will help you develop a strong foundation in information technology (IT). By the end of this book, you will be equipped to thrive in the dynamic environment of constantly changing technologies.

Chapter 8

"Electronic Communication Tools in Business" examines the tools of business communication. The exciting worlds of e-business and e-commerce are also explored.

Chapter 9

"How Can I Gather Information?" discusses what kinds of information are available "out there," how to access that information, and how to evaluate the information that you have gathered.

Chapter 7

"Electronic Communication Tools and the Internet II" takes an in-depth look at many different communication tools, Internet audio and visiual communication, and wireless devices.

Chapter 10

"Is It Okay If I Do That?" discusses the ethical and legal implications of posting, accessing, and transmitting data in the electronic age.

Chapter 6

"Electronic Communication Tools and the Internet I" explores Internet communication, including how information travels in cyberspace and different ways you can communicate electronically.

Glossary/Index

Our "Glossary" will help you unravel all the terms found throughout the book. Terms that appear in the Glossary are bolded and italicized within chapters. Can't find something? Turn to our detailed "Index" and you will be able to chart your own course to the topic you need.

To help you on your journey through *InsighTs: Succeeding in the Information Age*, we have developed a number of special guideposts and activity launchers.

CHAPTER OPENER

A full page itemizing the topics to be explored, and tasks you will have the opportunity to accomplish during the chapter.

Activity

Opportunities to apply what you have just learned, designed to enhance your knowledge and understanding of chapter contents.

Links to related sites on the World Wide Web, many with activities to do once you get there.

Learning Link

Interesting facts and pieces of information that will enhance your understanding of topics in the chapter.

A more in-depth technical examination of some of the technology, issues, or terminology discussed within the chapter.

News stories and other discussion topics that let you examine a situation in more detail as it relates to the topics in the chapter. A real opportunity to develop your critical thinking on a topic!

Information Technology is not just about working at a computer terminal all day. Our Career Profiles take a look at a variety of people in a myriad of jobs who all use IT to make them more productive.

WHAT DO YOU THINK?

This feature launches you into debates, discussions, and other examinations of issues raised within the chapter. Hold on to your hats for some lively debates!

Knowledge Check

Throughout each chapter you will find Knowledge Checks to help you review your knowledge and understanding of chapter contents.

CHAPTER SUMMARY

Each chapter ends with summary questions designed to assess your understanding of the chapter contents. You will be challenged to *think about* and *analyze* situations and to *apply* your knowledge to new situations. Finally, you will be given opportunities to *communicate* your findings in many ways.

A constant feature of *InsighTs* is the assessment of your skills and competencies developed throughout the book. Each chapter ends with this self-assessment.

INTRODUCTION: SETTING THE STAGE

Topics

➤ Competencies
➤ Portfolios
➤ Use of Computers in School

As you begin your study of information technology using *InsighTs: Succeeding in the Information Age*, you may find it helpful to consider what tools you can use to track your learning. Your teacher will track your progress using a variety of assessment tools. Two tools that can provide both you and your teacher with evidence that you are learning what you need to succeed in the Information Age are **competency checklists** and **portfolios**. In addition to this text, and the activities assigned by your teacher, your school computer will be an essential tool in your learning. This introduction concludes with a discussion about the rules that govern the use of computers and computer networks in most schools. Read on to learn how these tools and the activities in this text will give you the best chance of succeeding in this course.

Competencies

What Are Competencies?

Competencies are skills, knowledge, and behaviours that are used to determine a person's abilities, strengths, and weaknesses. Examples of competencies include writing skills, the ability to present in front of a class, knowledge of a certain group of definitions, the ability to change margins in a word processing document, and so on. The questions in the "Chapter Summary" sections at the end of each chapter in *InsighTs* and the "Competency Checklists" your teacher may give you are designed to help you determine the competencies you have achieved in the chapter.

If you conscientiously complete all of the activities in each chapter, you will be well prepared to answer the questions in the "Chapter Summary" sections and ready to check off the items in the "Competency Checklists" (see Fig. Intro.1 on page 2). As you complete the various assignments, check off the competencies you have mastered, noting the assignment in which the competency is demonstrated and the date you mastered the competency.

Fig. Intro.1 Sample Word Processing Competencies Checklist

Competencies	Assignment in Which the Competency Is Demonstrated	Date Mastered
Bullets		
Changing Case (upper to lower/lower to upper)		
Closing a File		
Cut		
Copy		
Data Entry		
Exiting from a File		
Font Type		
Font Size		
Footers—Your Name and the Date		
Grammar Check		
Graphics/Clip Art/Objects		

Competencies can be organized into categories such as "Understanding Information" and "Communicating." You will notice that the "Chapter Summary" sections in *InsighTs* are organized according to the competency categories shown in Fig. Intro.2.

Fig. Intro.2 Competency Categories

Understanding Information	Analyzing	Applying	Communicating
This category describes your knowledge and understanding of specific information. It includes learning facts and definitions of new words, understanding and explaining concepts, and understanding relationships among concepts.	This category describes your critical and creative thinking skills. These skills include your ability to ask questions and to look at different options, judge or evaluate these options, and make decisions. It also involves problem solving, interpreting and assessing information, and drawing conclusions.	This category describes your ability to make connections among experiences, concepts, and ideas, to transfer skills you already have to new or different situations, and to use the appropriate equipment and technology.	This category describes your ability to write, speak, or present ideas and information, your use of language and symbols, and your ability to communicate in different formats (such as letters, memos, and reports).

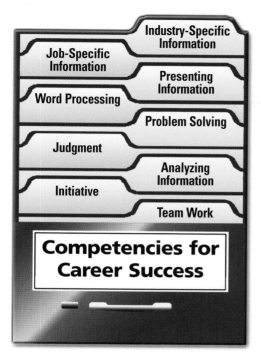

Fig. Intro.3

How Are Competencies Used?

The questions in the "Chapter Summary" sections will enable you to determine your information technology knowledge and skills. By tracking your own competencies, you will see where your strengths lie, how you have improved, and where you still need to do some work. You will be able to use your personal competencies lists to be sure you are achieving the knowledge and skills required to succeed in this course. Your lists will also be useful to you when you are preparing to apply for a job in the future.

Your teacher will give you opportunities to demonstrate your mastery of knowledge and skills in each of the competency categories.

Today, many companies are using competencies to help them decide whom to hire, which employees to promote, and which employees should receive raises. Companies that use competencies look at every job and prepare a list of skills and knowledge that an employee needs to do a particular job well. For example, a graphic artist would have to have knowledge of graphics software, the ability to use the software efficiently, the ability to design attractive art, and the ability to communicate with customers.

To find out how companies use competencies to hire and manage their employees, visit the Web sites for Accenture, Bank of Montreal, and The Conference Board of Canada on the *InsighTs* Student Page on <www.irwinpublishing.com/students>.

All competencies should be backed up with proof that you have demonstrated those skills and knowledge. You can attach a completed "Competencies Checklist" provided by your teacher to each of your completed assignments to show which competencies you displayed in that assignment.

Portfolios

Fig. Intro.4
Portfolios can be paper-based or electronic. They can take many forms, including disks, CD-ROMs, binders, folders, cases, and displays.

What Is a Portfolio?

An effective way of keeping track of your growing competencies is to keep all of your assignments and checklists together in a portfolio. Of course, for you to be able to access the work in your portfolio easily, you will have to keep it organized!

In a world that relies so heavily on changing information technology, having skills and keeping up with new knowledge is very important. People often need to showcase their competencies to schools or potential employers. Collections of work in a portfolio can show these skills and accomplishments. A *portfolio* is, in effect, an organizer in which people can put their materials and have access to them when they want them. Artists, for example, have collected samples of their work in portfolios for years as a means of illustrating the range and depth of their best and their most current work.

How Are Portfolios Used?

Portfolios have many uses. Some of the main applications include

- **to keep a personal record of accomplishments, achievements, skills, hopes, and thoughts**. Students who maintain portfolios can look at them to assess their skills based on the work they did and to see how their skills have changed over the year, as well as for their personal satisfaction.

- **to evaluate a student's work at the end of a course.** Many teachers and schools review student portfolios at the end of a course. Because portfolios contain work that was completed at the beginning of the course, during the course, and at the end of the course, they show a student's progress and improvement over the course of a school year.

- **to gain admission to a college or university**. Certain colleges and universities require that portfolios be submitted in order to gain acceptance into a program. Portfolios are useful to the college or university because they show what students are capable of producing, and what their work standards are.

- **to present to an employer in a job interview**. More and more often, employers are requesting that individuals applying for jobs submit portfolios along with their résumés, or bring a portfolio to a job interview. The material in the portfolio shows the employer what the applicant's work might look like. The employer can then see if the type of work the applicant does fits in with business requirements and standards.

Building Your Own Portfolio

This course requires you to create a portfolio to demonstrate the progress of your learning. Building such a portfolio is an ongoing process that will be guided by your teacher throughout this course. You will include in your portfolio samples of work you have completed throughout your course of study. The samples you collect should allow you to reflect on your work, track your personal growth, and identify the competencies you have developed through each activity you have completed. You may decide to revisit some of your work and make additional revisions.

When you decide what to put into your portfolio, you should not limit yourself only to materials that can be used for self-assessment or assessment by your teacher. What makes a student portfolio different from a notebook is that a portfolio also contains written thoughts or personal reflections by the author about his or her work. Therefore, when you are considering what to put into your portfolio, also include your thoughts and conclusions about what you are learning, and ideas and hopes you have for the future that may relate to information technology.

Fig. Intro.5
Portfolios may also include samples of work completed through group projects. Super Stock/1244/3423

Use of Computers in Schools

What Rules Govern Your Use of Computers and the Internet in School?

When you use the computer network at school, you are required to abide by the rules and code of conduct established by your school for use of the computer and the network. Many schools have established a Computer Code of Conduct or an Internet Acceptable Use Policy to govern use of computers. These agreements, signed by the user (and the user's parents if the user is under the legal age of majority), usually include guidelines relating to:

- **maintaining privacy of individuals**—rules governing gaining access to other students' accounts, files, or folders

- **using computer resources responsibly**—not related to criminal activity, commercial use, political lobbying, or playing games

- **refraining from use of obscene language, and sending, displaying, or locating offensive material**

- **refraining from excessive posting of information (*spamming*)**

Look at the Web sites for Toronto Catholic District School Board, Ottawa Carlton District School Board, and York Region District School Board on the *InsighTs* Student Page on <www.irwinpublishing.com/students> for examples of school board policies on the use of computers in their schools.

You will be given a number of opportunities to review and demonstrate your understanding of your school's particular set of rules and policies.

Fig. Intro.6

CHAPTER ONE

THE CHANGING WORLD OF MODERN INFORMATION TECHNOLOGY

Topics

- The World of Modern Information Technology
- The Impact of Modern Information Technology
- The Evolution of Computers
- The Internet
- The World Wide Web
- Infrastructure for Modern Information Technology
- What Next?

This chapter defines modern technology and discusses some of the impact that information technology is having on the lives of Canadians. You will explore the evolution of computers and the development of the Internet and the World Wide Web. You will also learn how some experts see information technology in the future and you will use that (and other) information to look into your crystal ball and make your own predictions for the future.

This chapter explores these questions:

- What is modern information technology?
- How does information technology affect the lives of Canadians?
- How did computers evolve?
- How did the Internet develop?
- What is the World Wide Web and how did it evolve?
- How are the Internet and the World Wide Web different?
- What infrastructure supports modern information technology?
- How is information technology changing?

In this chapter you have the opportunity to

- examine how information technology affects your everyday life
- explore the positive and negative effects of information technology on the lives of Canadians
- find out what information technology courses are available in your school
- explore the generations and evolution of computers
- think about the infrastructures that support information technology
- investigate the development of the Internet
- debate the topic of artificial intelligence
- create an information technology time capsule
- look at careers in information technology

The World of Modern Information Technology

What Is Modern Information Technology?

Data is raw, unprocessed information such as numbers, characters, or symbols. **Information** is data that has been processed so that it can be understood and used in decision making. For example, you may enter a series of numbers—your data—into a computer. The computer will then process these numbers according to instructions you give the computer program. You may, for example, instruct the computer to organize the numbers into a table or into a graph. Similarly, you may enter a series of words or sentences and then instruct the computer program to create a paragraph or bulletted list.

Information technology (IT) is a broad term that covers many different components. It is the use of technologies (such as the printing process, the publishing industry, telephones, radio, television, computers, electronics, and telecommunications) to process and distribute information—to *manage information*—among people and machines. Today, two main features characterize information technology:

- *electronic tools* that help people manage information (such as computers, communications networks, the Internet, and so on)
- the relationship between these tools and people's lives

Figure 1.1 illustrates the spectrum of modern information technology from people-oriented to machine-oriented. A *spectrum* is a *range* with two extremes at either end. In between, different options or combinations of those extremes are illustrated. Information technology is a spectrum, with various combinations of the relationships between people and machines across the spectrum.

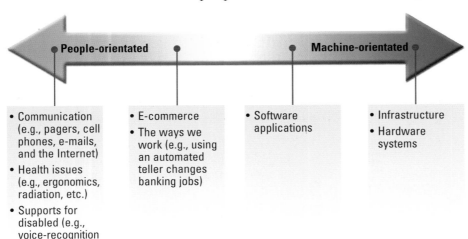

People-orientated   Machine-orientated

- Communication (e.g., pagers, cell phones, e-mails, and the Internet)
- Health issues (e.g., ergonomics, radiation, etc.)
- Supports for disabled (e.g., voice-recognition software)

- E-commerce
- The ways we work (e.g., using an automated teller changes banking jobs)

- Software applications

- Infrastructure
- Hardware systems

Fig. 1.1
Figure 1.1 represents the spectrum of modern information technology. The Institute of Information Sciences and Technology, a research and education organization in New Zealand, first developed the concept of information technology as a spectrum—"Information technology... is not a subject, but a spectrum."

People-oriented issues are those issues that concern people's interaction with information technology. For instance, the effect of computers on people's lives and health falls within this part of the spectrum. Advances in communication technology such as *pagers, cell phones*, and *e-mail* (electronic mail) have affected relationships among people by allowing them to communicate in new and different ways. Whether it is through *voice mail*, pagers, or e-mail, you may rely on information technology to keep in touch with your friends.

Machine-oriented issues are those that describe the way in which information technology equipment (such as computers, *modems*, communication devices, the Internet, etc.) actually work.

Notice that other topics appear between the people-oriented and machine-oriented ends of the spectrum. These topics deal with various relationships among modern information technology machines and people, and how those machines are applied and used.

The Impact of Modern Information Technology

How Does Information Technology Affect the Lives of Canadians?

The last 100 years—and in particular, the last 30 years—have seen amazing advances in information technology. Just think about new technologies you have seen invented in your own lifetime. These new developments have profoundly changed and continue to change the way we live our everyday lives.

Fig. 1.2

Despite the suggestion in the cartoon that children know much more about how to operate computers than their parents or grandparents, the number of older adults who are using computers, the Internet, and the World Wide Web is growing rapidly. Many seniors today use the Internet to invest, bank, plan holidays, shop, and play games. Seniors now use e-mail more frequently than young people, e-mailing friends and grandchildren.

Cartoon from *Boom, Bust and Echo 2000* by David K. Foot. Reprinted with the permission of Stoddart Publishing

Expert tutoring

Fig. 1.3
Rob Lewine/Firstlight.ca

 **Activity**

High Tech History Lesson

Part A

Speak to a parent, grandparent, or older neighbour. Find out what technology was like when he or she was your age. Ask the following questions:

1. When you were my age, what did you think the world would be like when you grew up?

2. What changes have you seen in technology?

3. What was considered "high tech" when you were my age?

4. What surprises you most about technology today?

Part B

Look at Fig. 1.3. With a partner, list as many information technologies as you can in the photograph. Compare your list with those of others in the class.

Part C

With a partner, make a list of as many information technologies as you can think of. At the end of this chapter, and again at the end of chapter 8, revisit this activity and add any technologies you missed.

Anne-Marie Romanko

Mechanical Draftsperson

The last time you used a plastic fork, did you think about how it was made? Computer technology plays a huge role in creating many everyday objects. Anne-Marie Romanko is a mechanical draftsperson, and works behind the scenes to create plastic injection moulds. Plastic injection moulds are metal forms into which liquid plastic is injected to create an object, such as a plastic fork, a car part, or parts of your computer case.

When a company wants to create a plastic part or object, it begins with a design of what the finished product will be, including the size and dimensions. That data is then sent to someone like Anne-Marie, who uses a special type of *mechanical software* such as CADKEY to design a three-dimensional model on the computer of a mould of the object. The shaping of a mould can be difficult—remember that the mould must be the inverse (or opposite) shape of the part! The mechanical draftsperson also has to consider how the plastic object will be removed from the mould without damaging the object. This factor, too, is worked into the design. Next, the design for the mould is surfaced. In this step, the computer model shows exactly how the metal surface will be cut by a machine to make the mould. Once the mould design is finished, the mould is cut from metal by a machine. Plastic is then injected into the mould to test whether the mould design works properly. If it works, the company can start manufacturing the plastic object.

In order to be a mechanical draftsperson, Anne-Marie completed an apprenticeship course, including hours of on-the-job practise. She began her career by taking a 42-week course called "Women in Metal Machining." Next, she went to college to complete a certificate in CAD/CAM (short for Computer-Aided Design/Computer-Aided Manufacturing—specialized engineering software used to design and manufacture products). Finally, she took a series of additional courses at her local college that were required for her apprenticeship while she was working for a mould company.

"The nice thing about my job is that I'm always challenged, and always learning," says Anne-Marie. "No two jobs are the same, so it lets me be creative in solving problems unique to making each object."

1. What education did Anne-Marie complete to get to her present job?

2. What did Anne-Marie do in order to complete her apprenticeship as a mechanical draftsperson?

3. What types of software does Anne-Marie use to do her job?

4. What competencies do you think are most important for a mechanical draftsperson? Why? Try to find one in each competency category (see page 2).

5. Suggest three objects that a mechanical engineer would design.

0-7725-2873-X

9 780772 528735

Fig. 1.4
Figure 1.4 shows the bar code on the back of this book.

Many of us rely on a number of technologies on a daily basis. Consider:

- Many of us wake up to radios that are programmed by a computer chip.
- Some of us rely on e-mail, pagers, cell phones, or voice messaging to keep in contact with others.
- Some of us use the Internet for research or entertainment.
- Many of us use automated bank machines, debit cards, credit cards, and telephone or PC banking to manage our finances.
- Cashiers scan bar codes. Universal Product Codes (UPCs) are the small markings made up of vertical lines, usually found on packages or price tags. They can be scanned to identify the price and item being sold.
- Magazines and books (including *InsighTs*) are designed and many of the illustrations are generated using computers.

Before modern information technology became widely available, students did their schoolwork very differently, as is shown in this case study.

Fig. 1.5
Before computers, libraries had chests of tiny drawers that held alphabetized cards to help visitors in the library locate a book. Each item in the library had several cards in the catalogue to represent it—one catalogued by title, one by author, and at least one by subject. These cardex files are still in use in many libraries.

Case Study

Biblio-Tech

It is 1975 and Samil is working on a report for his grade 12 History class. He goes to the local library, and looks through drawers and drawers of small file cards to find the names and locations of the right books. He writes notes from some of the books at the library, and signs several books out to take home. At home, Samil handwrites a rough draft of his report. He then types the report on an electric typewriter. Each time Samil makes a typing error, he has to stop, erase the error with correction fluid, wait for it to dry, and type over it. If he makes more than three mistakes, he retypes the entire page. He finishes the report, and hands it in.

1. How is finding information in your local or school library today different from the way Samil found information? How is it similar?

2. How has the use of a computer made preparing a report different from the process Samil followed?

3. Do you think information technology and computers have made the job of being a student easier or harder? Why?

InsighTs: Succeeding in the Information Age

Activity

Information Technology and Your Day

Make a list of the ways in which information technology affects your average day. Begin by thinking through everything you do from the time you wake up until the time you go to sleep. List each task you complete using information technology. At the end of your list, describe two ways in which your life would be different without information technology. Compare your lists and comments with the lists of others in the class.

Fig. 1.6
The disruption of our information technology can have serious effects. In August 2000, a fire in the Ostankino television tower in Moscow knocked out 30 television stations and a number of radio stations that relied on the tower to broadcast programs, and interrupted many other communications in the Russian capital.

CP Picture Archive
(Alexander Zemlianichenko II)

Information technology is also having a profound impact on the way business is conducted. Borders and time zones no longer bind companies. We work in a global community with trade taking place 24 hours a day, 7 days a week. The pace is often frenzied. To survive in this global economy, companies need to be able to adapt quickly to new and different technologies. They require employees who are literate in information technology to help them meet these challenges. Throughout this book, you will read career profiles of people who use information technology every day. You will see that many of these individuals have already worked through numerous changes in the way they perform their jobs. They will undoubtedly have to continue to adapt to new information technologies.

SITE SEEING

Started in 1997, Zi Corporation is a Canadian company based in Calgary, Alberta. It is a leading provider of software and educational products and services around the world. Zi has offices in Calgary, Beijing, Hong Kong, San Francisco, Shenzhen, and Stockholm. To learn more about this company and what it does, visit the *InsighTs* Student Page on <www.irwinpublishing.com/students>.

The development of more powerful computer networks, the Internet, the World Wide Web, e-mail, and modems (devices that make it possible for computers to communicate over telephone lines) also changed the way individuals work. Networks allow people to share documents and sometimes even work on the same document at the same time. E-mail and fax machines allow people to transact business within companies and with companies around the world much more rapidly than before. Increasing numbers of workers are working on computers in their homes rather than going to offices.

Designers send art and designs over the Internet to their clients for vetting, and photo services send photographs over the Internet rather than through the mail. Banks can update client accounts in seconds.

Fig. 1.7
Today, millions of Canadians use automated teller machines (ATMs; also called automated banking machines, or ABMs) to do their banking.

Juan Silva Productions/The Image Bank

Case Study

You Can Bank On It

It is 1970 and Broneslava has gone to her local bank branch to deposit her pay cheque. She presents the teller with her bankbook and the cheque. If Broneslava has not filled out a deposit slip by hand, the teller fills it out. Using an adding machine, the teller calculates the new balance in the account. The teller then writes the new balance into Broneslava's bankbook by hand and initials the change. After Broneslava leaves, the teller manually calculates the new balance in her file. At the end of the month, a bank clerk at the branch updates the bank's records by hand using an adding machine and paper journal.

1. How has technology changed the job of a bank teller today from the one in the case study?

2. Identify three advantages to having bank accounts organized on computers.

Activity

Information Technology: Pros and Cons

The changes in information technology have potential to help and, if applied poorly, the potential to harm society.

1. In small groups, brainstorm ways that information technology has supported our society. For example, experts suggest that because of the convenience and low costs of the service, more people keep in touch with friends and relatives via e-mail than they did by telephone.

2. Brainstorm ways you think information technology has been poorly used by society. For example, many people argue that the increased computerization of telephone marketing has made us victims of technological harassment in our own homes.

3. In small groups, consider some of the ethical challenges the development of information technology presents and continues to present (such as loss of privacy, changes in the types of jobs available for people, etc.).

Create a table with the headings Pros, Cons, and Ethical Challenges, and categories such as Privacy, Education, Medicine, Family Life and Leisure Time. Have one member of your group record your group's ideas.

4. When you have finished brainstorming, compare your group's table with those of others in the class. Enter any points you missed on your table.

You may want to keep a copy of your table in your portfolio for future reference, especially for chapter 10, when you learn more about some of the ethical and legal issues surrounding information technology today.

What Courses Are Available to You?

Taking courses is the best way to develop competencies that will prepare you for technology-related careers in all industries. The first step in developing your skills and knowledge is to explore your options for enhancing your learning. Courses, diplomas, and certificates are available at colleges and universities in your community, through the Internet, and in your own school.

 **Activity**

Investigating Technology Programs in Your School

Interview a teacher in your school to determine what other computer or information technology courses are available. Prepare a report that describes:

- the names of the courses offered
- the grade level of the courses offered
- a brief summary of the course content
- prerequisite courses you must take in order to enroll in those courses

Knowledge Check

1. Describe how information technology affects Canadians.
2. Describe one advantage of information technology in your life.
3. Describe one disadvantage of information technology in your life.

Case Study

The Challenges of Information Technology

The article describes what happened when the telephone system in downtown Toronto, Ontario, malfunctioned.

Toronto Phone Service Disrupted By Bell Canada Fire

TORONTO, ONTARIO, CANADA, 1999 JUL 16 (NB)

by Grant Buckler, Newsbytes

Telephone service and Internet access in downtown Toronto have been disrupted by a small fire at a Bell Canada central office in downtown Toronto which led to power being shut off for several hours. A Bell spokesman told Newsbytes that the company hoped to restore power using a backup diesel generator by about 1:00 today.

Bell Canada spokesman Don Doucette said a short circuit caused a small fire in a power box at the central office at 220 Simcoe St. at about 7:00 a.m., setting off fire alarms and the sprinkler system in the building. The fire department responded and shut off

power to the building. Although the central office has battery backup systems, these can power the switching systems only for three to four hours, and ran out of power at about 10 a.m.

"Normal power cannot be restored until the fire department is satisfied any danger is past," Doucette told Newsbytes, "but a diesel generator should allow Bell to begin restoring service shortly."

Telephone service was lost in much of downtown Toronto, as was Internet access for many customers. There have also been problems with cellular service, which Doucette said was caused by people turning

to their cellphones as a substitute for landline phones and overloading the system.

The Toronto Stock Exchange said some securities firms are being prevented from placing and confirming orders, obtaining trading data and communicating with the exchange, and its derivatives floor near the central office has been closed due to problems connected with the fire.

Reported by Newsbytes.com <http://www.newsbytes.com>.

Copyright 1999 Newsbytes News Network

1. What types of technology did the Toronto fire affect?

2. The Toronto Stock Exchange reported that some security firms were unable to make trades because of the technology problems from the fire. Describe what other types of businesses might have been affected by the fire.

3. For what purposes do people and businesses depend on technology?

4. Do you think we are too dependent on technology? Why or why not?

5. What can people do to become less dependent on technology?

The Evolution of Computers

How Did Computers Evolve?

The very large first- and second-generation computers were known as **mainframe** computers (**mainframes**). They were expensive and were used by companies to handle high-volume processing, (e.g., to process financial transactions and maintain a company's accounts). A mainframe is a large and expensive computer that is capable of supporting hundreds, or even thousands, of users at one time. Some large institutions still use mainframe computers. For example, in order for a bank to allow thousands of customers to make financial transactions at once, a mainframe is necessary.

A *computer* can be defined broadly as a mechanism for doing calculations—for computing. Today's computers bear almost no resemblance to the early versions of computers. The earliest computers were not electric. They were designed to calculate numbers and were only able to perform very simple tasks. Modern computers do much more. They organize information, allow us to communicate with others, and perform tasks for us.

The evolution of computers may be divided into six stages or generations. With each generation, computers became smaller, faster, and more powerful. Figure 1.9 on page 18 provides an overview of the main developments in each generation.

 **Activity**

Fig. 1.8
Picture shows IBM mainframe from 1954.
Courtesy of IBM Archives

Researching More About the History of Computers

Select a key word from Fig. 1.9. Visit the sites for The Computer Museum History Centre, The Machine That Changed the World, The History of Computing, and The Virtual Computer History Museum on the *InsighTs* Student Page on <www.irwinpublishing.com/students> to find more information or pictures for each of your key words. Before you begin your search, you may want to read the section on "key word" searches in chapter 9 on pages 254-256. Share your information with your class.

Fig. 1.9 A Brief History of Computing — MAIN DEVELOPMENTS

Mechanical Era (1820s–1942)	First Generation (1943–1953)	Second Generation (1954–1962)	Third Generation (1963–1972)	Fourth Generation (1972–1984)	Fifth Generation (1984–1990)	Sixth Generation (1990–Present)
The **mechanical era** was characterized by the use of machines to solve mathematical problems.	**First-generation computers** used electronic switches in the form of vacuum tubes, which opened and closed approximately 1000 times faster than mechanical switches. Information was input into computers using punch cards. Information was stored on magnetic tape.	The **second generation of computing** saw three new features.	The **third generation of computers** featured large gains in speed and power.	The main innovation of the **fourth generation of computing** was the introduction and development of the microprocessor, a single chip that could process data, store information in memory, accept input data, and produce output.	The **fifth generation of computers** is defined by parallel processing. Parallel processing is a means by which more than one processor can be used to perform different parts of the same task at one time. Working on networked computers increases the speed at which computer users can complete a task.	Two characteristics define **sixth-generation computing:**
Machines created during this era used mechanical switches (small levers similar to a light switch) to add, subtract, multiply, and divide.	Because of the number of vacuum tubes required, the smallest computers were the size of an entire room. As well, they were prone to overheating because of the large amounts of energy necessary to run the vacuum tubes.	Transistors replaced vacuum tubes. Transistors were much smaller and worked much faster than vacuum tubes, resulting in smaller and faster computers.	Integrated circuits that contained thousands of transistors and connecting wires on one computer chip, slightly larger than a quarter, were created. With the integrated circuit, a single computer chip was able to perform many tasks.	This development led to smaller computers available at lower prices, resulting in the birth of the personal computer. By the end of the fourth generation, personal computers were increasingly available and people began to see value in owning them.	The growing range of software made computers more and more useful to people. As computers continued to become less expensive, more people were able to afford their own personal computers.	Improved processor designs increased the speed of the central processing unit (CPU).
These machines had no memory.	Computers in this generation performed only mathematical calculations, solving problems that modern-day calculators perform.	The first high-level programming languages were created. These languages, which generally use familiar English words, made it easier for programmers to create complex programs.	Computer chips, which allowed computers to store more information than previous computers, and to process information more quickly, were developed.	The creation of additional programming languages led to the availability of easier-to-use software, such as word processing, spreadsheets, and games.	This generation saw the Internet continue to expand and improve, making it possible to network computers more efficiently over longer distances.	Improvements to networking included the growth of wide area networks (WANs).
	These machines had very little memory; they were able to save the equivalent of only about 20 words.	Magnetic rings called cores were introduced to store information inside the computer. The rings had to be magnetized by sending electrical current through them. The internal memory of a computer was formed by thousands of these cores.	Operating systems software was developed that controlled the overall activity of the computer by controlling hardware, running software, and managing information.	These computers were still very slow and far less powerful than today's computers. Information was stored mainly on cassette tapes or large floppy disks.		These improvements may lead to the continuing development of artificial intelligence in future generations.
						At the turn of the twenty-first century, the number of transistors and speed of microprocessors doubled approximately every 18 months. Components continued to shrink in size and became faster, cheaper, and more versatile.

Fig. 1.10 Pre-Mechanical Era
The abacus, developed approximately 5000 years ago, is considered by many to be the first computer. An abacus is a rack of sliding beads or pebbles that allows users to compute numbers—adding, subtracting, multiplying, and dividing—by sliding the beads along poles on a frame, using no electricity at all. In the top section of the abacus, each bead or pebble represents 5x some power of 10. In the bottom section, each bead or pebble represents 1x some power of 10.

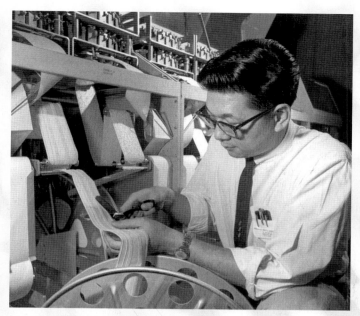

Fig. 1.11 Third/Fourth Generation
Until the late 1970s, information was input into a computer with perforated tape or cardboard punch cards. Each tape or card had holes in a specific pattern representing code that a computer could read. Here perforated tape that registered the previous day's long-distance calls is cut, ready to be forwarded for processing, 1965.

© Bell Canada

Fig. 1.12 Fifth Generation
Miniature circuits and memory chips made many products smaller, cheaper, and better. Note the size of this chip compared to the needle. Each memory chip could store enough information to fill a 75-volume encyclopedia in about a second!

Joel Gordon/PICTOR

ZAK MEADOW

You kids think you have it rough. Well, let me tell you! In my day...

Fig. 1.13 Sixth Generation
© Marc Ngui

The Changing World of Modern Information Technology

Kevin Atkinson Robotics Programmer

"When I began my career," says Kevin Atkinson, "I didn't start off thinking that I would want to program robots. It just happened!"

Kevin Atkinson graduated with a university degree in mathematics. He started programming computers four years ago. At his first job, he mainly created business application software for Windows *operating systems* (software that controls the operations of a computer and accompanying devices).

Next, Kevin took a job at a company that worked with industrial machines used mainly in factories. Just after starting the job, he was asked to create software for a robotic arm. "It was a 'sink or swim' situation," Kevin says. "I was given a manual on programming robotic arms, and had to teach myself."

His first assignment required him to create a computer program that would make a robotic arm pick up mechanical parts from a tray one by one, insert the parts into another machine that would test them, then place them in separate trays for defective parts and good parts.

A robotics programmer's job can be very stressful. "The first robotic arm I worked on was worth about $25 000," Kevin explains. "If the program I created did not work properly, the arm could bump into a wall, and the robot would be destroyed. It can get very costly if you're not careful! When I was creating Windows programs, the worst thing that could happen was the program would crash and inconvenience the user. When programming robots, thousands of dollars can be lost if the robot is broken. If the robot malfunctions on the job, it can cost a large company millions of dollars in lost time and defective products."

Today, Kevin works as a consultant in Windsor, Ontario. His company creates software that allows robots to connect to other devices, including other robots and computers. The software makes it much easier and faster to change a robot's function. It also allows machines to communicate with one another through a network.

Kevin really enjoys his job. "It's a real kick to see that you made a program that actually makes a robot move, and do something useful."

1. How did Kevin get into the robotics industry?

2. What competencies do you believe would be most important for Kevin to have in order to do his job? Why?

3. Do you think you would enjoy a career in robotics? Why or why not?

To learn more about the application of robots in industry, visit the *InsighTs* Student Page on <www.irwinpublishing.com/students>.

With each generation of computing, computers performed increasingly complex tasks, carried out tasks faster, in less space and with less energy. The development of more efficient networking (systems by which computers are connected to one another) made it easier to connect computers locally (in the same building) and globally (with other computers around the world). These trends are likely to continue throughout coming generations. As computers become even smaller, faster, and easier to use, we will likely be able to (and want to) have them with us at all times. We may, for example, use them as eyeglasses or as a watch. They will also be able to do more for us and perform more useful tasks. Anything is possible—what do you think?

Learning Link

By the end of the 1990s, many desktop or home computers had more processing power than the computer used to put the first person on the moon in 1969.

The Pentium III processor, released on February 26, 1999, contains 9.5 million transistors on a chip the size of a small cookie!

The Pentium 4 processor, released in November 2000, contains 42 million transistors and runs at speeds of 1.4 GHz (gigahertz) and 1.5 GHz.

Activity

Use Your Crystal Ball

In small groups, brainstorm what you think will characterize the next generation of computers. Have one group member record your guesses. Keep your predictions in your portfolio, so that you can refer to them at the end of this course and again when you complete your high school courses. Keep your predictions in mind and make a note in your portfolio if any of them come true.

Knowledge Check

1. What was the first non-electronic computer? Describe its function.
2. What were the major innovations of first-generation computers over the mechanical era?
3. What were the major innovations of second-generation computers?
4. What is a mainframe?
5. What were the major innovations of third-generation computers?
6. What were the major innovations of fourth-generation computers?
7. What were the major innovations of fifth-generation computers?
8. What is a microprocessor?
9. How did microprocessors change computers?
10. What were the major innovations of sixth-generation computers?
11. What trends can you identify over the first six generations of computing?
12. What competencies would a "computer expert" need at each generation?

The Internet

How Did the Internet Develop?

ARPANet

The *Internet* as we know it today is actually a very large *wide area network (WAN)* connecting computers and networks around the world. It makes it possible for millions of computer users to connect to one another via telephone lines, cable lines, and satellites.

The Internet was "born" in the late 1960s when the Advanced Research Projects Agency (ARPA) of the US Department of Defense linked together mainframe computers to form a communications network. The Agency's main objectives were to create a communication system that could survive a nuclear attack or natural disaster and to provide communication links to its users in remote locations. This early version of the Internet was known as *ARPANet*.

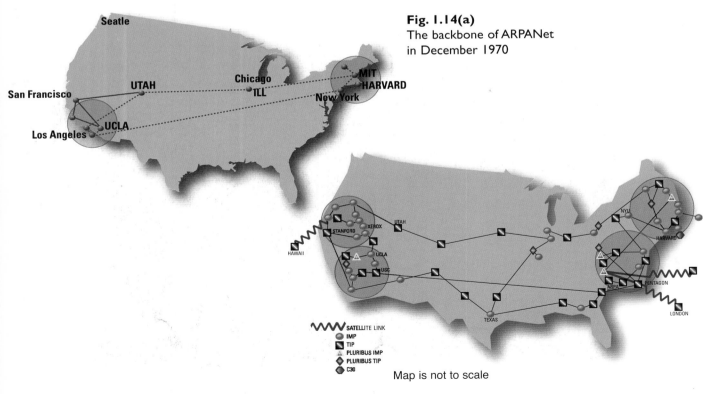

Fig. 1.14(a)
The backbone of ARPANet in December 1970

Map is not to scale

Fig. 1.14(b)
Backbone of ARPANet by the early 1980s

Fig. 1.14(a) shows the backbone of the early ARPANet. *Backbone* is a term used to describe a structure that handles the major traffic in a networked system—much like a major highway and traffic intersections handle traffic in or near your community. A *network backbone* is a "cyberspace highway" made up of high-speed cables and switching stations (intersections for network traffic).

ARPANet, MILNet, and NSFNet

Users of the ARPANet used the network to share scientific and engineering information but quickly discovered other uses for the network. The most popular use was e-mail. These developments encouraged the expansion of the network into Europe in the 1970s and its continued growth in the 1980s.

In 1983, the ARPANet split into two parts—ARPANet and MILNet. Various defence agencies and the military used *MILNet*. ARPANet continued to serve as a research and development network. ARPANet quickly transformed into an international communication tool for the academic community.

Fig. 1.15
By 1979, this scientist was using computers and the ARPANet to track the radiation from the nuclear power plant at Three Mile Island in the United States.
© Roger Ressmeyer/CORBIS, April 3, 1979

The Changing World of Modern Information Technology

By the mid-1980s, the speed of the ARPANet backbone was no longer sufficient for the high demands of the academic and research communities. At this time, the National Science Foundation (NSF) created a new high-speed network, *NSFNet*, designed with two main objectives:

For more about supercomputing, go to the National Center for Supercomputing Applications, a unit of the University of Illinois at Urbana-Champagne, on the *InsighTs* Student Page on <www.irwinpublishing.com/students>.

- to interconnect supercomputing centres so they could access one another's resources (*Supercomputers* are mainframe computers that are capable of very fast processing. They are used for tasks such as worldwide weather forecasting, oil exploration, and weapons research.)
- to give academic and research centres access to one another for purposes of exchanging information

ARPANet and NSFNet were linked to each other, but NSFNet had a faster backbone. Any additional expansion of this networked community was primarily through the NSFNet. By the early 1990s, NSFNet fully replaced the aging ARPANet.

In the later 1980s and early 1990s, the development and growing use of personal computers fuelled the growth of the Internet. As increasing numbers of people purchased their own computers, there was a growing demand for "anytime, anywhere" access to information through computer networks. But NSFNet was restricted to academic users only. It did not serve business and individuals. Telecommunications companies, such as Bell Canada, AT&T, and Nortel, responded to the growing demand by building high-speed backbones and new networks that used the same protocols (much like speaking the same language) as the NSFNet.

Learning Link

A **protocol** is an agreed-upon format for transmitting data between two or more devices. In networking, it is a set of formal rules describing how to transmit data across networks.

During these years, the *TCP/IP* (*Transmission Control Protocol/Internet Protocol*) network protocol became the accepted means of communication across networks. TCP/IP was available for free and its widespread use contributed to the rapid growth of the Internet as a network of many networks throughout the 1980s and 1990s. Business or personal users could set up Internet accounts with one of many telecommunications companies and *Internet service providers* (*ISPs*)—companies that provide users with access to the Internet, usually for a fee. During the later 1980s and early 1990s, the most popular use for the Internet was e-mail and file sharing.

Visit the *InsighTs* Student Page on <www.irwinpublishing.com/students> to get up-to-date information on the status of Canadian networks. Find out what the CA*Net Institute is, what groups of people CA*Net III is meant for, and how it will benefit all Canadians.

Canarie Inc. (a not-for-profit corporation) sponsored by members, partners, and

Canada's federal government has a mission to accelerate Canada's Internet development. It has proposed the development of a high-speed backbone that would provide every Canadian home and school with high-speed access by the year 2005. Visit the Canarie site on the *InsighTs* Student Page on <www.irwinpublishing.com/students> to learn more.

Knowledge Check

1. What type of network is the Internet?
2. What was the name of the earliest version of the Internet? What was the reason for its development?
3. What is a network backbone?
4. Who created the NSFNet and why?
5. What caused the expansion of the Internet in the 1980s and 1990s?
6. What is TCP/IP?

The World Wide Web

What Is the World Wide Web and How Did It Evolve?

The birth of the World Wide Web (WWW) and, in particular, the development of Web browser software led to skyrocketing Internet growth and exciting new uses for the Internet.

"I see the highway but I can't seem to find an on-ramp."

Fig. 1.16
The Internet is sometimes called the Information Highway.

Tim Berners-Lee developed the World Wide Web in the early 1980s at the European Laboratory for Particle Physics (CERN) in Geneva, Switzerland. Today, the WWW is more commonly known as the *Web* or *W3*.

The *World Wide Web* is a collection of millions of *hypertext* documents. Hypertext documents are most commonly written in a *Web authoring language* called *HTML (HyperText Markup Language)*. These documents can contain built-in applications and links to databases in addition to text, sound, graphics, and animation. *HyperText Transfer Protocol (HTTP)* is the set of rules that govern how documents written in HTML are interpreted and displayed through a browser.

To view Web pages on the Internet, users require a Web browser. A Web browser is a program that will interpret hypertext documents on the Web and display them on screen.

Berners-Lee wrote the first Web browser program shortly after he proposed the creation of the WWW in 1979. In 1983, a Web browser called NCSA Mosaic was developed at the National Center for Supercomputing Applications and distributed for free to the public. Soon after this distribution, the number of users on the Web increased dramatically. As the number of users grew, new and innovative ways to use the Internet and the Web developed.

Find out what the current status is for the NCSA Mosaic browser and more about Tim Berners-Lee and what he is doing today. Visit the *InsighTs* Student Page on <www.irwinpublishing.com/students>.

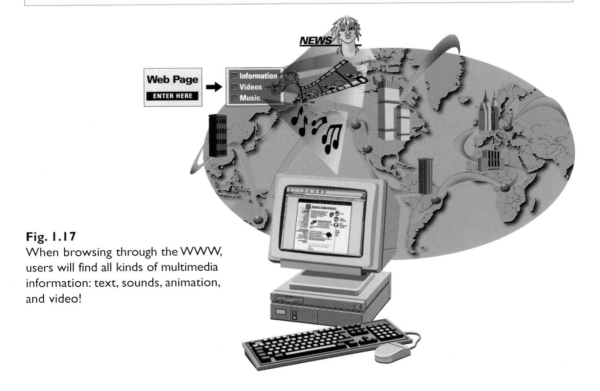

Fig. 1.17
When browsing through the WWW, users will find all kinds of multimedia information: text, sounds, animation, and video!

Hypertext documents contain hyperlinks. These links lead users to another World Wide Web site or another place within the same document. Hyperlinks are usually highlighted or underlined text, or pictures. You will recognize a hyperlink because your cursor, when positioned over a hyperlink, will change from an arrow to

You may be wondering why so many of the phrases associated with the Web begin with "hyper." The dictionary defines "hyper" as high strung, excitable, and highly excited. The word is sometimes associated with people who switch attention from one topic to another at a moment's notice. Web documents provide the opportunity for users to search for information in this way, by providing links to other documents that users can choose in whatever order they want, whenever they want. This method allows users to find quickly the information they are looking for without having to read everything on a particular page.

a hand. When selected, a hyperlink will move a user to another location on the same document, to another document on the same computer, or to a document on a computer in another part of the world!

Web pages are identified by addresses known as **URLs** *(universal resource locators)*. A Web site URL begins with "http" to tell your browser that the file being referenced by the URL needs to be interpreted a certain way (using the Hypertext Transfer Protocol or http) for you to be able to view it. Fig. 1.18 illustrates the main parts of a Web site address.

Fig. 1.18
Anatomy of a Web Site Address

A Web site address is also referred to as a universal (or uniform) resource locator or URL.

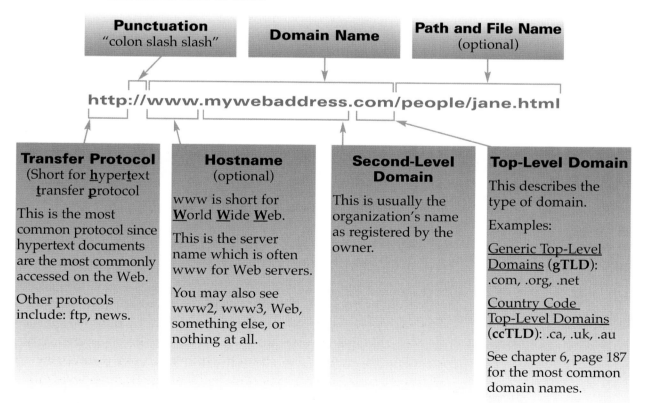

Punctuation
"colon slash slash"

Domain Name

Path and File Name
(optional)

http://www.mywebaddress.com/people/jane.html

Transfer Protocol
(Short for **h**yper**t**ext **t**ransfer **p**rotocol

This is the most common protocol since hypertext documents are the most commonly accessed on the Web.

Other protocols include: ftp, news.

Hostname
(optional)

www is short for **W**orld **W**ide **W**eb.

This is the server name which is often www for Web servers.

You may also see www2, www3, Web, something else, or nothing at all.

Second-Level Domain

This is usually the organization's name as registered by the owner.

Top-Level Domain

This describes the type of domain.

Examples:

Generic Top-Level Domains (**gTLD**): .com, .org, .net

Country Code Top-Level Domains (**ccTLD**): .ca, .uk, .au

See chapter 6, page 187 for the most common domain names.

How Are the Internet and the World Wide Web Different?

The Internet Society Web site has a number of links to sites that provide historical information about the Internet. To expand your understanding of the history of the Internet and the World Wide Web and the purpose of the World Wide Web Consortium, visit the *InsighTs* Student Page on <www.irwinpublishing.com/students>.

People often speak of the Net and the Web as the same thing, but there is a difference between the two. The Internet is the collection of networks of computers and storage devices linked together by cables and/or satellite. The underlying structure of the Internet is a set of backbone connections (major highways) and routing tools (major traffic intersections) that control the way pieces of data find their way to their destinations.

Learning Link

"Surfing the Net" describes the action of travelling on the Internet looking at Web sites. The term was coined in 1992.

Fig. 1.19
The Internet: a network of many networks

The Web, on the other hand, is the total collection of information on linked hypertext documents. People require the Internet structure to navigate the Web much like they require major highways and roadways to travel from destination to destination.

Knowledge Check

1. Who invented the World Wide Web? When?
2. What happened in 1983 that caused the number of users on the Internet to increase?
3. How is the World Wide Web different from the Internet?
4. How can you tell if a word or picture on a Web page is a hyperlink?
5. What is the language of hypertext documents?
6. What was the name of the first Web browser program?
7. What does "URL" represent? Using an example, identify the four major parts.
8. What is an Internet backbone?

Infrastructure for Modern Information Technology

What Infrastructure Supports Modern Information Technology?

Learning Link

Until the beginning of the twentieth century, writing and the printed word remained the primary means of communication, and information travelled on trains and ships at the same rate as people did.

Each new change in information technology has required the development of mechanisms that could transmit information effectively to more people over longer distances and at faster rates. In short, information technologies require an *infrastructure*—a structural foundation—that enables the technologies to work. Cities require the infrastructure of roads, sewers, and power and water supplies to function successfully. Today, the development of the personal computer, the Internet, and the World Wide Web has resulted in profound changes in how information is delivered. By the end of the twentieth century, five of the major communications industries—traditional media (newspapers, magazines, books, film, radio, television, CDs, cassettes), home electronics, information packagers and distributors, the computer industry, and telecommunications—were beginning to converge to create a combined infrastructure for delivering information.

The telecommunications industry includes land telephones, cellular telephones, pagers/mobiles, AM/FM bands, cable networks, broadcast networks, computer networks, communications satellites, the Internet, and the www.

Advances in cable television, computers, and telecommunication technologies provide the backbone necessary to support the rapid processing and managing of information over increasingly long distances. One of the main backbones for sharing information today is communication satellites orbiting the Earth. Another is fibre optics. Fibre-optic systems carry information via light pulses along ultra-thin glass fibres. Many telephone and telecommunication networks have or are converting to fibre optics. A fibreoptic cable can carry 1000 times as many telephone conversations as can a traditional wire cable. Fibre-optic systems today permit exceptionally high signal rates and long distances between repeaters (amplifiers) in a cable.

Knowledge Check

1. What is an infrastructure?
2. Identify three technologies that resulted in changes in the way information is delivered today.

3. Why are telecommunications companies interested in using fibre-optic systems?

What Next?

How Is Information Technology Changing?

As the number of users of information technology grows, new and innovative ways to use modern information technology develop. Advances in technology occur virtually every day, and the speed of change is constantly increasing. As you have read, our daily lives have been affected drastically by changes in information technology over the past 30 years. Your high school life is very different from the high school experiences your parents and teachers had! It is difficult to predict what changes will occur next. One can predict with certainty that the next year will bring faster computer chips, smaller and lighter portable computers, new and more powerful software, faster portable modems, and compact storage devices (such as minidisks) that can hold increasingly large amounts of information.

A number of people called "futurists" predict changes to technology and society. One well-known futurist named Richard Worzel predicts that within 20 years, we will wear our computers, similar to the way we wear watches. He believes that these wearable computers will be linked to systems similar to the Internet, providing people with a constant flow of information, 24 hours a day. Another futurist, Neil Gershenfeld, believes that our clothing will one day be net-worked to a computer, allowing it to send and receive information about our bodies and activities. Yet another futurist, Ray Kurzwell, predicts that by 2099, we will be able to download information from the human mind into computers. If this actually happens, you could have all the thoughts and knowledge in your brain copied onto a hard drive!

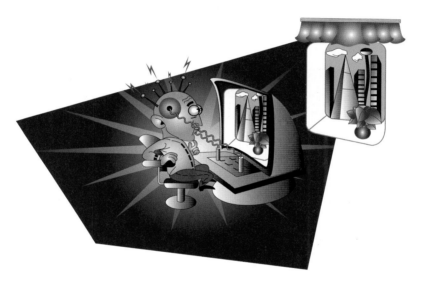

Fig. 1.20
Perhaps one day we will be able to look out the window and download the image in our minds to our computer.

Each of these futurists also describes the development of *artificial intelligence*. Artificial intelligence is the term used to describe computer programs that allow machines to imitate the thinking, learning, emotions, and decision-making processes of people. At the beginning of the twenty-first century, computers can still only perform actions that carry out specific tasks made up of steps laid out by software programmers. As you will learn in the case study below, a foundation for artificial intelligence may already exist.

WHAT DO YOU THINK?

Nanotechnology is the process of building molecule-sized machines called "assemblers." These assemblers can be programmed to produce larger machines (called *Nanobots*) made up of these molecule-sized pieces. The process is similar to the way human cells multiply to create a whole person. This idea was put forth in 1992 by Dr. Eric Drexler. Drexler believes that many of the world's problems could be solved by creating Nanobots that could create scarce materials or work inside the human body to kill disease.

1. How would anyone know what is real and what is not in a world where machines can reproduce anything down to its molecules? Would it matter?

2. What would stop criminals or dishonest researchers from creating physical evidence they desire to prove their case or thesis?

3. What other dangers can you foresee resulting from this type of technology?

4. What benefits can you foresee resulting from this type of technology?

To find out more about nanotechnology, visit the *InsighTs* Student Page on <www.irwinpublishing.com/students> for an article in *Micscape* magazine, a British publication, and for access links from the Foresight Institute, a California-based non-profit educational organization dedicated to providing information about new technology.

For more about the exciting changes in information technology, see chapters 6, 7, and 8.

Time Capsule

A time capsule is a collection of information about life during a certain time period that has been gathered, sealed, and preserved for a certain length of time (usually 100 years). Time capsules generally contain information about the everyday lives of people that cannot usually be found in a book, such as examples of people's work, cards, drawings, and photos. When opened, these pieces of evidence provide a snapshot of the time in which they were created.

This activity requires you to prepare a time capsule in the form of a report that reflects today's use of information technology. Imagine that 100 years from now someone your age will open the time capsule you create. He or she may have no idea what our technologies looked like or what they were used for. As a result, you have to explain everything in detail.

You will contribute your own personal views, opinions, and observations. You may include pictures and illustrations if you wish. Your time capsule must contain the following sections, each with a subtitle, that addresses your understanding of the topic:

- examples of information today
- how information technology makes people's lives easier today
- how businesses use technology today
- how schools use and teach technology today
- my personal predictions for technology in the next 100 years

Fig. 1.21

Your teacher will gather all the time capsules, seal them in an envelope, and place them in a safe place to be opened when you graduate.

AIBO, the Robotic Dog

In 1999, Sony launched a limited edition of the world's first robotic dog, **AIBO**. This creature was developed with the goal of creating a robot that could coexist with people, and it opens up limitless possibilities for interaction with humans. The first two letters of the word **AIBO** stand for "artificial intelligence." This robot is said to have artificial intelligence because it has the ability to learn, and has emotions. "BO" comes from "robot" and "AIBO" sounds like the Japanese word for "pal." AIBO looks somewhat like a dog, but is made of plastic and metal. It is called an "autonomous robot" because it acts in response to things that happen to it, and by its own judgement. It displays emotions and learns by communicating and interacting with human beings.

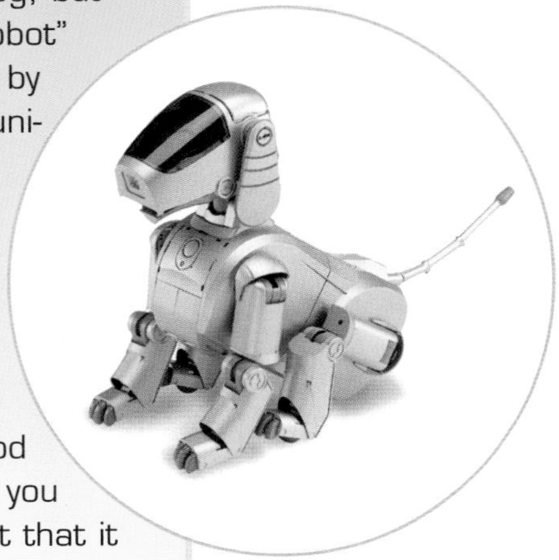

AIBO learns from its experiences and surroundings. It matures much like people do, going through the stages of a toddler, a child, a young adult, and an adult. A newborn **AIBO** is not very good at walking, and usually cannot do any tricks. The most important thing that **AIBO** needs in order to mature is a balance of daily experiences. Reinforcing good behaviour with praise will result in learning. For instance, if you scold **AIBO** while it is looking at a ball, it will soon figure out that it is not a good idea to look at a ball.

While playing or communicating with people, **AIBO** expresses joy, sadness, anger, and fear through movements, sound, and by lighting up its eyes. For instance, if **AIBO** is in a bad mood it will not do as it is told. On the other hand, if **AIBO** is in a good mood, it will show you one of its favourite tricks.

AIBO's head has a sense of touch. You can communicate with **AIBO** by petting or quickly tapping its head. It hears sounds through a pair of stereo microphones. It can see through cameras in its eye area.

Fig. 1.22
AIBO
Courtesy Sony Canada

1. Do you think **AIBO** could replace a real dog? Why or why not?

2. Do you believe that **AIBO** is able to learn? Why or why not? How is its learning different from yours?

3. Do you believe **AIBO** has emotions? Why or why not? How are its emotions different from yours?

To find out more about AIBO, visit the Sony Web site on the *InsighTs* Student Page on <www.irwinpublishing.com/students>.

CHAPTER SUMMARY

Understanding Information

1. What functions were the earliest computers able to perform?

2. How did people input information into first-generation computers?

3. What characterized the third generation of computing?

4. In which generation of computing were operating systems introduced?

5. What is a microprocessor?

6. How are mainframe computers used?

7. Beginning with ARPANet, identify some of the major networks that were developed during the evolution of the Internet. For each, describe its initial purpose.

8. Where did the Internet get its name?

9. Who invented the World Wide Web?

10. Why do so many World Wide Web terms begin with "hyper"?

11. List three predictions made by futurists about the future of information technology.

12. What is artificial intelligence?

13. Describe the job of a robotics programmer.

Analyzing

14. Briefly describe the main developments of the sixth generation of computers and their significance.

15. In what ways is an abacus similar to a computer? How is it different?

16. What were some of the factors that made computers accessible to people?

17. What are some of the similarities and differences between switches, vacuum tubes, and transistors?

18. How did microprocessors revolutionize personal computers?

19. Why do you think information technology can be used to help you learn in your other classes?

20. Why do you think the number of Internet users grew after the free distribution of the NCSA Mosaic?

21. Examine each of the Web site addresses below. Identify the i) transfer protocol, ii) hostname, iii) second-level domain, iv) top-level domain, v) path and file name

    a) <http://www.irwinpublishing.com>

    b) <http://yahoo.ca>

    c) <http://www3.mycompany.org/main/default.html>

    d) <http://www.web.MyCollege.uk/biology/level2/intro.html>

e) <http://YourSchool.org/students/grade9projects/>

f) <http://musiccentral.com/downloads/list.html>

22. Analyze three ways in which technology has improved people's lives.

23. State one way in which the misuse of technology has made people's lives more difficult.

24. How might artificial intelligence affect your life by the time you are an adult?

Applying

25. Draw a timeline to represent the six generations of computing.

26. How has technology changed in the last 20 years?

27. What types of jobs could never be replaced by technology? Why not?

28. Technology has had a huge impact on the daily lives of Canadians over the past twenty years. What, in your opinion, is the biggest change to the way people live resulting from technology?

Communicating

29. Describe the difference between people-oriented and machine-oriented issues in information technology. Use examples.

30. Choose three of the predictions made by the futurists quoted in this chapter and comment on what impact they may have on your life.

31. Make your own prediction for a development you think will take place in information technology. Describe why you think that development might happen. Describe what impact the development might have on people's lives.

Assessing Your Competencies

32. Using the software competency checklists provided by your teacher, check off the competencies that you have mastered during the course of this chapter. Note the competencies that require more attention and review.

33. Interview a classmate to determine the competencies he or she has acquired during the chapter. Also share some of the new skills you have acquired.

CHAPTER TWO

WHERE DO WE BEGIN?

Topics

➤ Anatomy of a Computer
➤ Hardware
➤ Computer Storage
➤ Peripheral Devices
➤ Software
➤ Connecting Computers
➤ Minimizing Security Threats

Have you ever wondered how computers work? Get ready to find out. In this chapter, you will first explore the internal and external parts that make up a computer's hardware. Then, you will find out what software is all about. You will also learn what a desktop actually is and how computers communicate with one another. After examining the computer's hardware and software, you will understand how the two components work together to give you the results you want. Finally, you will examine the issue of security and will learn what viruses are and look at some methods you can use to protect yourself against them.

This chapter explores these questions:

- How do computers work?
- What is hardware?
- How do computers store information?
- What are peripheral devices?
- What is software?
- What is a desktop?
- How do computers communicate with one another?
- How can you maintain privacy and confidentiality?
- What are viruses?
- How can you protect your computer against viruses?

In this chapter you have the opportunity to

- explore how the components of computers work
- look at different ways to save information
- investigate careers in information technology
- assess and compare software programs
- research various types of computers available from a local retailer
- identify recent viruses and their potential effects

Anatomy of a Computer

How Do Computers Work?

In chapter 1, you learned how computers evolved to where they are today. Now, we will look at what makes them work.

Essentially, computers complete tasks given to them by users. They work by carrying out the four *functions* shown in Fig. 2.1.

Fig. 2.1 The Four Functions of Computers

Input	Storage	Processing	Output
The computer collects information or instructions from you. You can provide the computer with **input** by keying using a keyboard, pointing and clicking a mouse, pointing a stylus, or speaking into a microphone.	The computer saves—**stores**—information or instructions in its memory.	The computer interprets and **processes** the data you input. It adds, multiplies, divides, finds, or manipulates data or text to complete a task you have given it.	The computer displays or produces information that has been processed. The **output** might be something you see on the screen (such as an answer to a mathematical problem), something you hear (such as a "ding" when you have made an error), or something you ask the computer to print.

In order for a computer to perform these functions, *hardware* and *software* are necessary.

Hardware

What Is Hardware?

Hardware is any part of a computer you can touch. There are two categories of hardware:

- **inside the computer**—all the components of the computer system contained inside the computer case
- **peripherals**—those components that are attached to the computer through cables or wireless technology

We will start by looking inside the computer.

Fig. 2.2 Inside a Computer

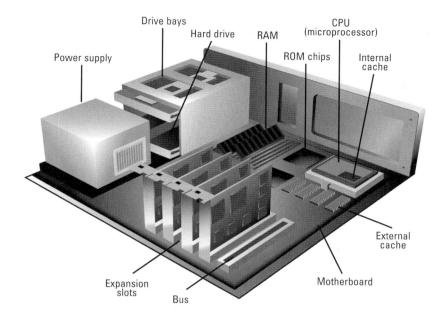

Labels in figure: Power supply, Drive bays, Hard drive, RAM, ROM chips, CPU (microprocessor), Internal cache, External cache, Motherboard, Expansion slots, Bus

power supply—brings the electricity to the computer through the power cord

motherboard—the main circuit board of the computer to which all components are attached. It contains metal tracks through which electricity flows, electronic devices, and transistors that control the flow of electricity.

CPU (central processing unit)—also called the *microprocessor*, the CPU is the main computer chip that processes instructions, processes data, and manages the flow of information in the computer (See Quick Byte on page 41).

external cache—memory that is external to the CPU and is used for high-speed storage of recently used information. It is sometimes called *L2* or *level 2 cache* because it is the second place the CPU looks to find recently used data or instructions.

internal cache—memory that is inside the CPU that is the first place the CPU looks to find recently used data or instructions. It is sometimes called *L1* or *level 1 cache*

expansion slots—sockets in the motherboard into which expansion cards can be added for additional memory or *peripheral devices*, e.g., sound card, *modem*, etc.

hard drive—a disk drive that holds, reads from, and writes to the *hard disk*, which is the *memory storage space* in the computer. It is used to store software and data files.

storage devices—spaces in the computer case where *disk drives* are housed. A computer can have several disk drives that are located in the drive bay. Usually, one disk drive is for 3.5" *floppy disks*. Others are for *CD-ROMs, DVDs (digital video/versatile disks)*, or *CD Rewritables*.

bus—a set of *conductor wires* that transports data among the components of the computer through an electronic path. Think of the bus as an invisible highway for electrons to carry information to and from components inside the computer case. The *bus width* is the number of *bits* (see A Quick Byte on page 40) of information the bus can transport at one time. The bus width is similar to the width of a highway—the more lane width there is on a highway, the more traffic can pass without a jam. The more bits the bus can carry, the faster information will travel from component to component on the motherboard.

RAM (random access memory)—also called *user memory*, RAM is temporary memory that stores information for the length of time a computer is left on or a program is left running. The data you see on your monitor while using your computer is stored in RAM. Once the computer is turned off, any information in RAM is lost unless you saved it to another location (e.g., hard disk, floppy disk).

ROM (read only memory)—also called *factory memory*, ROM is computer memory on which information has been stored at the time of manufacture (i.e., instructions needed on start-up). One or more ROM chips are attached to the motherboard.

Binary code, the fundamental language code that the computer understands, is represented by a series of Os and 1s. Why Os and 1s? Computers are machines that only understand two states: OFF and ON. The OFF state is represented by O; the ON state by 1. Every piece of information that is entered into a computer has to be digitally encoded as a series of Os and 1s in order for the computer to understand it.

To learn more about "binary," visit The Binary Homepage and the Webopedia page on the *InsighTs* Student Page on <www.irwinpublishing.com/students>.

Bits and Bytes

Just how much room does it take to store information? It all boils down to *bits* and *bytes*.

- A ***bit*** is the short form for <u>bi</u>nary dig<u>it</u>. A bit is the smallest unit of data a computer can use. A single bit can hold only one of two values: 0 or 1. More complex information can be stored by combining several bits.

- A ***byte*** is the unit of memory needed to store one character such as a letter, number, or punctuation mark. It takes 8 bits to make up 1 byte.

The amount of memory your computer has is referred to in

- kilobytes (KB) or 1000 bytes*. One kilobyte is capable of storing 1000 characters.

- megabytes (MB) or 1 000 000 bytes. RAM is usually measured in megabytes.

- gigabytes (GB) or 1 000 000 000 bytes. Hard drives are usually measured in gigabytes. An 8 GB hard drive can hold the equivalent of 24 000 000 pages of information.

*   1 KB is 1024 bytes exactly. However, people usually refer to K in its approximate value of 1000.
    Just as a <u>kilo</u>metre is 1000 metres, a <u>kilo</u>byte has come to be accepted as containing 1000 bytes.

How CPUs Work

CPU speed is measured in megahertz (MHz). The higher the number, the faster the CPU processes information. For example, an 800 MHz CPU processes twice as fast as a 400 MHz microprocessor.

Every time you input information into your computer, the CPU processes those instructions using four tasks.

- *fetch*—The CPU gathers—fetches—the code for an instruction and places it in the **instruction cache** (temporary memory where the instructions are stored).

For more information about the latest CPUs or microprocessors, visit the *InsighTs* Student Page on <www.irwinpublishing.com/students>.

- *decode*—The CPU **decodes**—interprets—the instruction in an area of the CPU chip called the **decode cache** and determines which functions are to be performed.

- *execute*—The CPU processes—carries out or executes—the instructions and sends the results to their proper destinations.

- *store*—The CPU sends the results of the instructions to the proper memory location to be retained—stored—for further instructions.

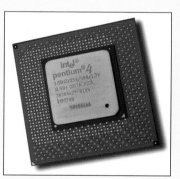

Fig. 2.3
Intel is a major manufacturer of computer chips, including the Pentium processor. This is a photograph of the Intel® Pentium® 4 processor.

Photo courtesy of Intel Corporation

Knowledge Check

1. What is "input"?
2. What is "output"?
3. What is meant by "processing"?
4. What is "hardware"?
5. Using Fig. 2.2, create a chart that summarizes the components inside a computer.

6. Name and describe the four tasks that a CPU performs to process information that has been input by a user.
7. Why do computers use binary code?

Computer Storage

How Do Computers Store Information?

How many times have you studied for a test from notes you took in class? Or flipped through a textbook looking for a specific piece of information? Your notebook and textbook are examples of information storage devices. A storage device is any device into which data can be entered and held, and from which the data can be retrieved at a later time.

When using computers, special storage devices allow you to save your work, as well as software, games, and other information. Some storage devices are part of the computer itself. Others are peripherals (see discussion of peripherals on pages 46-51). The type of storage device you use depends on what type of information you are storing. You must think about how much storage space you need, and how easily or quickly you need access to the information. The most common storage devices are summarized in Fig. 2.5.

ZAK MEADOW

©2000 MARC NGUI

Y'know, I don't think this is the best solution for your memory problems.

Fig. 2.4
© Marc Ngui

Fig. 2.5 Common Computer Storage Devices

Storage Option	Advantages	Disadvantages
Hard Drive (usually C: drive)	• extensive storage space • very easy to access information • fast access	• Once it is full, you either have to purchase another hard drive or delete files. • expensive • not removable or portable
3.5" Floppy Disk (usually A: drive)	• small, light, and easy to carry • inexpensive	• little storage space (1.44 MB) • easily damaged by magnets, heat, cold, or liquid • slow to save or read information
CD-ROM (for reading CDs only) and CD-Writer RW (for reading and saving onto CDs)	• Use a CD-ROM drive to read commercial CDs and CD-R disks made with CD-Writers. • Use a CD-Writer RW to read all CDs, record onto CD-R disks, and erase and record CD-RW disks. • significant storage space (600+ MB) • sturdy, not easily destroyed • small, light, and easy to carry • reads data quickly	• more expensive than floppy disks (but stores much more) • If you have already saved information on a CD and want to erase that information in order to copy new information on the CD, you need to purchase special CDs and have specialized software.
DVD (digital video/versatile disk) and DVD Writer	• extensive storage space (4.7 GB to 17 GB) • sturdy, not easily destroyed • small, light, and easy to carry • reads data quickly	• relatively expensive • requires special software and disks to copy over data
Removable Drives (Jaz®, Zip®, SyJet®)	• significant storage space (varies between 100 MB and 2 GB) • easily portable • read and save data relatively quickly	• expensive • easily damaged by magnets, heat, cold, or liquid
Online Storage To see an example of an online storage service, visit the *InsighTs* Student Page on <www.irwinpublishing.com/students>.	• can be accessed from any computer through a modem or other Internet connection • Files can be shared with others with the click of a mouse. • Most providers offer from 25 MB to 50 MB of storage free of charge. A few offer 100 MB of free storage.	• may not be secure, not suitable for confidential files • If the online storage provider goes out of business, the files are lost. • Files can only be accessed while you are online.
Removable Drive	• allows a hard drive to be easily attached and removed from a computer like a floppy disk • almost as spacious and fast as regular hard drives	• very expensive

Save Me!

Jennifer needs to save a lot of computer files. She needs help in determining the best storage options. She has the following storage devices available: a hard drive with 5 GB of space available, 20 floppy disks, 1 Zip Disk (a disk with 250 MB), and 1 CD. For each item in the list below, identify which of Jennifer's storage devices you think would be the best possible storage option and why. Set up your ideas in a chart like this.

Item	Storage Device	Reason
Science Lab Report		
Video Game, etc.		

- word-processed science lab report that she is still working on (10 KB)

- video game that she plans to use every day (7 MB)

- antivirus software that she plans to use every week (8 MB)

- presentation from history class that she will not use again (2.1 MB)

- ten music files that she does not plan to listen to often (each file is 10 MB)

- weekly journal from English class that she is still working on (46 KB)

- project from geography class that she will not use again (27 KB)

Learning Link

Although Canada uses the metric system of measurement, the computer industry in North America continues to use Imperial measures. Disk drives, floppy disks, printers, and other computer components are therefore designed to work with Imperial measurements (e.g., 3.5″ disk drives, 15″ monitors).

A 3.5″ floppy disk that can hold 1.44 MB is capable of storing approximately 1.4 million characters, or about 3000 pages of information.

Compressing Your Files

Large files can be *compressed* or "zipped" using a special type of "zipping" software that compresses all the information so the information fits into a smaller space in the storage device. The process is similar to taking a T-shirt and tightly folding it up so that it fits into a soup can. The same software that is used to zip the information is usually required to open it.

Fig. 2.6

Fig. 2.6 is a sample WinZip file that was compressed using the WinZip program. All files compressed with WinZip can be identified by this icon which is the same as the program icon. To unzip the files using the WinZip program, simply double-click on the icon. This single file is currently 123 000 bytes large. After the file is unzipped, it will become a group of files taking up 148 000 bytes.

Fig. 2.7

A compression program that is popular with Mac users is called Stuffit. You can identify Stuffit files because they have the extension **.sit** (see page 89 for more about file extensions). Fig. 2.7 shows the icon for the Stuffit program.

Stuffit can also produce .sea files (self extracting archives). The Stuffit expander application program is not needed to decompress these files, as is the case with .sit files.

Activity

Buying a Computer

Steve is in the process of shopping for a computer. He is worried because he knows very little about computers, and cannot understand the advertisements. He has located two computers he can afford, both at the same price. Help Steve to make a selection. In your own words, explain the difference between Computer A and Computer B.

- Computer A: 64 MB RAM with a 10.2 GB hard drive, 100 MHz bus, and 533 MHz processor

- Computer B: 128 MB RAM with a 20 GB hard drive, 133 MHz bus, and 800 MHz processor

Peripheral Devices

What Are Peripheral Devices?

In addition to the hardware that makes up the computer itself, *peripheral devices* can be attached by cable or wireless technology to the computer to perform specific functions. Peripherals are plugged into special sockets at the back or side of your computer called *ports* using appropriate cables. This section illustrates some common peripheral devices.

Monitors are devices that provide a visual display on a screen. There are two common types of monitors: CRT (cathode-ray tube) similar to a small television screen, and LCD (liquid crystal display), also known as a flat panel monitor.

Fig.2.8
A CRT monitor and LCD monitor

Fig.2.9
A modem

Modems are devices that allow a computer to transmit data over telephone lines by converting digital signals to analog signals and vice versa. Modems can be internal (inside the computer case attached to the motherboard) or external (contained in separate boxes and plugged into the computer).

Fig.2.10
Expansion card

Expansion cards contain chips that add new features to a computer. For example, a *graphics card*, or a *sound card* give the computer the ability to digitize video or sound so that the computer can reproduce graphics or sounds. The number of expansion slots on a computer indicates the number of expansion cards that can be added.

Printers are devices that print text or illustrations on paper, providing hard copy for users.

Pointing devices control the movement of a cursor or pointer on a display screen. The most common pointing device is the **mouse**. Mice work by being rolled along a hard, flat surface. The name "mouse" comes from its shape. As you move the mouse, the pointer on the display screen moves in the same direction. Mice come with one, two, or three buttons. Normally, the left button (or single button on a Mac mouse) is used to click on icons or menus, and to select and drag items on the screen. The right button is usually used to call up a window of commands or shortcuts. (On a Mac, press the Ctrl key and click the mouse.) The uses for the buttons depend on the type of software you are using.

Learning Link

A "mickey" is a unit of measurement for tracking the movement of a computer mouse equivalent to approximately 1.25 mm.

SITE SEEING

For more about the history of the mouse, see the *InsighTs* Student Page on <www.irwinpublishing.com/students>.

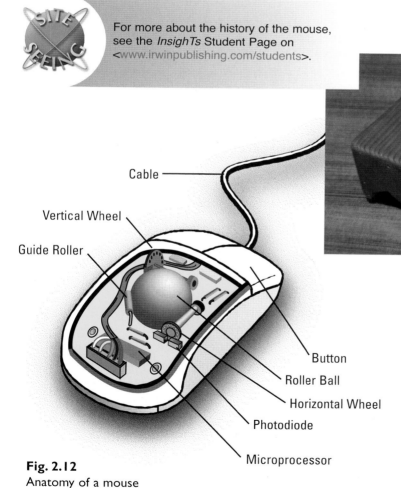

Cable

Vertical Wheel

Guide Roller

Button

Roller Ball

Horizontal Wheel

Photodiode

Microprocessor

Fig. 2.12
Anatomy of a mouse

Fig. 2.11
The first mouse. Douglas Engelbart of Stanford Research Institute in Menlo Park, California, invented the mouse in 1963, but it did not become widely used until 20 years later.
Courtesy Bootstrap Institute

Trackball

Touchpad

Fig. 2.13
Mice found on portable computers:
trackball and touchpad

Portable computers have mice that are a part of the computer itself. A *trackball* mouse looks like a ball that has been lodged into the computer. Users roll the exposed part of the ball with their fingers to move the cursor, and use buttons located next to the ball to click or drag. A *touchpad* (or acupoint) is a small square located near the keyboard. Users slide their fingers across the square to move the cursor, and use nearby buttons to activate commands. A third device looks like a pencil eraser, which the user pushes to move the cursor on the screen, pressing nearby buttons to activate commands. Another option is a *pen pad* or *digitizing tablet*, a pointing device that uses a special pen to move the cursor and provides some programmable features when used with specialized software packages.

When you press your mouse button, you signal to your computer that you want to do something, similar to the Enter key. The software that comes with your mouse, the software you are using, or the operating system interprets the message and carries out the task. Most mice communicate with a computer through a cord attached to a port on the back of the computer. There are two ways in which mice can connect to computers without a cord:

- *Infrared mice* send *infrared signals* to a receiver attached to the computer's mouse port. These mice do not require a cord, but the mouse must stay in the receiver's line of sight (nothing can come between the mouse and the receiver).
- *Radio mice* use low-power radio signals to send information to the computer. They are useful if you want to work away from the computer, such as when making a presentation.

Joysticks are levers that move in all directions and control the movement of a pointer or other display symbol. A joystick is similar to a mouse, except that with a mouse the cursor stops moving as soon as you stop moving the mouse. With a joystick, the pointer continues moving in the direction the joystick is pointing. Joysticks are used mostly for computer or video games.

Fig. 2.14
A joystick

(a)

Keyboards consist of typewriter-like keys that enable users to enter information into a computer.

Speakers are attachments that allow sound to come out of the computer. In some cases, they are part of the monitor or built into the computer case.

(b)

Fig. 2.15
Keyboards

Fig. 2.16
Speakers

 **Activity**

Peripheral Visions

Part A

Some peripherals are used for input, others for output, and some can be used for both input and output. Using the list of peripherals above, work with a partner to determine which of the devices are used for input only, which are used for output only, and which can be used for both. Summarize your findings.

Part B

Using a catalogue from a computer retailer or the Internet, locate two peripheral devices that are not part of the list above. Cut out the photos and descriptions of those peripheral devices. With a partner, create a display on a sheet of cardboard identifying these peripheral devices, what their purposes are, and whether they are used for input or output. Where possible, present your findings in digital format using a word processing program.

Case Study

The Nose Always Knows!

Imagine playing a racing video game, and actually being able to smell the rubber burning as you turn corners in your racecar. You may be able to enjoy this type of "scentertainment" in the very near future! In March 2000, DigiScents™, an American company, launched a new peripheral device called the iSmell™ Personalized Scent Synthesizer. The device was a speaker-sized box that plugged into a computer and received codes from software to mix and send out a scent using a set of oils stored inside the box.

Unfortunately, the company lost its funding in April 2001 and went out of business. Nevertheless, it will undoubtedly not be long before digital scents will be programmed into Web sites, video games, or any application software. For example, a Web site for a pizza chain could actually emit the smell of freshly cooked pizza every time a user with the appropriate digital device logs on!

1. In a small group, discuss how the iSmell™ device worked. Identify whether it was an input or output peripheral device.

2. With your group, generate as many possible uses for a digital scent device as you can. Consider how businesses might use it, how individuals might use it, and what specific applications it might have. Key a letter to a company outlining your ideas.

3. Discuss with the group whether you think this type of technology will become popular. Record your answer with reasons for later discussion.

4. What type of person would be most likely to purchase a digital scent device? Why? With your group, design an advertisement for the device that would appeal to that person.

5. With your group, make a list of all the advantages and disadvantages you can think of for this new peripheral technology. Consider some of the ethical issues the technology might raise.

6. Use your imagination to generate a list of peripheral devices that you think might be invented in the future. Describe each, and identify their function. Pick one and illustrate it.

7. Compare your group's results and conclusions with those of other groups in the class.

1. What are peripherals? Give three examples.
2. What is the purpose of expansion slots? Give an example of how you might use them.
3. In a chart in your notebook, describe three types of pointing devices.
4. How can mice communicate with a computer without a cable?

Software

Computers will not serve you if they consist only of hardware—no matter how efficient, fast, or sophisticated that hardware is. To carry out the four functions of the computer discussed at the opening of this chapter, computers must also include software. Without software, you can turn your computer on, but it will do nothing. It will not even recognize what the characters you key on the keyboard mean!

What Is Software?

Software is a set of electronic instructions that tell a computer what to do. There are two types of software—**operating system software** and **application software**.

Operating System Software

Operating system software controls the overall activity of a computer. Operating systems (O/S), sometimes called *platforms*, are similar to a hotel concierge. Concierges talk to all incoming guests, direct them to where they need to go, and monitor where they stay in the hotel. The role of the operating system is to recognize information coming in from a keyboard or mouse (similar to the concierge's role of greeting guests and finding out what they need), send information to the screen or printer (ensure the guests get to their destinations), keep track of directories and files on disks (monitor where everyone and everything is), and control all peripherals.

The operating system is also responsible for running software and for security, ensuring that unauthorized users do not enter the system. Because of its role in making everything happen, the operating system is the most important piece of software on a computer.

Fig. 2.17
The job of a computer operating system is like that of a hotel concierge.

Many different operating systems exist. Figure 2.18 on page 52 briefly examines five of the most common systems.

FIG. 2.18 SUMMARY OF FIVE COMMON OPERATING SYSTEMS

	MS-DOS (Microsoft Disk Operating System)	Windows 3.1, 95, 98, ME	Unix	Linux	Windows NT, Windows 2000	Mac O/S
Description	MS-DOS displays lines of text on the screen. Users perform tasks by keying short commands.	Windows displays information on a screen using graphics called a *GUI (graphic user interface)*. Users use a mouse to point and click to perform tasks. Windows is multitasking (can run several programs at the same time), but is not suitable for many users on a network at the same time.	Unix is mainly used by businesses and universities, not by individual users on home computers. Unix is multitasking and multi-user (can have several different people using the system at the same time). Like MS-DOS, basic Unix uses a text display, not GUI, and requires that users perform tasks by keying in short commands. It is possible to layer graphic display, making it appear similar to Windows.	Linux is a descendent of Unix, and is very similar to it. Linux is more compact, and can easily be used on personal computers. A GUI, such as X-Windows can be added as a shell that allows the user to interact with Linux in a way that is very much like Windows or the Mac O/S.	These Windows versions are used primarily by businesses as an alternative to Unix. Like other versions of Windows, they display information on screen using graphics, and make use of the mouse. These versions are a true multi-user system.	Similar to Windows, Mac O/S also displays information on a screen using graphics. Users use a mouse to point and click to perform tasks. Like Windows, it is multitasking, but is not a multi-user system. Macs can be networked and are suitable for multi-use.
Advantages	• relatively little disk space required	• widely used, so files can be exchanged with many other people • largest amount of software available, including MS Office, many video games, etc.	• rarely crashes • powerful, making it ideal for complex applications, such as engineering • does not waste disk space • unlimited ability to change and customize the desktop • excellent system security • ideal for multi-user networks	• free • rarely crashes • does not waste disk space • unlimited ability to change and customize the desktop	• runs almost all software for all Windows versions • rarely crashes • ideal for complex applications, such as engineering • does not waste disk space • unlimited ability to change and customize the desktop • good system security • ideal for multi-user networks	• large amounts of software available • superior graphics capabilities • rarely crashes • cross-platform applications available and user friendly
Disadvantages	• frequently crashes • not powerful • little software available • cumbersome to use as commands have to be correctly keyed in • inefficient file system that is difficult to use and understand	• frequently crashes or freezes • expensive • Disk space is wasted due to an inefficient file system. • limited ability to customize desktop appearance • not suitable for networks	• expensive • limited software available for use on this operating system • uses a great deal of hard drive space	• limited software available for use on this operating system	• more expensive than other Windows operating systems	• expensive • Disk space is wasted due to an inefficient file system depending on hard drive capacity.

Different operating systems may have different sets of rules. As a result, software created for one operating system will not always work on another. For example, software created for Windows will not be understood by Mac O/S.

Application Software

Application software is designed to allow users to perform—to apply—a specific task such as calculate numbers, enter text, or play a game. Application software is also referred to as software, an *application,* or a *program.* This type of software is often categorized by its function. Here are some common application software packages:

- *Utility software* is used to maintain your computer and make sure it runs efficiently. Examples of utility software are McAfee VirusScan and Norton Utilities.

- *Application suites* are "all-in-one" business software packages that usually contain a word processor, spreadsheet, and database. Some also include presentation software. Examples of application suites are Corel WordPerfect Suite, AppleWorks (originally Claris Works), Microsoft Works, and Microsoft Office.

- *Word processing software* is designed to create written documents such as letters and reports. Word processing software provides users with tools to change the size and appearance of words, edit the text, check spelling, and a number of other features. Examples include Microsoft Word and WordPerfect.

- *Spreadsheet software* is designed to allow users to enter numbers and perform mathematical functions. Examples include Microsoft Excel, Lotus, and Quattro Pro.

- *Database software* is designed to organize a collection of records or related files, such as class lists and report card data. Examples of database software include Microsoft Access, FileMaker Pro, and PeopleSoft.

- *Presentation software* is designed to allow users to produce slide shows with animations, graphics, and sound effects. Two commonly used presentation software packages are PowerPoint, Corel Presentations, and Director.

- *Desktop publishing software* is designed to create specialized products such as brochures, newsletters, and newspapers. This software is similar to word processing software, but allows users to more easily combine text, graphics, and complicated layouts. Examples include Microsoft Publisher, Adobe PageMaker, and Quark XPress.

- *Graphics software* is designed to create graphic images or manipulate photographs or pictures. Examples of graphic software include Corel DRAW, Adobe Photoshop, and Illustrator.

- *Internet browser software* allows users to read Web sites. Commonly used Internet browsers include Microsoft Internet Explorer and Netscape Navigator.
- *Computer games* include Solitaire, Duke Nukem, NHL Allstars Hockey, Quake, and Snood.
- *Communication software* facilitates communication among computer users. Examples include First Class and Outlook which provide e-mail and conferencing capabilities.

You will learn how to use some of the application software packages listed above in the chapters that follow.

You can *toggle* (rapidly switch between two open software applications) by clicking on ALT/TAB or click on the buttons on the taskbar (if you can see them).

 **Activity**

Software Showdown

Part A

Find out what operating system is used in your classroom. List the advantages and disadvantages of this operating system (see Fig. 2.18).

Part B

1. Read three or four software reviews from current computer magazines or the Internet. Make a list of the criteria used by the reviewer.
2. Choose one review and list the characteristics of the software recommended by the reviewer.
3. Choose a software application on your computer at school. Try out the software. Write a review of the software you tried using the criteria from question 1 (maximum one page).

OPTIONAL

As a class, set up a database to record the reviews you completed. Select common fields that will make up your database, including: name of program, company, type of software, use, target age group, cost, how the programs work, good points, bad points, and rating. NOTE: You may want to do this activity in chapter 5 when you learn more about *databases* and how to create one.

Creating Application Software

We all rely on application software to use the computer. How does it all begin? Software begins with a design. A person called a *software designer* develops a plan for what the software will do, how it will accomplish its tasks, and what users will have to do in order to communicate with the software.

Programmers bring the software design to life by creating a detailed set of instructions in a *programming language*—a specialized language used by programmers.

Next, the program is compiled and translated into *machine language* (binary or digital code) that the computer can understand.

Source code is the basic building block of all software programs. It is the program instructions in their original form. Initially, a software programmer writes a program in a programming language, such as C or Java. This form of the program is called the source code. For the program to work, the source code is translated into machine language, the language that a computer can understand. This translation is done using a special software utility called a *compiler*. Source code is readable by humans. Machine language is not. Once in machine language, the code cannot be easily translated back into source code. When you purchase software, it comes in machine language. This language means that your computer can run the software, but you cannot read the program or change it. This fact prevents people from being able to easily duplicate software.

Once the programming is complete, the software is tested for "bugs" (mistakes in the programming that cause the software to malfunction).

After testing, corrections are made to the software by programmers to ensure that the software works properly.

Over time, software developers and manufacturers make improvements and corrections to software. When software is released, it is given a *version number*. This number allows users to determine which is the most recent software. For example, Corel Suite 8 means that this particular version of Corel Suite is the eighth release. A document created in an earlier version of software can almost always be recognized by later versions of that software, but not the other way around. For example, if you created a document in Word 2000 and tried to open it while using Word 95, your computer might not be able to read it.

Adam Mock Game Software Developer

Have you ever wondered how a video game is made? Adam Mock, a video game producer at a company named VR-1 Canada, is the person to ask.

After graduating from the University of Windsor with a degree in communications, Adam began his career in the video game industry as a tester for a company called Gray Matter. "Testing games is not as much fun as most people think," Adam explains. "You have to play the same game over and over, and try to find any bugs that may exist in the software. Every time you come across a bug, you have to try to replicate it so you can pinpoint the problem."

A tester then generates a report of all the bugs and how to reproduce them. The list is given to the development team to be corrected, and then is given back to the tester for more testing.

Adam concludes, "It can be very tedious but testing is a very important part of the development process!"

After approximately eight years in the industry, Adam progressed to his current position of producer.

"I really enjoy my job at VR-1," Adam explains. "I have the opportunity to work with a lot of extremely talented and creative people and it's very gratifying to see a finished product come together from start to finish."

Most video game companies act as manufacturers. They have a team of employees, who design, program, and complete artwork and animation for games. The games are purchased by publishers and Internet service providers (such as Sega, Nintendo, Microsoft, or America Online) that then distribute them to retailers and consumers under their own names.

A video game starts with a design that describes all the aspects of how the game will be played. The design includes descriptions of the characters, what movements they will be able to make, maps of the virtual playing environment, how points will be scored, and so on. Once a company decides to create a video game, the producer creates a project plan. The project plan identifies the team that will work on the game (including artists, animators, programmers, and testers), the schedule for completion, and key dates. As a producer, Adam is responsible for the project plan, and for ensuring that everyone on the project team finishes his or her work on time. He also works with the company that will be distributing the game to make sure the game meets its expectations.

"A video game takes a long time to complete," explains Adam. "Depending on how complicated the game is, it can take anywhere from a year to three years from the time the design is approved. One of the more difficult parts of my job is making sure we finish things on time and in working order. Sometimes, a single bug can cause delays, and that means I have to re-work the rest of the schedule."

Adam offers some advice for those who want to be a part of the video game world: "Companies are looking for dedicated and creative people who are capable of multiple aspects of the development process. So if you're a programmer you might want to take some design or animation courses. And if you're an animator or a designer, you may want to take a programming course."

1. How did Adam Mock get his start in the video game industry?

2. Describe the main responsibilities of a video game producer.

3. Based on the responsibilities of a producer, what do you think are the three most important skills or competencies for Adam to have?

4. What type of training or courses should you consider if you want to work in the video game industry?

Knowledge Check

1. What is software? Name the two types of software and give one example for each.
2. In your own words, describe what an operating system is.
3. How is operating system software different from application software?
4. Explain why a particular piece of software will not run on all computers.
5. Describe the process involved in creating a piece of software.
6. What is source code?

What Is a Desktop?

There is often confusion surrounding the term "desktop." Some people, for example, refer to any personal computer system as a desktop. The term *desktop* actually refers to the primary screen you see as soon as you start your computer (if your operating system has a graphic user interface), or when you've turned the computer on but have not opened any software applications.

An interface is a set of commands you use to communicate with a computer program. A *command-driven interface* is one in which you enter commands. A *menu-driven interface* is one in which you select command choices provided by the computer.

The *user interface* is one of the most important parts of any software application because it determines how easily you can make the program do what you want. A powerful software program with a poorly designed user interface has little value. Graphic user interfaces (GUIs) that use windows, icons, and pop-up menus are used by many operating systems.

The appearance of a desktop will vary depending on the operating system, the interface that has been installed by the user or the user's organization, and the creativity of the user. There are, however, several common items that appear on most desktops.

Fig. 2.19 Typical features of a Desktop

Windows

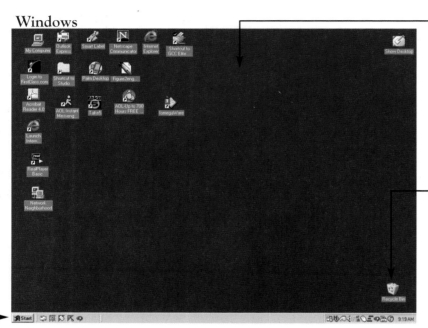

The *wallpaper* is the background of the screen. Some computers are set up with a solid colour, but a creative user can set a patterned background. Wallpaper simply makes the desktop more attractive to the user.

Icons are the little pictures on the screen that represent software or functions. You activate icons by clicking on them with a mouse. Examples of icons include the Trash or Recycle Bin, software applications icons, and My Computer.

Mac

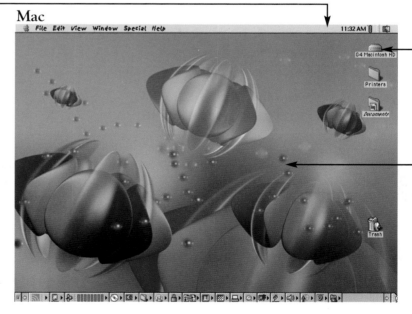

The *taskbar* is the line that appears across the bottom, top, or along the side of the screen. It may contain a start button, the time, and a series of other icons that represent features and software available on that particular computer. Along the screen top, Macs have a Menu Bar that functions similarly to the Task Bar. The Application Menu shows which programs are running.

There are two more features common to most desktops.

- A *window* is a rectangular area on the screen that displays the contents of a disk, *folder*, *directory*, or *document*. Windows appear when you open documents or click on icons.

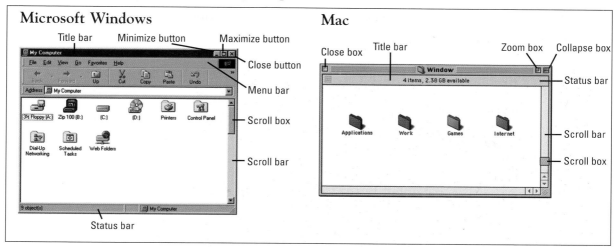

Fig. 2.20
The common elements of a window

- The *screensaver* is the pattern or animated screen that appears on the monitor when the computer is left idle. By varying the colours and patterns on the screen, screensavers give the monitor a break when an application is open but is not being used. The original purpose of a screensaver was to protect the monitor. In older monitors, if an application was left open but not used for a long period, the screen image might be "burned" onto the monitor's screen. By using a screensaver, the pattern changed every few seconds, making sure the monitor was not destroyed.

 **Activity**

My Desktop

Knowledge Check

1. What are the two meanings for the term "desktop"?
2. What is a "user interface"?
3. Describe one difference between a Windows desktop and a Mac desktop.
4. What is a window?
5. What is a screensaver?

Draw a picture or take a screen capture of your desktop at school. Label all the icons and features that appear on it, explaining what they represent or do. You may have to experiment by moving your cursor over each icon so the labels appear, clicking on the icons, opening software applications, and trying things out to complete this activity. Be adventurous!

Connecting Computers

How Do Computers Communicate with One Another?

A stand-alone computer is any computer that is not attached to a network. It cannot share its files or equipment with other computers, unless it is connected to the Internet. With the right hardware (modem), software, and an Internet connection, a stand-alone computer is capable of sharing both files and equipment (e.g., printer).

Putting two stand-alone computers side by side will not result in communication between them. In order for computers to share information, they have to be connected with a cable and specialized software, or set up to communicate with infrared signals. When two or more computers are connected so that they can communicate or share resources, they become a *network*. The advantages of networking computers include:

- **access to information**—By networking computers, information can be transmitted directly from one computer to another. Networking allows many people to share files and software in several ways.
  - All users on a network can access software from a central location.
  - All users on a network can access shared files.
  - A user can connect to a network from another location, then access all of his or her files and shared software.
- **access to equipment**—Computers on a network can share hardware. For example, a group of computers can be networked to one printer, so all users can print to that location. Networks also allow computers to share modems and *projection devices* (similar to overhead projectors that project images from a computer to a wall or screen).

Types of Networks

There are two types of networks.

- A *local area network (LAN)* consists of a group of networked computers that are all located in one building, such as a school or classroom. A LAN can be as simple as two computers networked in order to share a printer, or as complex as an entire office building with hundreds of computers networked together so that users can share software, hardware, peripherals, and information.
- A *wide area network (WAN)* is a group of networked computers located in a variety of locations in a large geographic area. For example, some school boards have all the computers from each school in an entire city networked together through a WAN. WANs can be set up to transmit information between computers by telephone line or satellite.

One Network or Many?

The Internet is like a single network because it allows millions of networks to communicate with one another. It is actually a collection of networks, and it is possible for computers on different networks to communicate because they all follow a single set of rules. The rules lay out the form messages must take and the procedures to follow to contact another computer.

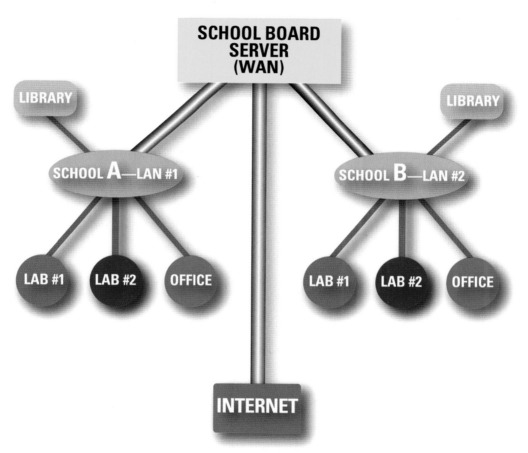

Fig. 2.21
Two LANs and one WAN

Whether you are setting up a LAN or a WAN, different ways of setting up the communication can be used. Networks are typically arranged in one of two ways.

- The *client/server network* arrangement designates one computer the "leader" of all the other computers in the network. The leader is called the *server*. The server is usually bigger, faster, and more powerful than the other computers, and can run the network operating system software. All the other computers in the network, called the *clients* or *nodes*, connect to the server through a *hub*. Like the hub of a wheel, the hub is a central device that connects several computers together or several networks together. It allows the computers to share the server's processing power and store information. Each client must have a *network interface card (NIC)* to be a part of the network. The NIC is an expansion card that allows the computer to act as a client or node in the network. Usually, any network that has more than a dozen computers uses this type of arrangement.

- The *peer-to-peer network* arrangement allows all the computers to be treated equally without a server. The disadvantage of this arrangement is that the network becomes very slow if more than ten computers are part of the network. Peer-to-peer networks also only allow for computers that use common operating systems and software to be networked.

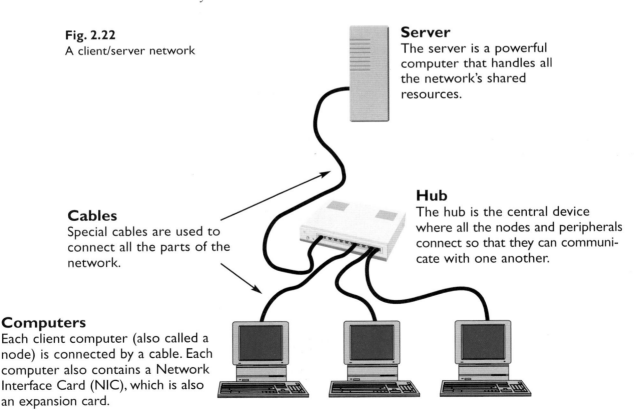

Fig. 2.22
A client/server network

Server
The server is a powerful computer that handles all the network's shared resources.

Hub
The hub is the central device where all the nodes and peripherals connect so that they can communicate with one another.

Cables
Special cables are used to connect all the parts of the network.

Computers
Each client computer (also called a node) is connected by a cable. Each computer also contains a Network Interface Card (NIC), which is also an expansion card.

All networks consist of two or more pieces of hardware connected together by cables. The **network topology** is the physical layout of the cables that connect the nodes and peripherals of the network. Three basic types of topologies exist.

- In the **bus topology** arrangement, all nodes and peripherals are attached to one main cable. One broken connection will bring down part of or the entire network.

- In the **star topology** arrangement, all nodes and peripherals are connected to one hub at the centre of the network with separate cables. One broken connection will not affect the rest of the network.

- In the **ring topology** arrangement, all nodes and peripherals are connected in a circular chain. One broken connection will bring down the entire network.

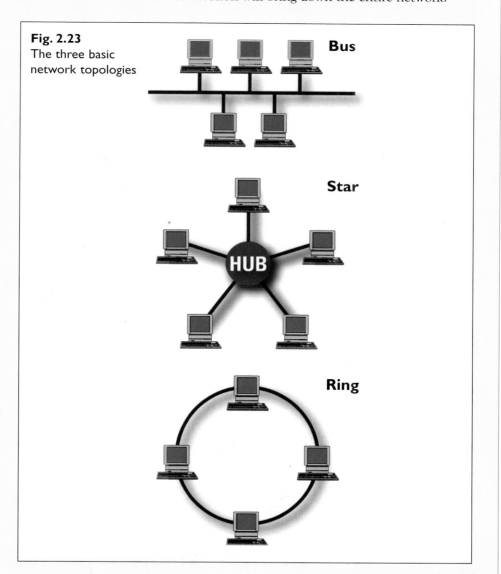

Fig. 2.23
The three basic network topologies

Bus

Star

HUB

Ring

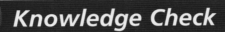

Knowledge Check

1. What are the advantages of networking computers together?
2. Identify one disadvantage of networking computers together.
3. Describe the difference between a LAN and a WAN.
4. Name and describe the two main network arrangements.
5. Name the three main network topologies.
6. Which network topology would you choose if you were responsible for creating your own network? Why?

Types of Computers

Many types of computers are on the market today. Different types of computers are sold for different uses. Figure 2.24 describes the most common types of computers.

Fig. 2.24 Types of Computers

Type of Computer	Description
Supercomputer	The most powerful computers available are known as ***supercomputers***. They are used mainly by large organizations (such as banks or research labs) to solve complex mathematical problems at rates exceeding 2.5 trillion operations per second. Supercomputers cost between $3 million and $30 million, and can be as large as an entire room.
Mainframe	Mainframes are the second most powerful computers. They are owned by large organizations (such as school boards, universities, or relatively large companies) that use them to support thousands of users at once or to solve complex mathematical problems at rates exceeding 125 million operations per second. They cost between $100 000 and several million dollars.
Personal Computer (PC)	PCs are relatively small and inexpensive computers, costing between $800 and $15 000. They are far less powerful than mainframes, but are able to run a variety of software applications. PCs are the type of computers people usually have in their homes.
Notebook Personal Computer	Notebook computers, sometimes called laptops, are portable computers that weigh less than 5 kg. They possess all the key components that PCs have, and perform most of the same functions.
Personal Digital Assistant (PDA)	PDAs are tiny computers that fit into the palm of the user's hand. These lightweight computers are portable, but have limited storage space. Two categories of PDAs exist: handheld and palm-sized. Handheld PDAs rely on keyboard input. Palm-sized PDAs can have an optional keyboard. Generally, users input information using a pen-like instrument called a stylus to write or draw on the computer screen.

Investigating Computers

In groups of two or three, research one PC and one PDA. You can visit your local computer store, use a flyer or catalogue from a local store, and use the Internet to get information. Prepare an oral presentation for your class that describes the following information for each computer. Gather pictures to show classmates as well.

- price
- size
- advantages
- disadvantages
- features (attachments, capabilities, type of software included or available)

Minimizing Security Threats

How Can You Maintain Privacy and Confidentiality?

Although computers help us keep in touch with the outside world and gather information, computers can also pose a threat by allowing the outside world into our homes and offices through our modems. They also provide a trail of information that is stored on a hard drive through e-mail, Internet browser histories (a list of Internet sites most recently visited), word-processed documents, and other files.

ZAK MEADOW

©2000 MARC NGUI

Now that's what I call a secure server.

Fig. 2.25
© Marc Ngui

You can ensure that information you want to remain private actually stays private, but it takes some care on your part. Some tips include:

- Choose passwords that are easy for you to remember, but difficult for others to guess. Use a combination of special characters (such as ~, $, #, @, and so on) along with words and numbers. For example, if your name is Jack, you could select a password such as ~Jack3.
- Do not share your password with anyone.
- Change your password often.
- Do not transmit confidential information over the Internet unless it is absolutely necessary. If you do have to transmit confidential information over the Internet, use data encryption. *Data encryption* is performed by special software that protects information transmitted between computers by scrambling the signals so that only the sender and intended receiver can interpret the signals.
- If you run a business or have a cable connection to the Internet, consider getting a firewall. A *firewall* is software that prevents other computer users or hackers from gaining access to the information on your computer while you are online. (*Hackers* are people who gain unauthorized access to computer systems usually for the purpose of stealing or corrupting information.)

- Do not save confidential files on shared computers unless you are prepared for others who use that computer to see the information.
- When you have visitors, turn off your computer monitor to discourage casual snooping. Add a password to your screensaver.
- Be careful about putting your computer too close to a window or open door to ensure confidential information is not seen by passers-by and to discourage theft.
- When you buy new equipment, do not toss the packaging by the curb with other garbage. Discarded packaging advertises to potential thieves what you have available.

WHAT DO YOU THINK?

In the fall of 2000, hackers successfully accessed some of Microsoft Corporation's program source code. However, a Microsoft spokesman stated that the hackers did not change the key source codes—a move that could have created chaos in the company's programs.

In small groups, discuss and make a list of the types of negative effects or damage that could happen to a company if hackers were successful in accessing a company's source codes and changing them.

Case Study

Biometric Security

Have you ever imagined having a computer that recognizes you by your fingerprint? This type of technology is already a reality. Companies that specialize in biometrics have developed products such as personal digital assistants (PDAs) that recognize users by their fingerprint, and telephone banking services that recognize customers by their voices.

A biometric is a measurable physical characteristic or personal trait that can be measured through automated means and used to recognize a person's identity. **Biometric authentication** (also called **biometric identification**) measures the unique biological characteristics of an individual. One of the most common biometrics used today is fingerprint information. Biometrics also include facial and voice recognition. A biometric can be used to protect secret data, such as a password, providing both security and convenience.

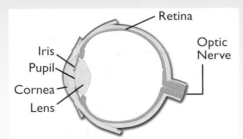

Fig. 2.26
The retina is the thin nerve on the back of the eye that senses light and transmits impulses through the optic nerve to the brain. Biometric identification of the retina uses blood vessels located along the outermost layer of the retina's four cell layers.

Retina identification is the most accurate of all biometric identification types, and also the most complicated. It works with retina scan devices that read through the pupil. The user must keep the eye within 1.25 cm of the capture device, and hold still while a retina scan reader determines patterns in the blood vessels. These patterns are matched to a person's identity.

The iris, the coloured ring around the pupil of the eye, can also be used for biometric identification.

Most biometric identification systems in development today keep biometric information secure on the user's computer. For example, suppose you wanted to make a bank transaction over the Internet using your PDA with biometric identification. You would place your finger on a special biometric identification template (a small scanning device) on your PDA. The template would read your fingerprint as a series of lines with measurements. The PDA would then match the fingerprint to a password stored in the PDA's memory. Only then would the password be sent to your bank over the Internet, allowing you to make your transaction. Encryption is used to protect the transaction. This process protects your fingerprint from being sent over the Internet, and helps to protect privacy. This biometric method also can prevent others from gaining access to confidential information on a PC or PDA. With this type of system, others cannot break into a computer because they cannot mimic or forge a fingerprint or retina. The chances of a hacker obtaining your password are greatly decreased, since the password can only be triggered on the user's computer using biometric identification. However, a very slim chance would exist that a hacker could obtain the password from the receiver's computer system.

At the present time, there are some disadvantages to this technology. First, the software and biometric devices are currently too expensive for most people to purchase. Second, some groups of people cannot use this type of technology. As people grow older, their fingerprints fade and are difficult to read. Third, physical injuries that cause changes to hands, faces, or eyes can make users unrecognizable. For example, if a user had an accident that severely cut his or her thumb, the fingerprint would no longer be recognizable, and the person could not access the technology.

1. What is biometric authentication? How does it work?

2. What is the main advantage to this type of technology? Why?

3. What are some disadvantages to this type of technology?

4. Aside from the manufacturers of biometric technology, what other types of businesses could benefit from the technology? Why?

5. What is the most accurate type of biometric identification? Explain how it works.

What Are Viruses?

Something is wrong with your computer—something awful. Strange letters and symbols are appearing in your word processing document. You've received unusual e-mails. You just noticed that half of your files seem to be missing. It looks like you have a virus.

Computer viruses are programs that insert themselves into program files and boot sectors (the *boot sector* is the area on each disk containing the program that loads the operating system, an essential process in starting your computer). Most viruses are activated when you run an infected program or open an infected file. They immediately start copying themselves by looking for new files and boot sectors to infect. Like real germs, the most successful computer viruses hide, reproduce, and wait for the opportunity to spread to another victim.

Like illnesses, viruses vary in how "sick" they make your computer. Some are quite harmless, simply causing odd messages to appear on your screen. Others are very destructive, and can destroy your hard drive or erase all your files.

Fig. 2.27

Here are the most common ways that viruses can get into your system.

- **disks and CD-ROMs**—Viruses can spread when you leave an infected disk in the drive and restart your computer.
- **Internet and e-mail**—Files found on the Web, *bulletin-board systems* (electronic message centres that serve specific interest groups and can be accessed by modem or through the Internet), and e-mail attachments can be infected and spread viruses when opened.
- **LANs**—Unless your entire LAN is protected by antivirus software, viruses can spread from infected files located on file servers and attached to e-mail.
- **people**—Mischievous people can save viruses onto an unsuspecting user's computer—either as a prank, or to inconvenience the user.

How Can You Protect Your Computer Against Viruses?

The best way to protect your computer is to make sure viruses cannot get to your computer in the first place. Here are some tips.

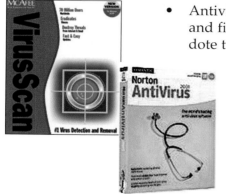

Fig. 2.28
Samples of antivirus software

- Antivirus software is available that will scan your hard drive and files on disk to locate viruses. This software acts as an antidote to the "illness" caused by the virus. It locates and destroys viruses it is able to recognize. Companies that sell this type of software have updates available on their Web sites. If you do not wish to buy and install this software onto your computer, you can download virus services from the Internet, usually for a fee. New viruses are detected daily, and these companies create virtual vaccines to destroy viruses and post the vaccines on their Internet sites immediately. Always keep your antivirus software up-to-date. Outdated antivirus software leaves you open to attack from new viruses. Most important, run your antivirus software regularly.

- Scan all disks and CD-ROMs you receive with antivirus software before using them.

Fig. 2.29 Write-protect tab

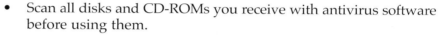

- Set the write-protect tab (the tiny, plastic sliding tab at the bottom end of the disk) by pushing it over on all disks when you are not saving to them. Setting the write-protect tab ensures that no additional information (such as a virus) can be added to the disk. Viruses that spread by infecting the boot sector of a disk are the most common type of virus, and some even periodically check the drive bay for an easy victim.

- Do not open e-mail attachments or run software or files directly from the Internet without downloading and scanning them first to determine whether they are infected (some antivirus software will check for viruses automatically). Although large companies usually check downloadable files for viruses, the World Wide Web can be dangerous.

- Do not enable macros in files whose source is suspicious.

- Back up your files onto disks or CD-ROMs regularly. Regular backups are important in case a virus attack destroys the files on your hard drive.

- Lock up your computer when you are not using it so it can only be accessed by a password. You may practise safe computing, but what about others who have access to your computer?

Activity

Investigating Viruses

Using the Internet or a recent computing magazine, identify three recent viruses. Describe how each of the viruses is transmitted, the symptoms created by each virus, and the damage, including costs, each virus can do to an infected computer. Compile your information into a chart or table with the headings "Method of Transmission," "Viruses," "Symptoms," and "Damage."

Up-to-date information on recent viruses is available. Visit McAfee, a leading antivirus software producer, and ZDNet, an e-zine (electronic magazine) with articles about technology-related issues, on the *InsighTs* Student Page on <www.irwinpublishing.com/students>.

Knowledge Check

1. In what way do computers pose a threat to a user's security?
2. What can you do to make your password more secure?
3. What is data encryption? Why is it important?
4. What is a firewall? Why is it important?
5. What is a virus?
6. What are the most common ways that a virus is transmitted?
7. Name and describe three strategies you can use to protect yourself against viruses.

Chapter Summary

Understanding Information

1. What is input? Give an example.

2. What is output? Give an example.

3. What is a CPU? What is another name for a CPU?

4. Draw a diagram that illustrates the hardware inside a computer. Label all parts.

5. What are peripheral devices? Give three examples.

6. What is a network interface card? What is its purpose?

7. Name and briefly describe the five types of computers identified in this chapter.

8. Describe five things you can do to maintain privacy and confidentiality when working on a computer.

9. What can you do to make a password as secure as possible?

10. What is biometrics?

11. Identify six things you can do to avoid a virus.

Analyzing

12. How are peripheral devices used for input or output? Use examples in your explanation.

13. Describe the difference between operating systems and application software.

14. Explain the function of an operating system. You may wish to create a diagram.

15. What are the similarities and differences between LANs and WANs?

16. Compare the three network topologies. Draw a diagram of each.

17. Compare your desktop at school to the ones pictured in Fig. 2.19. What are the similarities? What are the differences?

18. What is the benefit of zipping a large file?

19. Of the five types of computers described in Fig. 2.24, which type would you like to own? Why?

20. How are viruses spread?

21. Analyze what damage viruses can do to your computer.

22. How does encryption work?

Applying

23. Think of a task a person might do using a computer. Use that task to illustrate a computer's input, storage, processing, and output functions.

24. Imagine you have the same brand of word processing software at home and at school, but at home you have a newer version. How will the difference in versions affect your ability to bring electronic files home to complete your homework?

How will the difference affect your ability to bring files from home to school?

25. Weigh the advantages and disadvantages of networks. What advice would you give to a small business that is thinking of networking its computers?

26. Compare the storage options described in this chapter. Which storage devices would be most appropriate for:

   • a very large graphic file (50 MB) created by an advertising agency for a movie poster

   • your geography assignment (40 KB)

   • six songs recorded digitally (40 MB)

   • ideas for a history project that you will be working on with the other five members of your work group (18 KB)

27. In your opinion, should all companies invest in a firewall? Why or why not?

Communicating

28. In your own words, describe how a CPU works.

29. Identify what you think is the most important peripheral device for you to have. Explain why you feel this way.

30. If you were given the opportunity to create software, what would you design? Why?

31. If you were to work on a software development team, which job would you want to have? Why? Describe some of the tasks you would have to perform to do that job. What do you think are the most important competencies to have for that job?

32. Describe the type of software application you think will be most useful to you while you are a student. Explain your choice.

33. Create diagrams to illustrate client/server networks and peer-to-peer networks.

34. Explain why you would or would not feel secure and safe transferring information over the Internet.

35. Explain how biometrics affects security.

36. In small groups, discuss why you think people create and spread viruses.

Assessing Your Competencies

37. Using the software competency checklists provided by your teacher, check off the competencies that you have mastered during the course of this chapter. Note the competencies that require more attention and review.

38. Interview a classmate to determine the competencies he or she has acquired during this chapter. Also share some of the new skills you have acquired.

CHAPTER THREE:

BEFORE YOU CAN CREATE DOCUMENTS

Before you begin keying a document, there are some important things you should know and be able to do. By the end of this chapter, you will know the proper way to key quickly and accurately, understand the importance of ergonomics, and know the features and functions common to most software programs used in business. You will also learn how to name your documents, use folders, organize files, and maintain your disks, and will learn what features and functions are common to most word processing programs. You will also learn about editing and proofreading keyed documents.

Topics

➤ Getting Organized
➤ Ergonomics
➤ Office Productivity Software
➤ Managing Your Files
➤ Word Processing Software

This chapter explores these questions:

- How do people key so quickly and accurately?
- What is ergonomics?
- What can we do to improve our working environment?
- Which programs do what?
- What features are common to most office productivity programs?
- What functions are common to most office applications software?
- How do I manage my files?
- What features are common to most word processing software?

In this chapter you have the opportunity to

- practise proper keying technique
- debate the future of using your hands to do the keying
- investigate how ergonomics affects your health
- assess an area of your school to see if it is ergonomically sound
- investigate career opportunities using your software skills
- explore the common features of office productivity programs
- practise using the common functions in a word processor
- evaluate the use of the mouse versus the keyboard to access functions in programs
- develop strategies for naming files you create
- manage your files—create, move, rename, delete
- defragment a disk drive
- create bulleted and numbered lists
- proofread and key edited text

Getting Organized

Before we investigate productivity software programs and when to use them, we need to look at proper data entry techniques and ergonomics.

How Do People Key So Quickly and Accurately?

Being able to key accurately and quickly without looking at the keys is an important skill that will serve you well in the world of information technology, improving your personal productivity.

Keying Without Looking at the Keys

The *QWERTY keyboard* is the most common keyboard. It has four rows of alpha/numeric keys. The middle row of alpha keys is the *home row*. Your fingers should always hover over the following keys in the home row, ready to move to other keys when needed:

- Under the left hand—the A, S, D, and F keys
- Under the right hand—the J, K, L, and ; keys

Fig. 3.1
The home row on the QWERTY keyboard

InsighTs: Succeeding in the Information Age

When keying, your fingers should be curled like the legs of a spider (Fig. 3.2). This position gives you the maximum in reach and flexibility, allowing you to key quickly and accurately. Your arms should hang loosely at your sides, and, to prevent carpal tunnel syndrome, your wrists should not be bent, either up or down.

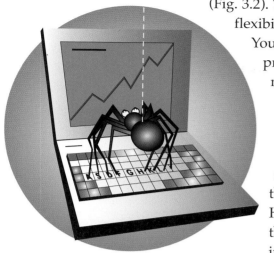

Fig. 3.2
Curl my fingers how?

Each finger has a job to do. Examine Fig. 3.3. Each of the keys on the keyboard is colour coded according to the finger that should be used to strike that key. Learning to key properly is a skill that requires hours of practice and dedication. However, by practising this skill, and adhering to the colour coding shown, your keying will improve in both speed and accuracy, and your ability to make the most of your computer programs will be greatly enhanced.

Activity

Blind Keying

In order to improve your keying ability and technique try this fun activity.

Fig. 3.3
Using the correct fingers for the different keys improves your speed and accuracy.

Using a file folder or piece of paper, cover your hands so that the keys and your fingers are not visible. Close your eyes and, if possible, turn off your monitor—no peeking allowed! Have a partner dictate to you a series of words or sentences, one letter at a time. Your partner needs to tell you when to press the Shift, space bar, Enter key, etc.

Turn your monitor back on and check your work for accuracy. Switch with your partner to see how he or she does.

Practise this way on a regular basis to improve your keying memory. You will become more productive when you do not rely on your eyes to tell you where the keys are.

To Key or Not to Key? Speech Recognition Software

For a number of years, software manufacturers have been striving to perfect *speech recognition software*. Essentially, the software works with your existing word processing program, a sound card, and a microphone to convert your speech into text on the screen. The accuracy of the programs in recognizing words has improved from 90% a few years ago to over 95%. The programs still do not recognize one in twenty words.

As the programs improve, they are gaining in popularity, particularly in the medical and legal fields where specialized language is used on a daily basis. They also help to combat the stresses of repetitive strain injuries and act as an aid to people with disabilities.

So why learn to key? Speech recognition software programs are meant to complement data entry skills, not replace them. It is necessary to "train" the programs to recognize your voice and pronunciation of words. On average, programs today require 20 to 30 minutes of dictation just to get them up and running. Users must learn to use the *tutorials* and *quick-reference cards* in order to become proficient at dictation and navigating through the programs.

1. Create a chart listing the pros and cons of using speech recognition software.

2. In small groups, discuss the "training" of speech recognition programs and the challenges you would anticipate in ensuring accuracy in dictation. Report your group's thoughts to the class.

3. Do you think speech recognition programs may one day replace the need to learn to key quickly and accurately? Why or why not? Write an opinion paragraph outlining your thoughts.

 *Activity*

Investigating Speech Recognition Programs

Check out the speech recognition programs of Dragon Systems, IBM, Lernout & Hauspie Speech Products N.V. Inc., and Philips Speech Processing on the *InsighTs* Student Page on <www.irwinpublishing.com/students>.

Compare the products of each company and present your findings in a chart using the headings "Training Time and Method," "Dictation," and "Compatible Applications."

InsighTs: Succeeding in the Information Age

Fig. 3.4
"Blind users can access a computer using special software that provides either synthetic speech output or large print on the screen. Here a user is reinforcing her keying skills with a talking keying tutor program."

American Printing House for the Blind, Inc., Louisville, Kentucky

Knowledge Check

1. What are the keys that make up the home row? Why should your fingers always be positioned over these keys?
2. Describe how you should position your hands and arms while keying.
3. What are speech recognition programs and how do they work? Do they replace keying? Why or why not?

Ergonomics

What Is Ergonomics?

Have you ever spent hours working at a desk or computer, only to find that by the time you are finished working, your neck hurts? You probably figured out on your own that your sore neck is a result of poor seating or having your work at the wrong height, causing your back to be hunched over or stretched. Problems like these can be resolved by applying the principles of ergonomics. *Ergonomics* is the study of workers' interactions with their working environment. Ergonomic specialists study the ways in which work surroundings can be improved to keep workers comfortable and injury-free.

On average, repetitive strain injuries (RSIs) cost the Canadian economy $800 000 000 per year in lost wages, productivity, and health care costs.

Research has shown that certain ergonomic aspects of work environments (temperature, lighting, air, furniture, and equipment) influence workers' productivity, health, and days off work. When work environments are designed with ergonomics in mind, workers tend to be happier and healthier. When workplaces are not designed ergonomically, they can cause a worker injuries over time.

The most common category of ergonomic-related injuries is *repetitive strain injuries (RSIs)*, also known as *musculo-skeletal injuries (MSIs)*. MSI occurs when a person performs the same task over and over, damaging nerves, muscles, tendons, or other body tissues. The most common MSI in North America is *carpal tunnel syndrome* (CTS). Other ergonomic-related illnesses include eyestrain, headaches, fatigue (tiredness), allergies, backaches, and poor circulation.

SITE SEEING

For more information about ergonomics, check out the Web sites for The Canadian Standards Association, an organization that develops workplace standards and certifies organizations, and The Center for Office Technology, an association of employers and manufacturers dedicated to improving the work environment. Both of these sites can be found on the *InsighTs* Student Page on <www.irwinpublishing.com/students>.

CAREER PROFILE

Noreen Hayashi Ergonomics Specialist

Ergonomics is one of Noreen Hayashi's responsibilities in her work at one of the province of Ontario's human resources branches. She assesses work environments and recommends solutions to make them safer for the people who work there. She says the role of an ergonomist will become more important in the next decade as Canada's workforce ages.

"A large proportion of Canada's workforce (known as baby boomers) is over forty years old," she explains. "As people get older, their bodies become less able to adapt to poorly designed work environments, including equipment and furniture that do not match their jobs and body dimensions."

As a result, employers will have to come up with ergonomic solutions and good workplace design to ensure that these people are able to continue working, are comfortable, and are not injured. It costs employers more money when employees are injured than it does to improve the workplace to prevent injuries.

But it is not only older people who are at risk!

"I am shocked by how many children—as young as seven or eight years old—suffer from musculo-skeletal injuries, including carpal tunnel syndrome! They're using computers, but the equipment and chairs are not the right size for them or cannot be adjusted to their small bodies. Some new diagnoses such as 'Nintendo thumb' can arise from overusing video game hardware. Eventually, many children are injured."

When you enter the workforce, remember to thank people like Noreen for paving the way to a safer and healthier workplace for you.

• •

1. What competencies do you believe would be most important for an ergonomist to have? Why?

2. Why is it beneficial to employees to have an ergonomist on staff?

3. Why do you think a large organization would want to employ an ergonomist?

What Can We Do to Improve Our Working Environment?

The following are some steps we can take to minimize the possibility of injury when working in a computer environment.

Fig. 3.5
How not to sit if you want to avoid ergonomic-related health problems.

Fig. 3.6
This position is excellent for helping to avoid repetitive strain injuries.

Work Environment

- **temperature**—Temperature should be kept between 15°C and 22°C.

- **air circulation**—Plenty of air circulation (but not drafts from open windows) is important. Circulating air minimizes the amount of dust and bacteria in the air, keeping workers healthier.

- **cleanliness**—It is important that the work environment be cleaned regularly and thoroughly. Dust, mould, and other particles in the air can cause allergies and respiratory problems.

- **lighting and colour**—Lighting should be kept stable. Lights should not flicker, as flickering causes eyestrain. The colour of workrooms should be neutral and soft. Pure white, very dark, or shiny surfaces can cause fatigue.

Furniture

- **chairs**—Chairs should have five legs for stability. Seats should be adjustable and be between 37.5 cm and 52.5 cm from the floor. A firm back should allow the elbows to be bent at a 90° angle when using the keyboard. The seat should be padded enough to allow circulation, but firm enough to maintain good posture.

- **work surfaces**—Tables and desks should provide enough space for people to work without bumping into one another. Enough legroom should be available to allow people to change their seating position to avoid muscle and circulation problems in the legs. The edges of tables and desks should be smooth and rounded to avoid injury.

- **colouring**—Medium- and light-coloured surfaces help ease eyestrain when reading. Work surfaces should have a matte (not shiny) finish to reduce glare.

Computer Hardware

Recent research suggests that computer users should change position often. Slouching or leaning back periodically can be helpful in relieving stress, as long as you tilt the keyboard to maintain a neutral arm and wrist position. If possible, users should vary their tasks during the day to break up repetitive motions and routines, and take small 60-second breaks every 30 minutes.

Learning Link

- **monitors**—Monitors should have flat, anti-glare screens to reduce eyestrain. They should be positioned so that the top of the screen is at eye level, and at a distance of 45 cm to 60 cm from the face to reduce stress on the eyes and neck. Because monitors attract dust and repel it towards the user's face, they should be frequently cleaned to avoid allergies. When you are using the computer for an extended period of time, remember to rest your eyes by occasionally looking away from the screen.

- **keyboard**—The keyboard should be placed at elbow height. As well, it should be placed at an angle that causes the fingers to land on the home row (ASDF JKL;) and at a 90° elbow angle in order to prevent strain on the wrists. Carpal tunnel syndrome

can occur when keyboards are not adjusted properly. Several types of keyboards are available to meet different ergonomic needs. The standard keyboard is rectangle-shaped, with the letters QWERTY along the top row of letters. The angle of most QWERTY keyboards can be adjusted. Miniature and compact keyboards require less effort and reach. These kinds of keyboards are particularly useful for people with a muscular weakness. Keyboards with built-in pointing devices can help people whose reach is limited. Ergonomic keyboards are also available. They have a natural, curved shape and usually have built-in wrist rests. Many ergonomic keyboards allow the user to adjust the angle of the keys.

Knowledge Check

1. In your own words, what is "ergonomics"?
2. Why would an employer be interested in ergonomics?
3. What are four steps that can be taken to ensure that people working in an office will be safe and comfortable?
4. What is the most common ergonomic-related injury? What are the symptoms?

Activity

You Are an Ergonomics Engineer

Part A

1. Describe how office furniture and hardware can be ergonomically correct.

2. Obtain a copy of an office supply catalogue, or visit the Web site of a local office supply retailer.

3. Cut out or print copies of several ergonomic items. Be sure to label the items and identify the cost of each.

4. Create a collage on a large piece of paper or cardboard showcasing the ergonomic items you found. For each item, draw an arrow to the appropriate item in the collage and provide a brief explanation to identify what makes the item ergonomic. Mark the price of each item on the display.

ZAK MEADOW

I think we made it a little too comfortable.

Fig. 3.7
© Marc Ngui

Part B

Working in a small group, create a list of all the things that make a work environment ergonomically correct. Using that list, assess an area of your school (such as your computer lab, resource centre, or office) and comment on how well that area meets the ergonomic criteria on your list. Once you have completed your assessment, prepare a report for the class describing what you found.

Part C

Evaluate someone's work area from an ergonomic point of view. Prepare a report outlining any problems and suggesting possible low-cost solutions to the problems. Use the information you collected in Part A to assist you.

CAREER PROFILE

Shirley King Senior Secretary

Shirley King is a magician on the job. At least that is how the staff at Barrie Central Collegiate in Barrie, Ontario, sees her. As senior secretary, Shirley is involved in virtually every aspect of school life, from answering calls from parents/caregivers to working with teachers and support personnel to keep the school running efficiently. She supervises the office team, making sure all deadlines are met. She is an incredible resource person for everyone—teachers, custodians, community groups, administration, students, parents/caregivers, and school board personnel.

On top of all that, Shirley is responsible for preparing the principal's correspondence, reports for submission to the board, newsletters to parents/caregivers, and memos outlining all the procedures for staff to follow for examinations and report cards. As well, correspondence on a variety of subjects crosses Shirley's desk every day. She sorts and redirects the correspondence to the appropriate person in the school for him or her to handle.

Shirley uses office productivity software extensively in her job, including Word, Excel, and Outlook (e-mail). She downloads information from the student database, converts it, and then merges the data into diplomas, mailing labels, and yes, report cards. She also uses a special financial software package to manage school fundraising accounts. As well, she finds herself troubleshooting all kinds of hardware and software problems during the day.

Shirley uses a variety of other electronic communication devices in her daily routine, including the telephone, fax machine, voice mail, e-mail, and automated phone programs (see chapter 7) to let parents/caregivers know when students are not in class.

Secretaries draw from so many different skill sets—competencies—that it is hard to keep track. Shirley has continually upgraded her skills over her career, taking advantage of every course offered to her. "My work requires more skill, education, and knowledge than when I entered the workforce, but it is much more rewarding. I am able to do so much more and I have a sense of accomplishment with the work that I am able to produce."

Shirley has seen technology take its toll, however. "Everything is done by computer, but not without a price. We are expected to do more with less staff and the stress is quite evident."

● ●

1. List five of the many tasks that Shirley has to perform in her daily job as Senior Secretary at Barrie Central Collegiate. From your own experience in your school, list five more duties or tasks you have seen the Office staff perform.

For information about jobs in the secretarial/office administration field, see Secretaries, Recorders and Transcriptionists in Job Futures at Human Resources Development Canada on the *InsighTs* Student Page on <www.irwinpublishing.com/students>. Select a job at the site. What courses could you take to help prepare you for this job?

2. How has the job changed in the years Shirley has been in this and similar jobs? What implications do these kinds of changes have for students just learning about Information Technology?

3. What can you do to continue to upgrade your skills in the years ahead?

Office Productivity Software

Which Programs Do What?

People who use software every day must choose between a variety of programs to complete the tasks assigned to them.

In most businesses today you will find people using common software programs. Each of these applications has a specific purpose. You will have the chance to explore them further in upcoming chapters.

- *Word processing* programs allow users to format text and insert graphics and objects created in other programs (e.g., drawings or charts) to create professionally formatted documents. Many programs allow the integration of spreadsheets and databases with word processors. Later in this chapter, you will explore features and functions common to most word processing software.

- *Spreadsheet* programs allow users to work with numeric information to perform calculations (e.g., sums, averages, or customized formulas) and to create graphic representations of data.

- *Database* programs are used to keep track of information about customers, products, and employees, to name only a few examples.
- *Desktop publishing* programs are somewhat similar to some word processing programs. However, desktop publishing programs allow users to combine and manipulate text and graphics more easily to create such items as concert programs, flyers, and brochures.
- *Electronic presentation* programs allow users to present information using all elements of multimedia, that is, text, graphics, video, audio, and Internet hyperlinks.

Computer users can purchase these software programs individually or bundled together in integrated software packages. An *integrated software package* is a software program that combines some or all the programs listed above. The programs included are fully integrated, allowing users to easily insert files or objects from one program into another. Three examples of integrated software are the Microsoft Office Suite, the Corel WordPerfect Suite, and AppleWorks. These software packages contain a word processor, spreadsheet, and presentation program. Some versions also include a database.

What Features Are Common to Most Office Productivity Programs?

Integrated software package programs have similar features.

- If you are in a Windows operating environment, the *taskbar* at the bottom or along the side of the screen indicates which programs are currently open and running. The item on the taskbar that is highlighted is the one you are currently using. The Mac O/S does not have a taskbar. The Application menu shows which programs are running. Users can switch from one program to another using this menu, located in the upper right-hand corner of the screen.
- The *title bar* at the very top of the active window displays the name of the program you are working in and the name of the file you have open on the screen.
- In Windows, the *menu bar* is immediately below the title bar. On a Mac computer, the menu bar always remains at the top of the screen. Each item on the menu bar—for example, File, Edit, and View—has a pull-down *menu*. Each menu is activated when the user clicks on the menu item. This action usually results in the display of a *dialog box* that contains a number of functions

for the user to choose from to perform various tasks. Menu items with ellipses (...) after them indicate that further choices will be provided via dialog boxes.

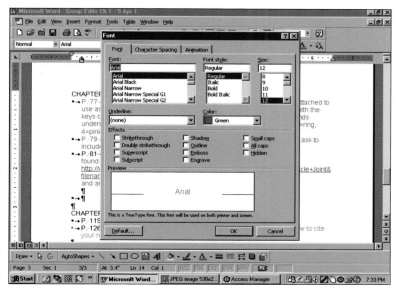

Fig. 3.8
A dialog box appears on the screen when you access different menus. Here we see the Format, Font dialog box.

- The *menu bar* on a Mac contains dialog boxes with functions for various program tasks.
- The *toolbars* contain a series of icons that activate the most frequently used features of software programs—for example New, Open, Save, and Print. In some programs, such as WordPerfect, one of the toolbars, called a *property bar*, changes depending on the tasks you are currently performing. For example, if you are creating a table, the table options and icons appear in the property bar. The icons that appear on the toolbars when you first install the program are the *default settings*, or preprogrammed settings, chosen because they are the most frequently accessed functions. You can add or delete icons from the toolbars by accessing the Tools menu and selecting Customize.

What Functions Are Common to Most Office Applications Software?

There are also a variety of *functions* that are common to the software programs listed on pages 83-84.

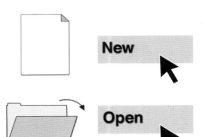

- **new**—Clicking the New icon opens a new document file on your screen, allowing you to begin entering a new file. Any previously opened documents remain open for editing and can be accessed through the Windows menu.

- **open**—Clicking the Open icon allows you to open a previously saved file or program from a disk (floppy, hard, or CD), or an accessible networked drive.

- **close**—The Close icon permits you to close the file, saving changes if required.

- **save**—The Save icon allows you to save the file over the previous version of that file, thus updating the file with any changes made to that point. You can also save the file under another name by accessing the Save As command in one of the pull-down menus. The Save As function allows you to keep the first version of the file and the updated version using two separate names.

- **print**—Clicking the Print icon activates the print command. **But beware!** In some programs, clicking the Print icon will print the entire file without giving you a chance to specify which pages you want to print. If you only want to print selected pages of a document, you need to select the Print function in the File pull-down menu and indicate which pages you want to print.

- **copy**—If you want to copy text, a picture, or other object from one part of a document to another, or from one document to another, use the Copy icon. In Windows you must first *highlight* the text or item(s) you want to copy by holding down the left mouse button and dragging the mouse to the end of the selection you want to copy. (The highlighted section will usually appear with a black background and white lettering on your screen.) Alternatively, you can press the F8 function or Shift key and press the right arrow key (→) until the selection is highlighted on the screen. Once you have highlighted the material you want to copy, click the Copy icon on the toolbar or right-click to access a pop-up menu.

  In Mac O/S, you may access a pop-up menu by pressing the Ctrl key and clicking the mouse button—there is no right mouse button on a standard Mac mouse.

  Clicking the Copy icon places a copy of the item on the computer *clipboard*—a *virtual* clipboard that is in the computer's memory—for use at a later time. The original item remains in the document you copied the material from and is still visible on your screen. Once the item is on the clipboard, you can paste it countless times until another item takes its place on the clipboard.

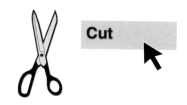

- **cut**—The Cut icon is very handy for deleting large blocks of text, pictures, or other objects. To cut something permanently, highlight what you want to delete and then press the delete button. To cut something from a document, first highlight the item to be cut, then click the Cut icon. This action places the item on the clipboard, but the item is gone from the document and is no longer visible on the screen. You can then either forget about the material you have cut or you can paste it to another location in the current document or another document.

- **paste**—The Paste icon is used in conjunction with the Copy and Cut icons. Click the mouse at the place in the document where you want the item on the clipboard to be inserted. Then click on the Paste icon. You can repeat this action as many times as you want until the item is replaced on the clipboard.

- **undo/redo**—These icons are a very handy feature in most office packages today. By clicking the Undo icon, you can reverse your most recent action. For example, you could get text back that you accidentally erased. **But beware**. For the Undo function to work in some programs, you have to click on the Undo icon immediately after the action you want to reverse. If you do anything after the action you want to undo before you click the Undo icon, the Undo icon will undo everything you have done, not just the one action. But then you can just click on Undo again as many times as necessary to get back to where you were before you performed the unwanted action. If you later decide you did not want to undo an action, click Redo. In that same example, you might choose to get rid of the text after all. These two icons have helped many a computer user out of what could be a costly error in terms of time and money!

 *Activity*

Using the Functions

Open your word processing program and try each of the functions listed on pages 86-87. If the icons do not appear on your screen, ask your teacher if you can customize the toolbars to add these common features. Key a paragraph on the screen so you can try the Cut, Copy, and Paste functions. See what happens when you undo a command and then redo it.

We take the clicking of icons for granted today. Apple Computers introduced the first computer mouse in 1983. Before the mouse, computer users used **function keys** to activate commands. Software manufacturers provided plastic templates to lay on top of the keyboard to help users remember what the function keys did. Some computer users still prefer to use keyboard commands to activate various functions. For example, changing the font appearance "on the fly" is easy by pressing Ctrl/B to turn on **bold** or Ctrl/I for *italics*. To select (Ctrl/A for a whole document; Shift and arrow key for part of a document) and copy text (Ctrl/C, Ctrl/V), your fingers need never leave the keyboard. Even though the mouse is a standard feature of computer systems today, some users argue that it slows them down, as they have to stop keying to click.

1. Survey your class to determine how many people use keyboard commands versus the mouse for common tasks like Copy, Paste, and font changes.

2. Make a list of common tasks and the keyboard shortcut for each.

3. Investigate your word processing software program menus to find the keyboard commands. Try the functions and see what you think. Do you think you would be a more efficient and productive computer user if you memorized the function commands and used them for certain tasks? Why or why not?

Knowledge Check

1. Outline the function and purpose of each of the following: title bar, menu bar, toolbar, and taskbar, or application menu in Mac O/S.

2. How do you access the functions on the menu bar?

3. How do you start a new document? What happens to the document you are working on if you start a new one?

4. What are default settings in a program?

5. How can you change the icons that appear on a toolbar?

6. What is the difference between Save and Save As?

7. Describe how you use the Cut, Copy, and Paste functions (either from the menu bar and the toolbar or using shortcut commands).

8. What functions do the Undo and Redo icons perform?

There are countless other features in software packages, but many of them are unique to the type of application you are using. Before we consider the other features and functions common to most word processing programs, we will examine how to manage the files you will be working on.

Managing Your Files

How Do I Manage My Files?

Learning Link

Computer users are often frustrated when they cannot easily share their word processing files with other users. A special file format known as **Rich Text Format** can solve this problem. Most word processing programs allow users to save in this format, which uses the extension ".rtf." When saved in this way, the file can be easily shared with other word processing programs in both Windows and Mac environments.

Types of Files

You will generally work with two main types of files.

- *Program files* are software applications. Most software application program files must be installed on the hard drive before they can be used. Some can be run directly from a disk or compact disc. Examples of program files include video games, word processors, and antivirus software.

- *Data files* or *documents* are files that can be opened or created in an application program. Examples of data files include a report keyed using a word processing program, a graph made in a spreadsheet program, an image made in a graphics program, and a picture taken with a digital camera and viewed through a graphics program.

What is a PDF File?

PDF is short for **Portable Document Format**. This popular document format was developed by Adobe Systems. When an individual or an organization wishes to distribute an electronic document and be sure that its format (layout of graphics and text) will remain as it was originally designed, it is best to convert the document into a PDF file. This type of document can be easily viewed on any computer that has the Adobe Acrobat Reader software installed (a free application available at the Adobe Systems Web site). Adobe Acrobat is now considered a standard application on most computer systems.

You can recognize the type of file you are dealing with by the *extension* on the file name. The extension is the last few characters (usually three) after the period. In a file name, for example, the extension ".exe" usually means that you are using a program file. A name such as "dog.exe" means that this is a program file, and more than likely it has something to do with dogs! Data file name extensions usually reflect the type of software that was used to create the document. For instance, a document created in Microsoft Word usually has the extension ".doc," whereas a document in WordPerfect has ".wpd." The Mac O/S operating system does not use extensions.

Instead, the operating system adds a four-letter code that is embedded or hidden in the file. When Mac O/S users share files with Windows users, they should add the appropriate three-letter extension at the end of the file name so that Windows will recognize the type of file.

The Name Game

Did you ever save something, then forget what you called it? There is nothing worse than having to hunt through dozens and dozens of files to find the one you want. By setting up some naming rules, you will be able to identify all of your files in a flash. Here are some tips.

Learning Link

Changing the extension by typing a new set of letters on the end of the file name does NOT convert the document to a different file type. It may even prevent you from opening the file in the program automatically.

To save as a different file type, use the Save As command and select the type of program in which you wish to format the document.

- Try to keep your file name to fewer than 15 characters so that it will easily fit in the display area for easy identification. Some operating systems limit the number of characters to eight. Windows 95 and all later versions will allow long file names.

- Select a symbol to divide sections of information. The underscore (_) works well.

- Include the initials of the author in two characters or less.

- Identify the subject of the document in five characters or less when sharing files.

- Identify the date the draft was completed.

- An extension (usually three additional characters after a period) shows the type of software that was used to create the document. Most software programs will automatically add an extension when you save a new file.

Confused? Here's an example: The document you are going to name is a science project completed by Nelson Chan on September 4, 2001, using Microsoft Word. Using the guidelines above, you could save the document with the name NC_sci_4SEP01.doc

 **Activity**

Naming Rules

Work with a group of three to four students to develop your own naming strategies for documents. Once you have listed three or four naming "rules," each group member should devise a list of three file names based on the rules the group developed. Exchange lists, and try to decode which document each file name represents.

A Road Map to Your Data: Folders and Paths

The next step is to put your documents in a logical place so that you can access them easily when you need them. Think of your electronic storage devices as filing cabinets. Organizing digital information effectively is all about using folders to create paths that make sense to you—not unlike paper folders you would use to set up a filing cabinet.

 *Activity*

Modern Filing

Electronic files are created by saving information on the computer. This activity requires you to create a document file using word processing software.

1. Begin by opening your word processing software, and start a new document. Key in your first name. Save this document by either clicking on the Save button at the top of your screen, or using the menu bar. Note that the file is being saved into the default folder or drive (the one that automatically comes up). Give the document file the name "Name1."

2. Now key in your last name. Repeat the saving process you used earlier. Notice that the dialog box does not appear this time. This is because the file already exists, and changes are being saved onto the existing file.

3. Next, create a copy of this file using the Save As feature. Do this by going to File on the menu bar, then choosing Save As. Key in a new name for the document file, "Name2." You now have two document files saved, both in the default folder or drive.

4. Create a chart in your notebook outlining when to use Save and Save As.

Save	Save As

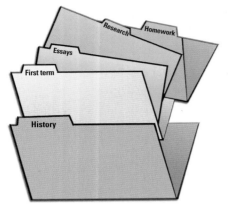

Fig. 3.9
Creating folders can help you organize your files according to subject or topic.

Using Folders

If more than one person uses a computer, a good first step is to create separate folders for each user. Then, each user can individually organize the contents of his or her personal folders.

One smart way to organize your files is to create separate *folders* for groups of similar documents or items that have a similar theme. You can create folders and subfolders inside of folders. For example, you may want to start with creating one folder for each course you take in school. Within each course folder, you could set up a second set of folders for each unit you will study. Within each unit, you could have folders for different types of files, such as essays, homework, and research.

 **Activity**

Folder Fun

Create your own personal folder that bears your name. Inside that folder, create another folder called "Course work."

There are several ways to create new folders. Here are two:

- Open a window on your desktop (e.g., My Computer or Windows Explorer) that shows the contents of the drive in which you want to create the new folder. Go to File on the menu bar, then choose New, then Folder. A new folder will appear. Name the folder by keying into the space beside it.

- When saving a document or file in a software application, look at the top right-hand side of the button bar on the Save As dialog box. You may see a button that has a picture of a folder (🗀) with a star on the upper-right hand corner. By clicking on this icon, a New Folder dialog box will appear, allowing you to name the folder.

The Path to Success

A *path* is the set of folders you have to follow to find a document. It is similar to a road map. A path begins with the name of the drive in which the file is contained. A backslash (\) separates the names of the drive and the folders. For example, if a document you were looking for was in the file path

A:\french\homework\vetements\chapeau.doc, you would look in the A drive, then open a folder called "French." Within the "French" folder, you would open a folder called "homework," then one called "vetements." The file called "chapeau" would be in the "vetements" folder.

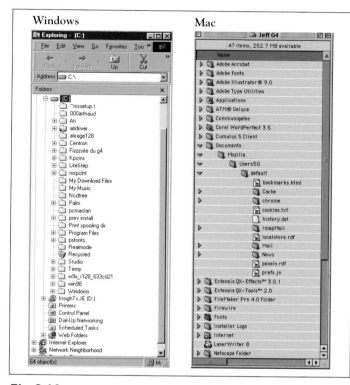

Fig. 3.10
Typical directory path

Keeping Things Organized

As much as you might hate cleaning your room, it sure makes it easier to find things once you have finished. To keep your computer organized, it pays to clean things up every few weeks. By following the checklist below, you will be able to keep your files and documents tidy and organized, ready for when you need them.

- Back up all important files by saving copies to another location (e.g. floppy, zip disk, alternate hard disk) so that if anything happens to the originals, you can still access them (it is better to be safe than sorry!).

- Delete files you no longer need to free up space on your hard drive.

- Move files to the appropriate folders.

- Archive all files you rarely use by saving them on labelled disks or CD-ROMs to free up space on your hard drive.

- Empty your Trash or Recycle Bin to remove unwanted files from your system.

Cleaning up files is not the only thing you need to do to keep your computer in tip-top shape. Similar to a car, your computer should be on a regular maintenance schedule to keep it running well.

Here are some useful maintenance tasks.

- At least once a month, scan your hard disk for disk errors using tools such as Windows Scandisk. This program is available to all Windows users and can be found in the Programs, Accessories,

ZAK MEADOW

Your desktop is a disgrace! There's to be no surfing until you tidy your files.

Fig. 3.11
© Marc Ngui

System Tools menu. It will look for and eliminate damaged files or file fragments and identify and mark "bad sectors" on a hard disk. Bad sectors can happen when the hard drive read-write head stops suddenly on a sector, such as when a disk is removed before the drive light goes off. When possible, the errors are repaired by the Scandisk software.

Mac users use Norton Utilities and Norton Anti-Virus to accomplish the same thing.

- Clean your monitor, keyboard, and mouse or trackball (several times a month).
- Clean the dust out of your computer case by opening it and carefully dusting, being sure you do not disturb any of the components (yearly).
- Ensure that cards (memory, video, etc.) in the motherboard are correctly inserted (if unexpected things happen, especially after moving your computer).
- Defragment your hard drive. Different operating systems will have different ways to do this. In a Windows environment, a regularly used computer should have its hard drive defragmented at least once a month (more often for applications that work with very large files, such as graphic design). See A Quick Byte on page 95.

Cleaning Tips

Clean your monitor using a glass cleaner and soft cloth that will not scratch the glass. The case can be cleaned carefully with a damp (not wet) cloth. Be careful not to wet the button and vents.

The keyboard can be cleaned in one of two ways. Spray cans of air can be purchased from computer retailers. These cans have special attachments that allow you to spray air in between the keys, pushing dust out. A second, less expensive method is to insert a Post-It™ note with the sticky side down in between the keys. The glue on the note will catch dust, crumbs, and dirt.

To clean a mouse, use a damp (not wet) cloth to remove dust and dirt from the outside case. Be careful not to get any moisture in the mechanical parts. The trackball should be removed and wiped with a dry cloth.

Defragmenting

Have you ever packed a suitcase for a trip? You probably carefully folded your clothing and organized the contents in your suitcase so that you could fit as many items as possible in the small space. Then you got to your destination and pulled out one or two items from the middle of the suitcase. Did you have trouble closing the suitcase again once you disrupted your original packing? Did you find that the items you some-how managed to pack earlier no longer seemed to fit in the same suitcase?

In some operating systems, the same sort of thing can happen inside your computer.

After you clean up your files by deleting unnecessary files, gaps remain between the files on your hard drive. This disorganization wastes a lot of memory, since the spaces between the files often cannot be used to store new information. New files are stored in chunks, filling these gaps, slowing down access time. You can solve this problem with a process called defragmenting. *Defragmenting* rearranges all the files saved on your hard drive in a tightly packed way, eliminating gaps and putting frag-ments, or pieces, of files closer to other similar fragments. Tightly packing your files in this way makes it easier to access fragments when you need them.

You should periodically defragment your hard drive to keep it running efficiently. The process is very simple.

- Close all applications software and disable your screensaver. To do this, right-click the mouse on the desktop, select Properties, then Screensaver. Select "none" in the screensaver selection menu, then click OK.

- Start your defragmenting software.

- A message will appear on the desktop when the defragmenting is complete. At that time, enable the screen saver by re-selecting the screensaver of your choice instead of "none."

Knowledge Check

1. Why is it important to have a strategy for naming your computer files?
2. What is a folder? How is a folder used?
3. What is a path? Give an example.
4. What does it mean to archive a file?
5. Why is it important to back up your important files?
6. How often should you perform mainte-nance tasks on your computer? Why?
7. What methods should you use to clean the hardware of your computer?

Word Processing Software

The word processor, like the typewriter before it, was designed with business in mind. Word processing software programs are used to input, process, save, edit, and revise written communications to produce professionally formatted documents.

What Features Are Common to Most Word Processing Software?

Like office productivity software packages in general, word processing software programs have a number of features and functions in common. Every software package has been programmed with default settings for many features. When you start your word processor, for example, the font, font size, paragraph alignment, tabs, and margins are already set. Each of these features will be discussed in more detail in the sections that follow.

Page Sizes/Orientation

There are two common *paper sizes* used in business throughout North America—letter size and legal size. Letter-size paper is $8\frac{1}{2}''$ x 11" and legal-size is $8\frac{1}{2}''$ x 14." Notice that both sizes of paper are given in Imperial measurements, not metric.

We also refer to *page orientation* when we set up documents. A page that is longer than it is wide has a *portrait orientation*. A page that is wider than it is long has a *landscape orientation*. In most programs, you can switch the page orientation in the Page Setup menu.

Once you have determined the size and orientation of the page you want to use, you need to select your margins.

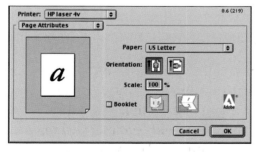

Fig. 3.12(a)
Portrait page orientation

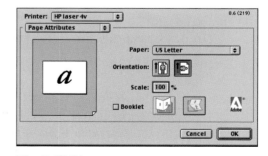

Fig. 3.12(b)
Landscape page orientation

Margins

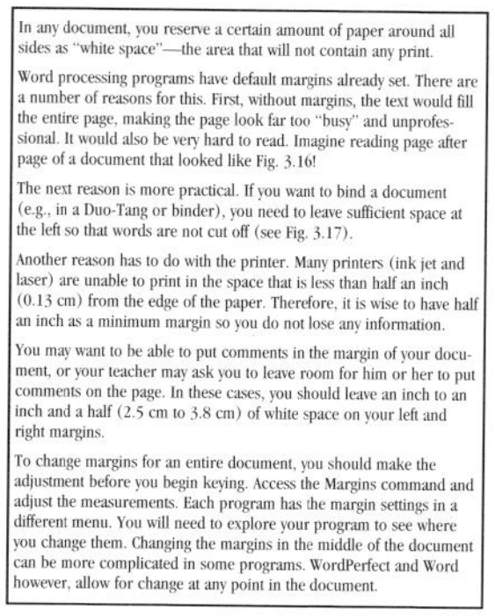

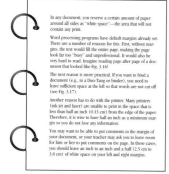

Fig. 3.13

Fig. 3.14

In any document, you reserve a certain amount of paper around all sides as "white space"—the area that will not contain any print.

Word processing programs have default margins already set. There are a number of reasons for this. First, without margins, the text would fill the entire page, making the page look far too "busy" and unprofessional. It would also be very hard to read. Imagine reading page after page of a document that looked like Fig. 3.13!

The next reason is more practical. If you want to bind a document (e.g., in a Duo-Tang or binder), you need to leave sufficient space at the left so that words are not cut off (see Fig. 3.14).

Another reason has to do with the printer. Many printers (ink jet and laser) are unable to print in the space that is less than half an inch (0.13 cm) from the edge of the paper. Therefore, it is wise to have half an inch as a minimum margin so you do not lose any information.

You may want to be able to put comments in the margin of your document, or your teacher may ask you to leave room for him or her to put comments on the page. In these cases, you should leave an inch to an inch and a half (2.5 cm to 3.8 cm) of white space on your left and right margins.

To change margins for an entire document, you should make the adjustment before you begin keying. Access the Margins command and adjust the measurements. Each program has the margin settings in a different menu. You will need to explore your program to see where you change them. Changing the margins in the middle of the document can be more complicated in some programs. WordPerfect and Word, however, allow for change at any point in the document.

Lining It All Up

Once you have set your margins, you are ready to start keying your text. Word processing software allows you to key without having to press the Enter key at the end of each line. The software will begin a new line as needed. The words will continue to *wrap around* from one line to the next as you key. The only time it is necessary to press Enter or Return is at the end of a line or paragraph when you want to start a new line or paragraph.

When you start keying in a word processor, you will notice that the *default alignment* is at the left. In other words, the lines of text are even (*justified*) at the left-hand margin and jagged (**unjustified**) at the right-hand side, ending where the words end. There are four alignment options in a word processor—left, right, centre, and full/justified. You can choose the option you prefer by clicking the appropriate icon at any time in the paragraph you are working on. Note, however, that the alignment will stay that way until you change it again. If you change your mind later about the alignment you used, you can highlight the text you want to adjust and click the appropriate icon.

- **left**—Clicking on the Left icon will place lines of text so that the left side of the paragraph is even with the left margin. The right side of the paragraph is jagged, ending wherever the words end. The Left alignment is the most commonly used alignment.

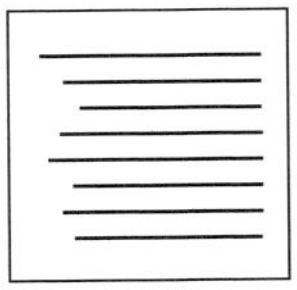

- **right**—Clicking the Right icon will align your paragraph so that the right-hand side is even with the right margin and the left side is jagged according to where the words begin. The Right alignment is the least used alignment.

- **centre**—The Centre icon allows you to centre lines of text or even full paragraphs horizontally within the current margins. For example, if the centre of the page is at three inches (7.62 cm), all lines will have half of the text to the left of the centre point and half to the right. This feature is very useful for many applications such as ensuring a title is exactly in the centre of the line.

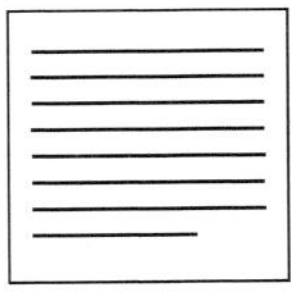

- **full justification** or **fully justified**—This icon formats paragraphs so that both the left and right sides are even (justified) with the margins. The software adjusts the spacing so that the edges remain even. To achieve this result, larger- or smaller-than-usual spaces may appear between words and letters. This alignment is used most often when creating newsletters where the text is in several columns.

left—Clicking on the Left icon will place lines of text so that the left side of the paragraph is even with the left margin The right side of the paragraph is jagged, ending wherever the words end. The Left alignment is the most commonly used alignment.

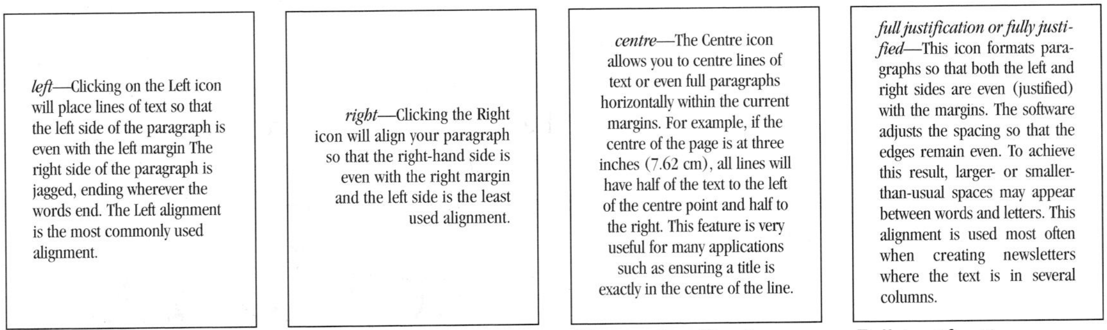

Left justification

right—Clicking the Right icon will align your paragraph so that the right-hand side is even with the right margin and the left side is the least used alignment.

Right justification

centre—The Centre icon allows you to centre lines of text or even full paragraphs horizontally within the current margins. For example, if the centre of the page is at three inches (7.62 cm), all lines will have half of the text to the left of the centre point and half to the right. This feature is very useful for many applications such as ensuring a title is exactly in the centre of the line.

Centre justification

full justification or fully justified—This icon formats paragraphs so that both the left and right sides are even (justified) with the margins. The software adjusts the spacing so that the edges remain even. To achieve this result, larger- or smaller-than-usual spaces may appear between words and letters. This alignment is used most often when creating newsletters where the text is in several columns.

Full justification

Fig. 3.15
The four alignment options

InsighTs: Succeeding in the Information Age

Designing a Recipe

Locate a recipe, either on the Internet or at home, for your favourite cookie.
Key in the recipe using the following formatting guidelines.

- Centre the title. *14 Font, Times New Roman* ✓✓
- Left-justify the ingredients. *– 12, Font, Times NR.* ✓✓✓
- Key instructions as a paragraph. ✓
- Right-justify your name as cook. ✓
- Save your recipe as Cookie. ✓

spelling / grammar 8/8

Changing the Look of the Text

To learn more about type—graphics, great articles on typography, design, and free font downloads—visit the *InsighTs* Student Page on <www.irwinpublishing.com/students>.

This next section deals with a number of the features found in the Format menu of your word processing software. Any time you change the look of your document, you are *formatting* it.

Word processing software has been programmed to use a specific font or typeface and font size. This font is the *default font*. To change the default font for a document you are about to key, you must access the Format, Font menu, and set the default font. You may decide you want to change only part of the document you are working on, or you may decide once you have finished a document that you want to change the font for the entire document. Highlight the part of the text you want to change and change the font on the toolbar or in the Format, Font menu.

Font styles come in two basic varieties—serif and sans serif fonts. *Serif fonts* (e.g., Times New Roman or Courier) have serifs or "tails" on the letters. They are more formal fonts, generally used for the body of the text. *Sans-serif fonts* (e.g., Arial) do not have the "tails" and are considered to be less formal and cleaner in appearance. They are generally used for headings. There are hundreds of each font variety in many programs. You can literally spend hours choosing the right font for your document—if you have that kind of time, that is.

Fonts sizes range from very tiny to very large.

Most business documents are keyed in a 12-point size (1 inch / 2.5 cm = 72 pts).

You can also choose to change the appearance of the font style by selecting one or more special font effects. On the formatting Toolbar or Property Bar, you will find three commonly used font enhancements—the **Bold**, *Italic*, and <u>Underline</u> options. Turn on the enhancement at the click of your mouse. Clicking again will turn off the enhancement. Alternatively, you can highlight the text, then change the style by clicking the icon or using Ctrl/B for bold, Ctrl/I for italics, or Ctrl/U for underline.

Activity

Open the Cookie file you saved earlier. Enhance the recipe document using different fonts, sizes, bold, italics, and underlining.

In the Format, Font menu, there are other options, such as:

~~Strikethrough~~   **Shadow**

Superscript letters/numbers   Outline

Subscript letters/numbers   SMALL CAPS

These options can enhance the work you are doing and are also useful when working with mathematical and scientific documents.

Line spacing is another important consideration when keying documents. Letters, for example, are keyed single-spaced. In other words, there are no blank lines between lines of text. Reports, on the other hand, are usually double-spaced, leaving a blank line between each line of keyed text. Line spacing can be set in the word processor in the Format menu. Some programs have preset spacing options (e.g., single, 1.5, double; see Fig. 3.16). Others allow the user to specify the exact spacing such as 1.75 or 2.2.

Line spacing is another important consideration when keying documents. Letters, for example, are keyed single-spaced. In other words, there are no blank lines between lines of text. Reports, on the other hand, are usually double-spaced, leaving a blank line between each line of keyed text. Line spacing can be set in the word processor in the Format menu.	Line spacing is another important consideration when keying documents. Letters, for example, are keyed single-spaced. In other words, there are no blank lines between lines of text. Reports, on the other hand, are usually double-spaced, leaving a blank line between each line of keyed text. Line spacing can be set in the word processor in the Format menu.	Line spacing is another important consideration when keying documents. Letters, for example, are keyed single-spaced. In other words, there are no blank lines between lines of text. Reports, on the other hand, are usually double-spaced, leaving a blank line between each line of keyed text. Line spacing can be set in the word processor in the Format menu.
Single spacing	1.5 spacing	Double spacing

Fig. 3.16
There are many changes you can make to text to make it stand out, including changing the line spacing.

InsighTs: Succeeding in the Information Age

Bullets or numbers? That is the question...

Students often ask whether a list should have bullets or numbers. The answer lies in the list. If your list is indicating steps in a process or items in order of preference, use numbers. Otherwise, use bullets, which indicate a list of items in no particular order.

So far, we have been focusing on full paragraphs of text. However, you may not want to have all of your text in full sentences, or you may want certain points to stand out. This text includes many examples of two of the options you can choose to achieve these effects—bullets and numbers.

Bullets and Numbers

- **bulleted list**—Most word processing programs allow you to use bullets—or symbols—to denote a list of items. In many programs, the bullets can be changed to illustrate graphically the type of list. For example, you might choose a bullet of a check mark (✔) for a checklist or a mouse (🖰) for a list of computer facts. To use bullets, you can either use the icon on the toolbar to use the default bullet setting or go into the Format, Bullets and Numbering menu to choose the form of bullet you would like to use from the Customize menu. If you want to bullet text you have already keyed, highlight the text involved and follow the same process. Regardless of the kind of bullet you choose, the list is formatted so that the text lines up at a pre-set tab mark with only the bullet at the left-hand side (Fig. 3.17) and the text wraps around to the tab mark, not to the left margin. This alignment looks much more professional and is easier to read.

- **numbered list**—A numbered list allows you to insert a list of numbered items within a document. The list can be a simple 1, 2, 3, etc., or be in the form of an outline. Again, the text associated with each item in the list is formatted so that the words wrap around to line up with the other words, not with the left margin, leaving the numbers clearly visible for the reader. To select a numbered list, you use the same process you would use to choose a bulleted list.

MY BIRTHDAY WISH LIST

- 🎁 Personal Digital Assistant with Internet connection to access e-mail account
- 🎁 Colour ink jet printer
- 🎁 High speed DSL Internet access
- 🎁 19" flat screen monitor
- 🎁 New surround speaker system for computer with sub-woofer for DVD movies
- 🎁 Mini-microwave to make the popcorn
- 🎁 Cordless optical mouse with remote capabilities

Fig. 3.17
A bulleted list with customized bullets

LIFE'S LITTLE INSTRUCTIONS

1. Loosen up! Relax. Except for rare life-and-death matters, nothing is as important as it first seems.
2. Show respect for all living things.
3. Don't bore people with your problems. When someone asks you how you feel, say "Terrific, never better." When they ask, "How's business?" reply, "Excellent, and getting better every day."
4. Don't delay acting on a good idea. Chances are someone else has just thought of it, too. Success comes to the one who acts first.
5. Live your life so that your epitaph could read, "No regrets."
6. Be bold and courageous. When you look back on your life, you'll regret the things you did not do more than the ones you did.
7. Never waste an opportunity to tell someone you love him/her.
8. Evaluate yourself by your own standards, not by someone else's.
9. Just to see how it feels, for the next twenty-four hours, refrain from criticizing anybody or anything.
10. Understand that happiness is not based on possessions, power, or prestige, but on relationships with people you love and respect.

Fig. 3.18 A numbered list

Creating Bulleted and Numbered Lists

On a blank word processing screen, key a list of items, such as your favourite music groups or leisure activities. Format your list so that it displays with bullets. Where possible customize the bullets to reflect the theme of the text.

Now key a list of instructions to demonstrate a numbered list. For example, explain how to make your favourite sandwich, or how to tie your shoelaces. Make sure you have at least one step that has a sub-step involved to see how the outlining feature works. Format the list so that there is a blank line between each bulleted item and numbered item.

Most word processing programs come with a wide variety of helpful features. The most common features are the Spell Check, Thesaurus, Grammar Check, and the Help menu.

Spell Check

In business and schoolwork, it is important that there be no spelling mistakes in documents. Today, word processing software is programmed to help you with your spelling. You have two options when it comes to using the *Spell Check* feature. If the feature is not set to automatically check your spelling, position your cursor at the beginning of the document or section you want to check. Click the Spell Check icon on the toolbar. Once you have clicked the icon, the software will start to check the document from the point at which you have placed your cursor. It will highlight words that the dictionary in your software does not recognize, showing you the word you have keyed and providing suggestions for the correct spelling. You have the option of choosing one of the program's suggestions or ignoring all of them.

Windows

Mac

Fig. 3.19
Screen shots of the box that appears when a word is keyed incorrectly and Spell Check is activated.

So you think a Spell Checker will look after your reports! Check out this little "poem."

Eye halve a spelling chequer
It came with my pea sea
It plainly marques four my revue
Miss steaks eye kin knot sea.
Eye strike a key and type a word
And weight four it two say
Weather eye am wrong oar write
It shows me strait a weigh.
As soon as a mist ache is maid
It nose bee fore two long
And eye can put the error rite
Its rare lea ever wrong.
Eye have run this poem threw it
I am shore your pleased two no
Its letter perfect awl the weigh
My chequer tolled me sew.

Fig. 3.20

The other option you have is to set the program to Spell Check as you key (see the Help menu in your program for instructions). If the dictionary does not recognize a word, it will underline it with a red wavy line, prompting you to check the word. In Windows, you can right-click on the word with your mouse and a list of possible suggestions will appear on the screen. If you want to select one of the suggestions, just position your cursor over the word and click. Correcting as you go is a helpful feature, especially when keying long documents. This can reduce the time needed to check the entire document at the end.

Word processing dictionaries are limited, so if you want to add a word the Spell Check has indicated as "incorrect" to the dictionary, move the cursor over the Add option and click.

The dictionary in your word processing program will influence the results of the Spell Check process. Most Spell Checks allow you to choose either American or British spellings. Either of these options can result in incorrect Canadian spelling. For example, if your Spell Check uses American spellings, words like "colour" and "favourite" will be marked as incorrect. Always check the dictionary version that has been set for your word processor to ensure that you use the appropriate one.

Beware: Many word processor users assume that if they use the Spell Check feature, they do not have to proofread their documents for spelling mistakes. This is not the case. The Spell Check occasionally misses mistakes. Even more important, the Spell Check will not catch the incorrect spelling of a word that has several spellings, such as "to," "too," and "two," or "there," "their," and "they're." As well, the Spell Check will not catch those errors you make when you key another—correctly spelled—word by mistake, for example, when you key "bet" instead of "get." Look at Fig. 3.20, which "passed" a spell check.

Thesaurus

"What's another word for...?" How many times have you asked yourself this question while working on a document? The ***Thesaurus*** is the feature you have been searching for. Most, if not all, word processors have a built-in thesaurus. Click your cursor on the word you want to replace, then go into the Thesaurus function in the Tools menu (in Word you then look under Language).

The Thesaurus will list the different ways that the word you want to replace can be used, that is, as a noun, a verb, etc., and give you a list of other words that might be appropriate for each category. **A word of warning,** however. Do not just choose any word from the list the Thesaurus suggests. Not all the words are necessarily an appropriate match for the word you want to replace, and you must check the context carefully. The English language is very complex. Do not assume that all of the words listed are truly interchangeable.

Fig. 3.21
Ensure you choose the correct alternative from words in the Thesaurus.

Grammar Check

Another automated feature in most programs is the *Grammar Check,* which is designed to check for common grammatical errors. This function compares the sentence structure in the document with a series of rules programmed into the software. If the Grammar Check detects a grammatical error or an overly long sentence, it will underline the section with a green wavy line. For example, the software will flag the end of a sentence that should have a question mark based on the way you have worded the sentence. You can correct the underlined section as shown, or ignore the suggestion given after right-clicking on the green wavy line.

Again you should **beware!** Do not automatically accept a Grammar Check's suggestion. The Grammar Check can be wrong. As well, the program may incorrectly interpret the intended meaning of your sentence. Always read the suggested correction carefully.

Help

One of the most useful features of any of the software programs discussed in this chapter and later chapters is the *Help menu*. Think of the Help menu as a book that you can refer to when you need assistance while working on an application. Learning to use this menu is an important skill for all computer users. There are three common parts to most Help menus—the Contents, the Index, and the Find features.

- **contents**—The Contents is similar to a Table of Contents in a book with its listing of chapter headings. Double-clicking on the chapter headings—or book icons—will open that "chapter" to show you the subheadings within the chapter. Continue to double-click until all the topics are shown. When you click on a topic, a dialog box appears on your screen with information and links to further, more detailed instructions. You can follow the Help instructions in your document without closing the Help window. This feature is very handy when you are not sure of the steps to follow.

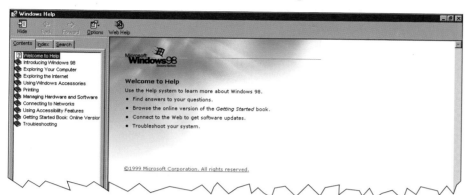

Fig. 3.22
Screen capture of the Contents page of the Help menu in Windows 98

- **index**—What do you do when you do not know where to look in the book? First, use the Index. The *Index* in the Help menu is just like the Index at the back of a book. It lists all the topic headings, but without page numbers (in a virtual book, the computer will go to the page for you!). Key the term you are looking for and the Index will list all the topic headings that contain that term. Double-click on the topic you want and the information dialog box appears on your screen.

- **find**—If you still cannot locate the information or assistance you need, there is one last alternative—the *Find* option. At first glance, the Find and Index sections of the Help menu look similar. There are, however, some important differences in the way they work. The Index lists only the topic headings in the Help program. Find will locate every instance of the word you key in its directory regardless of the section or topic the word is in. For example, the word "bullet" might only appear in one or two topic headings in the Index, but Find might locate 40 to 50 places where the word is used. One of these topics might be what you need to help you out. Some programs also include a feature in the Help menu ("Ask the Perfect Expert" in WordPerfect, for example) that allows you to key your search in the form of a question. For example, "How do I change the line spacing?" The program then looks at the words you have used and lists a variety of topics from which to choose.

Learning Link

In Word, the Index option allows you to do a topic or a key word search similar to Find.

Before You Can Create Documents

Need help with your word processor? Visit the *InsighTs* Student Page on <www.irwinpublishing.com/students> to check out the Microsoft Word Info Web site, a site sponsored by Alki Software Corporation, manufacturer of add-in products for Word. It has great tips for both Windows and Macintosh users. You will also find a link to a volunteer service provided by experienced users of Word and WordPerfect products that will provide answers within three days.

Regardless of the Help function you choose, it is crucial that you use the correct terminology and be as specific as possible. Computers are very literal and cannot read your mind!

Activity

Part A

Explore the Help menu in your word processing program. Describe the Help options available to you. Look for Contents, Index, and Find (or Search). How do they work? How do they differ? Use an example to help you explain.

Part B

Use your Help menu to locate information on the steps required to create bulleted or numbered lists in your word processor. Compare what you find with your notes.

Editing and Proofreading Documents

After you have input your text and have used your word processing software's Spell Check, Thesaurus, and Grammar Check, you are ready to edit and *proofread* your document. Errors in a document, no matter how small, are sometimes enough to turn off a potential client or result in mark deductions in a school report. Especially for long documents, you will find it best to proofread your *hard copy*—the copy you have printed out.

You will need to read for errors in keying, spelling, grammar, punctuation, and word usage. Watch particularly for letter transpositions (e.g., "form" instead of "from") and appropriate capitalization. Also check that nouns, verbs, and pronouns agree. For example, make sure you have not used a singular noun with a plural pronoun or verb, such as, "*two* things *is* certain," or "check with *a* classmate to see what *they* want to do."

You should also check for layout consistency. Are the margins even? Have you indented consistently? Did you use font enhancements (bold, italic, etc.) appropriately and consistently?

You should also proofread your document from the point of view of the person who will be reading it. Have you given enough information or too much information? Have you used jargon that may not be familiar to the reader or made assumptions about your reader that may not be accurate.

Once you have edited and proofread your document, key your changes. Remember to save regularly. Then proofread for a final check.

There are a series of standard editing and proofreaders' marks that you can use to help you in the editing and proofreading stages (Fig. 3.23). You will find that using these common marks will take the guesswork out of preparing documents from revised and edited hard copy.

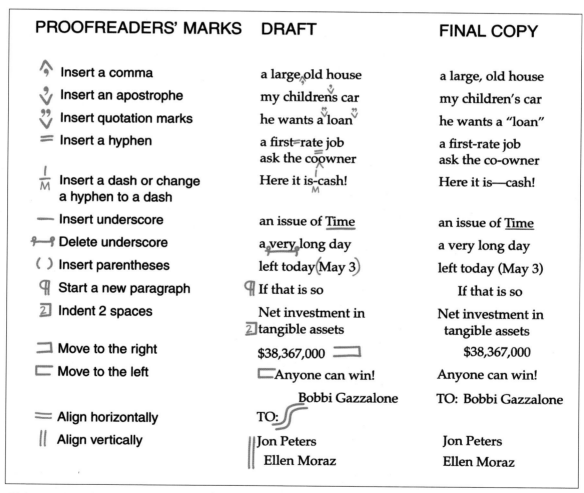

Fig. 3.23
Common editing and proofreaders' marks

Activity

Using Proofreaders' Marks

Rekey the paragraph shown in Fig. 3.24, making the changes indicated by the proofreaders' marks. Be sure to check carefully against the chart of marks to ensure you have made the right corrections.

Why Learn to Key?

A corse in formla keyboarding instruction should provide the students with the opportunity for developeing a skill in the correct techniques of operating computer the and for preparing him / her to use this machine as a tol for communication.

What do the students Say?

A survey of studnts recently enroled an in introductory course in keyboardingrevealed the following reasons for considering the optional course in school:

1. My assingments, which are keyed appear neater than my hand writing
2. We have a computer at home and I would like to now how to use it more effectiveily
3. I will need to key know matter what jobs I peruse in the future

---

Fig. 3.24

Knowledge Check

1. What are the two most common sizes of paper used in word-processed documents? What are the names used for these sizes?

2. What is the difference between landscape and portrait orientation? How could you remember which is which?

3. What is a margin on a document? How are margins determined?

4. In your own words, describe the difference between left, right, centre, and full justification.

5. What is "word wrap" and how does it work?

6. What are fonts and how do you change them in your document? How would you change the font in only part of a document?
7. What is the difference between serif and sans serif fonts? What are two examples of each type of font?
8. What are the three most common font enhancements? How do you activate these features on the toolbar? How do you change the appearance of text after it is keyed?
9. Describe the difference between single and double spacing in a document.
10. What are bulleted and numbered lists? What is the difference? How can you customize a bulleted list?
11. How does Spell Check work and what are some of its limitations?
12. What is a Thesaurus and how does it work? What are some of its limitations?
13. How does Grammar Check work? What are some of its limitations?
14. Describe the elements of the Help window—Contents, Index, and Find (or Search). How do they differ?
15. What are the steps you should take to ensure that your documents are error free and ready to submit? Why is this so important?

CHAPTER SUMMARY

Understanding Information

1. List and describe the main types of ergonomic-related injuries.

2(a) What are the basic components of office productivity software packages?

2(b) List and describe five of the common elements/features found within each of these packages.

3. What is an extension?

4. What is a file extension?

5. What is defragmenting?

6. Why is defragmenting important?

Analyzing

7. Describe some of the dangers an organization might face if it does not consider ergonomics when designing offices.

8. Why is it necessary to follow the hand position guidelines described in this chapter when keying?

9. Explain the difference between program files and data files. Use examples.

10. Describe two things you can do when naming your files that will help you keep your work organized.

Applying

11. How can schools benefit from understanding ergonomics? Present your ideas in a one-page, double-spaced report.

12. After you have keyed the report in question 11, trade papers with one of your classmates. Edit and proofread the hard copy of his or her report using the proofreaders' marks in Fig. 3.23. Revise your own report once it has been peer-edited.

13. Describe some strategies you can use to ensure that you are able to find electronic documents when you need them.

Communicating

14. Investigate three formatting features of the word processing package you use in class that were not covered in this chapter. Prepare a two-page keyed report outlining which three features you investigated, how to use them, and where you could see them applied in this or other courses.

Assessing Your Competencies

15. Using the software competency checklists provided by your teacher, check off the competencies that you have mastered during the course of this chapter. Note the competencies that require more attention and review.

16. Interview a classmate to determine the competencies he or she has acquired during this chapter. Also share some of the new skills you have acquired.

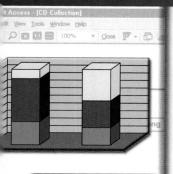

Topics

➤ Word Processing and Business Documents: Letters and Reports

➤ Spreadsheet Software

➤ The Database

CHAPTER FOUR:

HOW DO I GET MY DOCUMENTS TO LOOK THAT GOOD?

By the end of this chapter, you will understand how professionals use office productivity programs to get their work done. You will have opportunities to explore your word processing, spreadsheet, and database software, and to examine a variety of business documents that can be created and enhanced with these tools. In addition, you will use these office productivity tools to complete assignments that really do look that good!

This chapter explores these questions:

- How do you format a business letter and report?
- How does a spreadsheet work?
- How do you convert data to a chart or graph?
- What is a database?

In this chapter you have the opportunity to

- analyze letters received at home
- create a cover letter for part-time job
- key an edited and proofread letter, applying these skills
- key a business report
- enter data into a spreadsheet
- enter formulas and functions
- format a spreadsheet
- determine the most appropriate format for representing data
- create your own charts
- brainstorm organizations and places that collect personal information
- explore the database software in your school and create a database for your CD collection
- design the structure for a database and an input form for a small service business
- investigate career opportunities using office productivity skills

Word Processing and Business Documents: Letters and Reports

How Do You Format a Business Letter and Report?

No matter what kind of company you decide to work for, or what type of work your office does, written communication will be an important part of getting the work done and maintaining the flow of information. Before typewriters were introduced into office environments, correspondence and reports were handwritten. Typewriters changed the way offices functioned because they allowed written work to be prepared much faster and appear more professional. Computers brought about a second revolution in the way offices work. Although they require a whole new skill set, they allow for even faster production of effective, professional-looking business documents, and a fast and easy way to share information with others.

One of the most commonly used forms of communication among businesses is the letter.

Learning Link

You will remember from earlier chapters that the computer industry continues to use Imperial measurements in many areas, including paper sizes.

"Letterhead" refers to writing paper with pre-printed information at the top. It usually includes the name and address of the person or company using it. It may also include the person's or company's telephone number, fax number, e-mail, and Web site address.

Business Letters and Their Parts

Even with the widespread use of e-mail as a form of business communication (see chapter 6), the letter is still one of the fundamental documents that every person should be comfortable keying. Although there are many ways to set up business letters, there are some generally accepted standards.

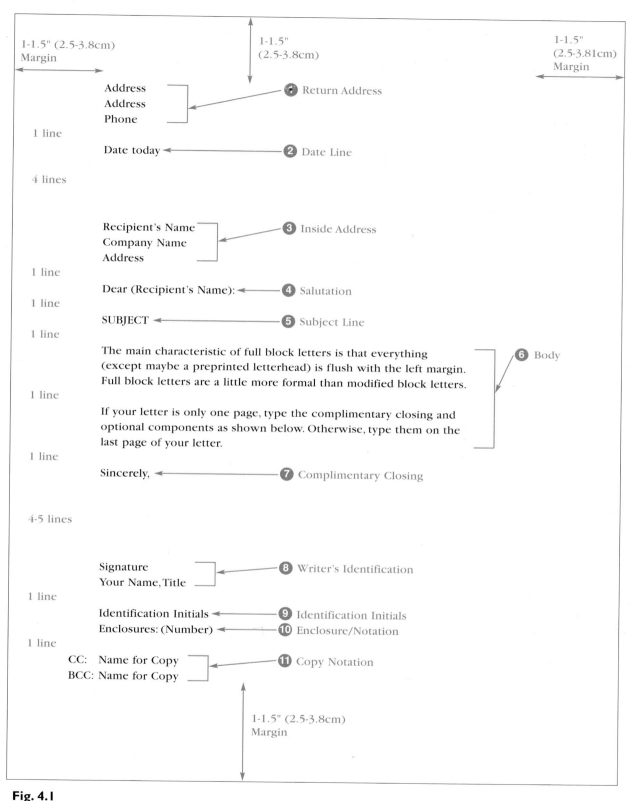

Fig. 4.1

Parts of a typical full block business letter. Derived from *Webster's Secretarial Handbook, Second Edition,* Copyright © 2000 J. Steven Niznik.

Let's take a closer look at the parts of the business letter shown in Fig. 4.1.

1. **return address**—The *return address* is necessary for the receiver of the letter to know where to send a reply. It is becoming common to include fax numbers and e-mail addresses in the return address. You key the return address 1"-1.5" (2.5 cm-3.8 cm) from the top of the page. If you have set a 1" (2.5 cm) top margin, you start the address 0.5" (1.3 cm) below that. Notice that the address does not contain your name. You key your name at the bottom of the letter below your signature. If you have set up your own letterhead (you will learn how to create your own letterhead in chapter 5) you do not key the return address again.

2. **date line**—Immediately below the return address is the *date line*. This line indicates the date the letter is keyed. The date should be formatted using the long date, for example, June 1, 2001 or 2 June 2001. You do not use the short date version (e.g., 06/01/01), as letters tend to be more formal in nature. If you are using letterhead, key the date below it, leaving a line or two in between.

3. **inside address**—The *inside address* is the name and address of the recipient of the letter. If you know the name of the individual in the organization to whom you are sending the letter, key it on the first line, along with the person's title. The company name appears on the next line, followed by the company's address, city, province, and postal code.

To look up a postal code, go to the Canada Post Web site on the *InsighTs* Student Page on <www.irwinpublishing.com/students>.

4. **salutation**—The *salutation* is the greeting within the letter. If you know the name of the person, use it. For example, Dear Mr. Jonsmagh or Dear Ms Keystone. If you do not know the person's name, use a generic salutation such as

   • Dear Sir or Madam

   • To Whom It May Concern

   • Ladies and Gentlemen

5. **subject line**—Key the subject of your letter on the *subject line*. Be concise, using one line or less. Key the subject in all UPPER-CASE letters or upper-lower case and underlined.

6. **body**—The *body* of the letter is where your message is placed. Use full sentences and choose clear, concise words to get your message across. Remember, business letters should waste no one's time. Single-space the paragraphs with a blank line between each paragraph.

7. **complimentary closing**—The choice of *complimentary closing* depends largely on the nature of the letter. Choose a formal closing for a formal letter. Some examples of closings are:
   - Respectfully yours (very formal)
   - Sincerely (very common, less formal)
   - Yours truly (neutral)
   - Cordially (more friendly)

8. **writer's identification**—The name of the letter writer appears four to five lines below the complimentary closing to allow space for the writer to sign the letter. Your title also appears here to help the recipient correctly address a reply, where necessary.

9. **identification initials**—If you have someone else key the letter on your behalf, that person's initials appear below the keyed name. There are a number of ways to show that someone else keyed the letter for you, including
   - JLE:tl
   - JLE/tl
   - tl

   The CAPITALIZED part of the initials represents the initials of the writer of the letter. The lower-case letters are the initials of the keyer.

10. **enclosure notation**—If you have included anything with the letter (resumé, invoice, brochure, etc.) you make a note of it here. If there is more than one enclosure, key the number of enclosures in brackets (2).

11. **copy notation**—*CC* stands for *courtesy copy*. This copy used to be a carbon copy in the days of typewritten letters. If you are sending a copy of the letter to another person, it is polite to let the person to whom the letter is written know that the other person has also received a copy of the letter. Key CC with the person's name at the bottom of the letter.

    BCC stands for *blind courtesy copy*. A BCC notation means that the recipient of the letter does not know that a copy of the letter has been sent to the person in the BCC line. How can the recipient not know? The BCC line only appears on the copy that the writer keeps and the copy that goes to the person on the BCC line. It does not go on the copy sent to the person to whom the letter is written.

Some of the letter parts outlined above are optional, depending on the type of letter you are sending. However, all business letters must have the return address, date line, inside address, salutation, body, complimentary closing, and writer's identification.

Learning Link

Each time you press a key on the keyboard, the keystroke takes up storage space.

Letter Styles

As you examine Fig. 4.1, you will notice that all of the letter parts are aligned at the left-hand side. This style of letter is called ***full block***. It has quickly become the most popular style of letter in the computer era because it requires fewer bytes for storage on disk. There are no extra indents or tabs to move letter parts over as there are in a block (Fig. 4.2(a)) or semi-block letter style (Fig. 4.2(b)).

In ***block letter style***, the return address, date line, complimentary closing, and writer's identification all start at the halfway point in the line.

Semi-block letters are a modification of the block letter style. In this style of letter, each new paragraph begins with an indent.

Your Name
Address
Address
Phone

Date today

Re: (To what this letter refers)

CERTIFIED
PERSONAL

Recipient's Name
Company Name
Address

Attention (Recipient's Name)

Dear (Recipient's Name):

SUBJECT

The main characteristic of full block letters is that everything (except maybe a preprinted letterhead) is flush with the left margin. Full block letters are a little more formal than modified block letters.

If your letter is only one page, type the complimentary close and optional components as shown below. Otherwise, type them on the last page of your letter. (For the components of continuation pages, click on the link below to go to page 2 of this letter.)

Sincerely,

Signature
Your Name, Title

Identification Initials
Enclosures: (Number)

CC: Name for Copy
CC: Name for Copy

Fig. 4.2(a)
Block letter

Your Name
Address
Address
Phone

Date today

Re: (To what this letter refers)

CERTIFIED
PERSONAL

Recipient's Name
Company Name
Address

Attention (Recipient's Name)

Dear (Recipient's Name):

SUBJECT

The main characteristic of full block letters is that everything (except maybe a preprinted letterhead) is flush with the left margin. Full block letters are a little more formal than modified block letters.

If your letter is only one page, type the complimentary close and optional components as shown below. Otherwise, type them on the last page of your letter. (For the components of continuation pages, click on the link below to go to page 2 of this letter.)

Sincerely,

Signature
Your Name, Title

Identification Initials
Enclosures: (Number)

CC: Name for Copy
CC: Name for Copy

Fig. 4.2(b)
Semi-block letter

The style of letter you use is your choice. However, many businesses have adopted one of these three styles as their standard. When you are an employee of an organization, be sure to find out which style is preferred.

Once you have developed your competency in composing and keying business letters, you will be able to present your message in a professional manner.

 **Activity**

Comparing Letters

Gather letters sent to members of your household over a period of time, and, *with your family members' agreement*, bring them to class. Compare the letter styles, and use what you learned earlier in this chapter to label the parts of each letter. Create a chart comparing the use of the letter parts. Which parts are common to all? Which other parts are used most frequently? Least frequently?

To Comma, or Not to Comma?

Another important part of a letter is punctuation. Within a business letter, there are two common options for punctuation—two-point (mixed) or open.

In two-point punctuation, you key a colon (:) after the salutation, and a comma (,) after the complimentary closing. For example, Dear Mr. Singh: and Yours truly,

In open punctuation, there is no punctuation after these letter parts, leaving these parts "open" and without clutter.

 **Activity**

Writing, Editing, and Proofreading Letters
Part A

Compose and key a letter applying for a part-time job at a local business. Research the name of the person to whom you should send the letter. Be sure to look up the full address of the organization, including the postal code. This letter should focus on how you can meet the employer's needs. Highlight the skills you have that could be applied to a position in that company. What makes you different from the other people who are applying for the same position? If possible, refer to a specific job opening. Refer to Fig. 4.1 to ensure that your letter presents you in a professional manner.

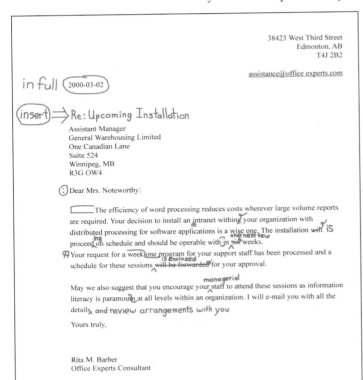

Fig. 4.3

Part B

Two steps in the letter-writing process that should never be overlooked are proofreading and editing. You should always edit your letters to be sure you have expressed clearly and accurately the points you want to make. You should also proofread for spelling and grammar mistakes. Errors in your letters or awkwardness in expression, no matter how small, are sometimes enough to turn off a potential employer or client.

Re-key the letter in Fig. 4.3, applying your knowledge of proofreaders' marks (see pages 106-108) and proper letter format.

Knowledge Check

1. In your notebook draw a sketch of a business letter indicating the essential parts of a letter—the return address, date line, inside address, salutation, body, complimentary closing, and writer's identification. Indicate on your sketch how many blank lines should appear between each part.

2. How do you write a proper salutation? What is not included in the salutation that might appear in the inside address?

3. What are four typical complimentary closings? When might you use each one?

4. What information is helpful in the writer's identification for the recipient of the letter? Why?

5. Describe the difference between a full block, block, and semi-block letter style.

6. Describe the difference between open and two-point punctuation.

Business Reports

Another way you share information and present your ideas in business is in a report. *Reports* are prepared in business for a variety of reasons, including

- to provide information
- to analyze information
- to propose a project
- to summarize a project
- to suggest actions to be taken and predict their outcomes

Regardless of the purpose of a report, reports take on a similar "shape" and are formatted in a standard manner. In this section, you will learn about the parts of a report and the ways in which a report can be formatted using the power of your word processing software.

Parts of a Formal Business Report

1. **title page**—All formal reports have a *title page* listing the title of the report, the author's name, the person or organization for whom the report was prepared, the date the report was submitted, and the organization to which the report was given. As students, you normally substitute the course name for the organization. There is no absolute rule regarding the setup of the title page. Figure 4.4 shows two formats you can follow.

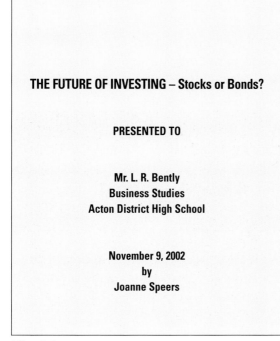
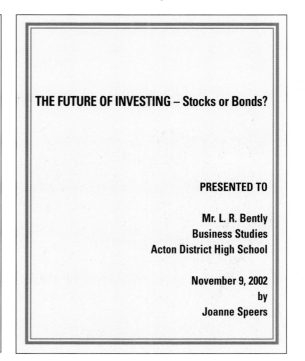

Fig. 4.4
Sample title page formats

How Do I Get My Documents To Look That Good?

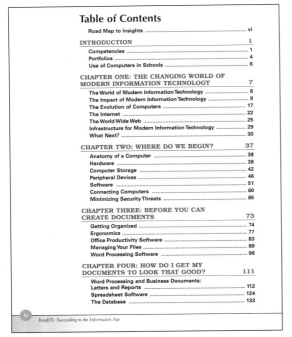

Table of Contents

Fig. 4.5
Sample table of contents

2. **table of contents**—The *table of contents* is a listing of each heading contained within the report and the page on which the heading appears. Typically, a Table of Contents is used only when the report is five or more pages in length. The headings in the table of contents should appear as they do in the report—both in words and in typestyle. This consistency helps the reader of the report locate the headings within the body. A typical Table of Contents is shown in Fig. 4.5.

3. **list of illustrations**—"A picture is worth a thousand words." One of the most useful tools in a report is the inclusion of illustrations, charts, graphs, and pictures to help writers communicate their ideas. These may be gathered during the research process, or created by the author in one of many software programs such as Excel, Quattro Pro, or Access. We will be exploring these programs later in this chapter. If you have five or more illustrations, you should key a List of Illustrations. Such a list gives the title of each illustration and the page on which it is found. If there is room, you can key the list immediately below the Table of Contents. Otherwise, include it on a separate page just after the Table of Contents.

Note: The title page, table of contents, and list of illustrations are best keyed after you have prepared your report, to ensure accuracy and consistency. Many word processing programs have the ability to automatically generate a table of contents.

4. **report text**—The report itself is made up of three sections: the *Introduction, Body,* and *Conclusions and Recommendations.*

5. **references**—References list the specific sources of information that were used to get information for the report.

Introduction

The *introduction* should provide the reader of the report with four pieces of information. Many report writers prepare the introduction after the report body is completed.

1. **purpose**—The statement of purpose should indicate what the report will accomplish. Is the report's purpose to inform,

suggest courses of action, or propose a new idea? The purpose needs to be stated clearly so there is no confusion.

2. **scope**—The scope indicates the amount of detail the report will go into. Is the report just an overview or is it an in-depth study that looks at every possible angle of the situation? You will find that using the headings within the report body will help you outline the scope of the report. The scope should give the reader a good idea of what the report covers.

3. **sources of information**—The author of a report needs to indicate where he or she got the information to compile the report. Did the author perform the research himself or herself, or was information gathered from secondary sources? If the data was gathered from secondary sources, what type of sources, in general terms, did the writer use?

4. **authorization**—This part indicates who requested the report in the first place and authorized the research to be done.

Body

The body of the report itself is a logical progression of ideas, "walking" the reader through the proposal, information, or suggestions for action. Typically, there is some background information provided to give the report a context or setting. Then the writer will proceed with the discussion of the subject. In all cases, the report is divided into logical sections using headings—the same headings that appear in the table of contents. Headings should be keyed in a consistent manner, both in typestyle and structure (e.g., indent, spacing). If you use questions for some section headings, use questions for all headings of the same level. You can also vary the appearance of the headings to give the reader visual clues as to the importance of the heading. Main headings might appear in UPPERCASE letters, with subheadings in upper/lower case (sometimes known as title case) and perhaps indented.

Conclusions and Recommendations

Skilled report writers will draw conclusions as the report proceeds, writing them at the end of each section. They then summarize their conclusions and recommendations in the final section of the report, Conclusions and Recommendations. Most business reports are requests for action and should state clearly what the author recommends as a result of the study undertaken.

References or Citations

References are all the written sources from which you got information for your report. Reference lists can include books, magazine articles, reports, CD-ROMs, videos, and Web sites. If you used several types of references (e.g., books and articles), you may wish to include subheadings that tell the reader what type of reference the grouping represents. Several styles of recording references are accepted. Usually, the information is listed, alphabetically, in the following order.

- author (last name first with a comma)
- title of book, article, and magazine name, report, or Web site
- city in which the item was published or produced
- name of publisher or Web site address
- year of publication

You will learn more about how to cite your references in chapter 9 (pages 263-264).

Keying Your Report

Before the development of word processing software, typists were restricted by the typewriter itself in the keying and formatting of a business report. They had only the line spacing, CAPS and underline features to help distinguish body sections and headings. As such, a business report would have looked like Fig. 4.6.

Today, however, we can use the features and capabilities of word processors to modernize the appearance of reports. Note the differences between the typed report in Fig. 4.6 and the word-processed report shown in Fig. 4.7. Font sizes and enhancements help to distinguish headings from body text. Line spacing, once restricted to single or double spacing can be varied within the report. Paragraphs no longer need to be indented when other features are employed. However, some features have remained unchanged.

- The title on the first page should start approximately 1" (2.5 cm) below the top margin to set it apart from other pages.
- The second and subsequent pages should have a header or footer containing the report title and page number. A horizontal rule may be used to separate the header or footer from the report body.
- Page numbering begins on the first page of the report body, *not* the table of contents.
- Pages that appear before the report body are numbered using Roman numerals, for example, (i), (ii), (iii).

USING ILLUSTRATIONS IN REPORTS

An illustration in a report should help your reader <u>absorb</u> the facts and ideas you are presenting. Used well, an illustration can convey facts and ideas that are difficult to put into words.

<u>Pretty or Punchy</u>

Illustrations should NEVER be used as ornaments. They should be as important as the text in the report. Be careful not to over-illustrate. Use illustrations ONLY when they will make a direct contribution to the reader's understanding of the content.

<u>Consider the Audience</u>

You would choose a different illustration of a laser beam for a high school science class than you would for a university level training document for doctors.

<u>Keep it Clear</u>

Many of the attributes of good writing – simplicity, clarity, conciseness, and directness – are equally important when creating and choosing illustrations.

<u>Types of Illustrations</u>

The most common types of illustrations are photographs, graphs, tables, drawings, flowcharts, organizational charts, and maps. Know which are the most appropriate for your purpose.

Your Name   Date

Fig. 4.6
Typed report

USING ILLUSTRATIONS IN REPORTS

An illustration in a report should help your reader <u>absorb</u> the facts and ideas you are presenting. Used well, an illustration can convey facts and ideas that are difficult to put into words.

Pretty or Punchy
Illustrations should NEVER be used as ornaments. They should be as important as the text in the report. Be careful not to over-illustrate. Use illustrations ONLY when they will make a direct contribution to the reader's understanding of the content.

Consider the Audience
You would choose a different illustration of a laser beam for a high school science class than you would for a university level training document for doctors.

Keep it Clear
Many of the attributes of good writing – simplicity, clarity, conciseness, and directness – are equally important when creating and choosing illustrations.

Types of Illustrations
The most common types of illustrations are photographs, graphs, tables, drawings, flowcharts, organizational charts, and maps. Know which are the most appropriate for your purpose.

Your Name   Date

Fig. 4.7
A modern report

Activity

Preparing a Report

Using the results of your ergonomic assessment of an area of your school (see chapter 3, page 82) prepare a report outlining both your findings and your recommendations for improvement. Prepare an appropriate introduction. Use headings to divide the report body into sections. Prepare a conclusion summarizing your main points. Refer to Figs. 4.6 and 4.7 for ideas on setting up the report. Remember to insert headers and footers on the report (refer to the Help menu in your program for specific instructions).

Knowledge Check

1. What are the essential elements for a Title Page on a formal business report?
2. Describe how a Table of Contents is prepared.
3. What is a List of Illustrations and when is it used?
4. What information should the Introduction of a report provide to the reader?
5. How are headings used within the body of a report? What should they look like?
6. What are the four constant features of a report—whether typed or word-processed?

How Do I Get My Documents To Look That Good?

Spreadsheet Software

How Does a Spreadsheet Work?

A spreadsheet is another software application that today's business student should learn to use competently. In simple terms, a *spreadsheet program* allows users to perform calculations, from very simple to very complex, on values entered into the program. These values can then be analyzed, graphed, and printed.

As you go through this section, you will want to use the spreadsheet yourself. Open your spreadsheet program and follow along, entering the data on your screen as you proceed.

Imagine that you are in charge of a school store and you have to prepare monthly reports on its sales. Your original data might look like Fig. 4.8.

Our School Store—September and October Sales

	September	October
Pencils, pens, paper	**$125.00**	**$37.00**
Gym shorts, T-shirts	**$228.00**	**$55.00**
Candy	**$48.00**	**$66.00**

Fig. 4.8

You might decide to use your computerized spreadsheet to enter formulas so that the software will automatically calculate the totals for you, identify the category with the highest sales, the category with the lowest sales, and the average sales for each month. You could then use this information to create a pie chart that shows the percentage of sales for each category. Read on to learn how.

The Spreadsheet Screen

Like word processing software, spreadsheet software includes a title bar, menu bar, and one or more toolbars with buttons that perform the functions within the program. Many of the buttons function the same as in word processing—for example, the New, Open, and Save icons on the standard toolbar. Buttons unique to the spreadsheet will be discussed in more detail later in this section.

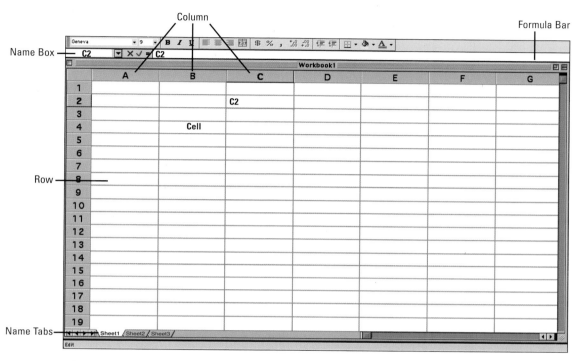

Fig. 4.9
Screen capture of an Excel spreadsheet

When you launch your spreadsheet program, the cursor will automatically go to cell A1.

While a word processor organizes data by paragraph, a spreadsheet organizes data into cells. The *spreadsheet workbook* or *notebook* is the file in which you create and work on your data. It consists of numerous worksheets or *spreadsheet pages*, each of which consists of a grid of vertical columns and horizontal rows. An alphabetical letter identifies each column. A number identifies each row. The location where each column and row intersect is called a *cell* and is identified by a *cell address*. For example, where column C crosses row 2, the cell address is C2. If you click your cursor in cell C2, you will see the cell name in the name box immediately above the worksheet grid (see Fig. 4.9). If you have been scrolling through a spreadsheet and cannot locate your cursor, just look in the name box.

Learning Link

Beside the name box is the formula bar, where you can see the formula as you key it and edit it, if necessary, at a later time.

At the bottom of the workbook, there are a series of name tabs for each worksheet. The names in these tabs remain as originally programmed until you rename them.

Your workbook can contain numerous worksheets and charts that are all related to the same topic. For example, for the workbook "Our School Store," you might want a separate worksheet for each school year, with sheets for graphs and charts as well.

Entering Data into Your Spreadsheet

Information entered into a spreadsheet cell is one of three types.

1. **labels**—*Labels* refer to the text information—all the words— used to describe the data in the spreadsheet. Numbers on the screen are relatively useless without some information to help users understand what the numbers mean. Labels can include the title of your worksheet, column headings, row identifiers, or words to describe the functions you have programmed the spreadsheet to perform (e.g., Total).

2. **values**—Any numerical data entered into a worksheet is a *value*. On some spreadsheet programs, you must be careful when entering values. In these programs it is important **not** to include commas, dollar signs, or other formatting characters. If you do so, the program may interpret the data as labels rather than as values. Such misinterpretation would make it impossible for the program to use the data to perform calculations. After the data is entered, you can format the cells as a type of number, date, or time. In other programs, such as Excel 2000, or Excel 98 for Mac, including dollar signs, commas, and other formatting characters does not create problems.

3. **formulas**—The real power of a computerized spreadsheet comes from the *formulas* you enter into cells.

Exponents	^ (e.g., 3^2)
Division	/
Multiplication	*
Addition	+
Subtraction	-

Fig. 4.10
Common operators in electronic spreadsheets

All formulas begin with an *indicator* such as an = sign, @ sign, or other character, depending on the program you are using. Not all software packages use the same indicator. The order of the elements or parts of a formula is known as the *syntax*. Formulas follow the order of operations learned in your mathematics classes—brackets, exponents, division, multiplication, addition, and subtraction. Some of the operators (mathematical

InsighTs: Succeeding in the Information Age

functions) used in a computerized spreadsheet just look a little different than they look in a mathematics book. In addition, spreadsheet formulas can include numbers, cell addresses, or cell ranges (e.g., B5..E9).

Suppose you were to set up "Our School Store" in a worksheet, including only the labels and values. It would look like Fig. 4.11.

Fig. 4.11

The true value of using formulas in a spreadsheet is the time saved when you change values. The formulas will automatically recalculate the answers!

Click on the cell where you want the answer for your formula to appear and key the formula. If you have to edit the formula later, click on that cell again, and make corrections in the Formula Bar.

Once you have entered the labels and values for "Our School Store" you need to enter a formula to calculate the total sales. To find the total of September sales, you could key the formula =B4+B5+B6 in Excel. In Quattro Pro, the formula would appear as +B4+B5+B6. In both cases, the program will add the three numbers from B4 to B6.

 Activity

Entering Values and Labels

Enter the values and labels for the "Our School Store" example in Fig. 4.11 into your own spreadsheet program. Use formulas to calculate the total sales for both September and October. Check the Help menu for the correct syntax (format) for the formulas.

Functions Unique to Spreadsheets

All spreadsheets have programmed *functions* that will perform the same calculation using a range of numbers, although, as you have seen, the exact format of the formula may vary depending on the function name. The most frequently used functions in spreadsheets are SUM, MIN, MAX, AVERAGE or AVG, and COUNT. A brief description of what each function does is shown in Fig. 4.12.

CHART OF FUNCTIONS	
SUM	calculates the total of the numbers/cells/range of cells
MIN	identifies the lowest value (minimum) in the range of values specified
MAX	identifies the highest value (maximum) in the range of values specified
AVERAGE or AVG	calculates the arithmetic mean of the numbers/cells/range of cells
COUNT	counts up the number of entries/values in the range specified

Fig. 4.12
Frequently used spreadsheet functions

 Activity

Substituting Functions

Substitute the function =SUM(B4:B6) for =B4+B5+B6 in the "Our School Store" spreadsheet. You will notice that the same result occurs but you did not have to key each cell reference separately. Imagine how much time this process would save you if you were totalling 100 cells in column B.

Learning Link

Arithmetic computing has come a long way since the Mark I in 1944, the first electro-mechanical calculator. The Mark I performed basic arithmetic, multiplying and dividing numbers in seconds. The drawback was its size—15.24 m long weighing in at 35 tons! Today, spreadsheets are used for everything from calculating company profits to income tax to loan payments.

InsighTs: Succeeding in the Information Age

Formatting Your Spreadsheet

Once you have entered the labels and values into the cells on your spreadsheet, you might want to format your spreadsheet so that it has more visual appeal. First, select the cells to be formatted. There are then a variety of options you can choose from. Some of the more popular ones are shown in Fig. 4.13.

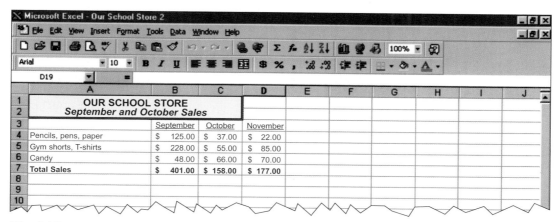

Fig. 4.13
Screen capture of a formatted spreadsheet

- Titles are centred across the columns in the spreadsheet.
- Titles are bold and/or italicized with a border around the cells and shading in the border area.
- Month labels are underlined.
- Total row is bold.
- All sales data, including totals, have been formatted for currency.

 **Activity**

Formatting Data

There are many options for formatting your spreadsheet data. Explore your software application and format the "Our School Store" data on your computer.

How Do You Convert Data to a Chart or Graph?

One of the most popular options in a spreadsheet package is the ability to turn your data into charts and graphs. Charts and graphs allow people to see patterns in data and to share data in simple form. The phrase "a picture is worth a thousand words" was never truer.

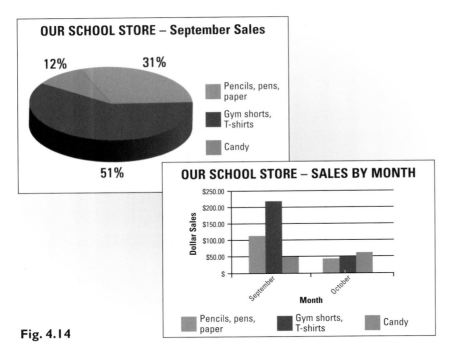

OUR SCHOOL STORE – September Sales

12%   31%

Pencils, pens, paper
Gym shorts, T-shirts
Candy

51%

OUR SCHOOL STORE – SALES BY MONTH

Dollar Sales

$250.00
$200.00
$150.00
$100.00
$50.00
$

September   October

Month

Pencils, pens, paper
Gym shorts, T-shirts
Candy

Fig. 4.14

Using the data from "Our School Store," you can create a pie chart for each month, a column chart comparing the two months, or perhaps a line graph to indicate sales by category. Figure 4.14 shows a pie chart for September sales and a column chart comparing the two months. In order to prepare charts and graphs so they accurately depict the information in your spreadsheet, it is necessary to understand the parts of a chart.

1. **title**—In any chart or graph it is important to include a *title* that describes the content of the chart so there is no confusion. In Fig. 4.14, the pie chart's title of "OUR SCHOOL STORE— September Sales" leaves no question in the reader's mind.

2. **legend**—In Fig. 4.14, both the pie chart and column chart have a *legend* indicating which colour represents which category of sales.

3. **data labels**—On the pie chart in Fig. 4.14, the percentage of total sales is used as the data label for each pie slice. Other options include showing the actual value from the spreadsheet, the label (instead of using a legend), or the label and percentage. Each spreadsheet package has slightly different *data label* options. If you included data labels on the column chart, you would place the value from the spreadsheet above the appropriate columns.

4. **x-axis**—The *x-axis* is the horizontal axis of a column chart. In Fig. 4.14, the x-axis indicates the months being compared.

5. **y-axis**—The *y-axis* is the vertical axis of a column chart. "Our School Store"'s column chart shows the Dollar Sales as the y-axis.

In all cases, it is important to use clear, concise wording on your charts. A picture may be worth a thousand words, but make sure the words you use are understandable!

Choosing Which Charts

There are no definitive rules regarding the choice of charts. The choices you make depend largely on what information you are trying to convey.

- *Pie charts* are very useful for showing the contribution of each value to the total. In "Our School Store" in Fig. 4.14, a pie chart was used to show the percentage of September sales for each product category.

- *Column* and *bar charts* are ideal for side-by-side comparisons of data. Column charts show vertical bars, whereas bar charts show bars horizontally on the graph. Using the column bar for "Our School Store" (Fig. 4.14) makes it easy to see the difference in sales for each category by month.

- *Line graphs* are ideal for showing the trend of data over time (see Fig. 4.15(a)). A line graph would be a good choice if you wanted to chart the value of the Canadian dollar over the course of a year.

- *Stacked column* and *bar charts* show the contribution of each value to a total across categories (see Fig. 4.15(b)).

More specialized charts and graphs can also be created. Refer to the Help menu in your program for more details.

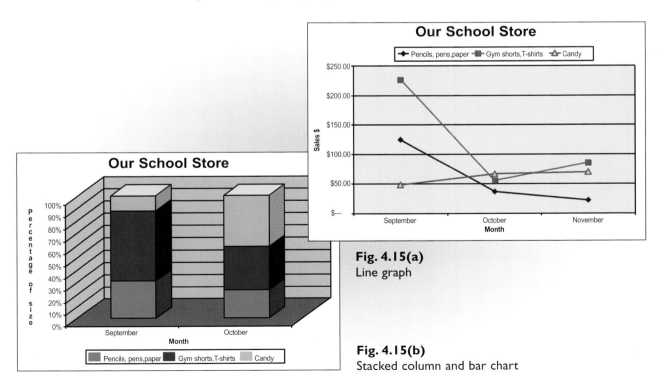

Fig. 4.15(a)
Line graph

Fig. 4.15(b)
Stacked column and bar chart

How Do I Get My Documents To Look That Good?

 **Activity**

Determining Format

Look at the line graph and stacked column and bar chart in Fig. 4.15. Which of the two formats do you think is the most effective given the nature of the data being represented? Why?

 **Activity**

Create Your Own Charts

Part A

Use the "Our School Store" file to create the following charts:

- pie chart for September's sales
- bar or column chart comparing September and October sales
- stacked and column bar chart for September and October sales

For each chart, write a brief description of what the chart shows.

Part B

Research the average scores for the current month for your favourite school or professional sports team. Which format do you think would be most effective for presenting your data? Why? Use your spreadsheet software to present your data. Would you use the same format to present the average temperatures for your area for four months? Why or why not?

Knowledge Check

1. What is a spreadsheet?
2. How are columns and rows identified?
3. What is a cell? How are individual cells identified?
4. What are the three types of information you can enter into cells? Describe each one.
5. What steps do you take to make numbers in a spreadsheet appear as currency? As percentages?
6. What is a function in a spreadsheet? What are four of the most commonly used functions?

7. What are some of the formatting options you have for information in a spreadsheet?
8. Describe the following parts of a chart/graph created from spreadsheet data: title, legend, data labels, x-axis, and y-axis.
9. When might you use each of the following types of charts/graphs: pie chart, column/bar graph, line graph?

InsighTs: Succeeding in the Information Age

The Database

What Is a Database?

A *database* is a collection of information about a particular subject or purpose, organized in such a way that users can retrieve information quickly and easily. One of the best known database examples is the telephone book. Each person or business with a publicly listed telephone number is shown, in alphabetical order, by city. Each entry in the phone book shows the person's last name, first name or initials, street address, and telephone number. Some directories also list the postal code.

Fig. 4.16
Sample of a relational database

The phone company, however, has much more information about each customer on file. For example, it has billing information showing how much a customer owes each month and when the last payment was made. In a product file, the company knows which of its services the customer uses—such as Call Display or Touch-Tone service. For a customer who uses the company's long-distance service, it has a file showing the telephone numbers dialled and the length of each call. The common thread throughout these files is the telephone number. Although the phone company collects different pieces of information and keeps them in different places, it can also pull all these pieces of information together to create a complete profile based on just a phone number. By defining how each file is related (the telephone number), the data only needs to be entered once. This kind of database is known as a *relational database*.

 **Activity**

Who Collects Personal Information?

Brainstorm all the organizations or places that collect personal information. What kind of information is collected? How do you think the people who collect the information organize the information? Is there any common thread that ties the information together? Compare your lists with those of other members of your class.

The Anatomy of a Database

Before creating a database, you must first understand the various components that make up the database.

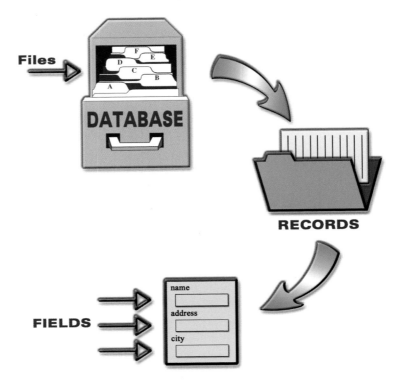

Fig. 4.17
A database file is made up of files, which are made up of records, each of which contains numerous pieces of information in fields.

1. **record**—A *record* is all the information relating to an individual item or person in a database. For example,
   - all the information collected about a person or organization by the telephone company
   - all the information collected about you by your school or school board
   - information about each CD in your CD collection (e.g., title, artist, year of release)

   Each record has its own unique number within the database. This is the ID number for that record. Records in Microsoft Access, for example, are shown in the rows as in Fig. 4.18. Notice that each record contains the same type of information. These are the fields.

2. **field**—Within each record are the pieces of information you have collected. Each piece of information is contained in a field. In Microsoft Access, *fields* are the columns in the table. Using your CD collection as an example, you might want to record the CD title, the recording company, the artist's name, and the songs on each disc. You might also want to include your own comments about each song. Each of these bits of information is entered in its own field or column.

3. **data type**—For each field, you must choose what type of data you will enter. Some examples of field data types in Access are text (the default data type), memo, date/time, and yes/no fields. Yes/no fields are useful for when you only want to enter one of two options. For example, you might want to record a person's language preference as English or French. "Yes" could be assigned to either language. If you are planning on performing any calculations on the data, you must define the data type as numeric or currency, depending on what the data will contain. By specifying the data type at the beginning (e.g., currency), you can streamline data entry into the database (e.g., dollar signs added automatically to the amounts).

4. **field size**—For each field in Access you must determine how many characters will be needed for the data being entered. The default Field Size is 50 characters. You can adjust the field size to accommodate your data.

Once you determine the field names, data type, and size for each field, you enter them into the table or form within your program. Again, each database program functions slightly differently so you must familiarize yourself with the program's requirements. Using Microsoft Access, your database might look like Fig. 4.18.

ID	CD Title	Artist	Song Title	Notes
1	Planet Out There	Some Guy	Got to Get Going	Great tune. Lots of bass.
2	Planet Out There	Some Other Guy	Escape!	What a blast. This guy has a great set of pipes.
3	Planet Out There	Whosat	What a Blast	Not so crash hot. Too many drum solos.
(Auto Number)				

Fig. 4.18
CD database, Access

Setting Up Your Own Database

One of the first computerized database uses was the US Census in 1951. In that year, the American government used the new UNIVAC (Universal Automatic Computer) to input and process data. UNIVAC was the first computer to use magnetic tape, reading both alphabetic and numeric data at 7200 digits per second.

Explore the database software in your school and determine the steps required to set up an address book for your friends and relatives. Set up the database with fields for first name, last name, address, city, province, postal code, telephone number, and e-mail address.

Entering Information into a Database

To enter data into the database, you key the data for each field within the table, and tab to the next field when finished. Most database packages will automatically number the records. When you fill a record, another is automatically started for you. The *record number* is indicated at the bottom of the screen—in our example in Fig. 4.19, the "1 of 3." There are navigating buttons beside the record number that allow you to move around from record to record.

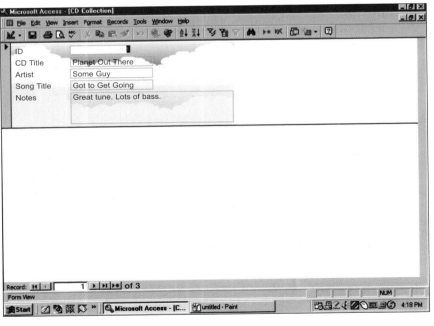

Some people are more comfortable entering information on a form within the database, rather than a table. A *form* is an electronic version of what you might see on a printed document used to collect data. Entering data is the same as in a table. Users tab from field to field and when a record is complete a new one is started on a fresh screen.

Fig. 4.19
Screen capture of CD information on database form

Planning a Database

Use a paper and pencil to plan a database for a small service business (e.g., hairdresser, personal trainer, lawn care, computer repair shop). Determine the fields (name, data type, and size) you would need to keep track of sales to various customers. Do not forget the different product categories you might sell. Once you have determined the necessary fields, use you database program to design a form in which to input your data.

Getting Information Out of a Database

There are two main ways of getting information out of a database.

- **queries**—A database can become quite large by the time all the data are entered into the records. If you want to retrieve only certain information, most databases allow you to design a query (or Find function) to do this. Suppose you want to find out how many songs "Some Guy" sang in your CD collection and which CDs the songs are on. You would design a query to find each occurrence of the artist "Some Guy," listing the song title and CD title, in your database in alphabetical order. In Microsoft Access the Query screen would look like Fig. 4.20.

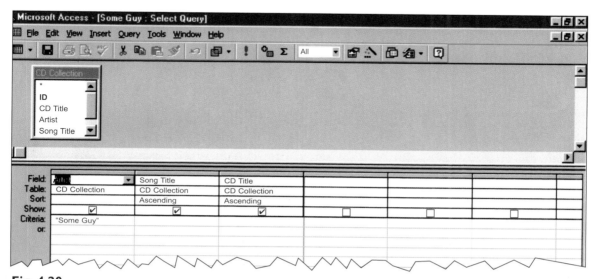

Fig. 4.20
Microsoft Access Select Query asking for records in the database for "Some Guy" as the Artist. The query will display only the records for that artist in alphabetical order by song title and CD title.

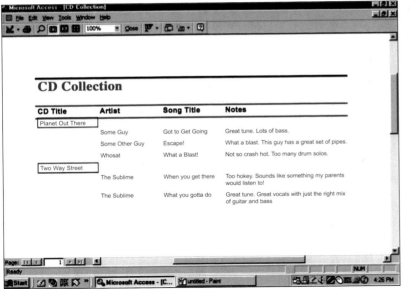

Fig. 4.21

- **reports**—The other way to retrieve information is in the form of a report. A report looks more like a word-processed document, but is created by the database program. In Fig. 4.21, the songs are grouped by CD title, in alphabetical order by artist.

Case Study

Big Brother Database Scrapped

For many years, Canada's federal government has been collecting information about every person in the country. In fact, the Longitudinal Labour Force File (LLFF) had up to 2000 facts on just about every citizen. This massive database linked data from Canada Customs and Revenue Agency (the tax department) with numerous social assistance agencies—health insurance claims, child-benefit payments, welfare claims, job programs, and employment insurance. Until 2000, that is. In response to growing concerns across the country regarding personal privacy, the Human Resources Ministry dismantled the database and returned the taxation data to the Revenue Ministry in the spring of 2000.

1. Research your school's or school board's policy regarding the confidentiality of data about students. Prepare a one-page written report outlining your findings.

2. For a 24-hour period, keep track of all the people you and your family interact with, Web sites you visit, or tasks you perform that require you to identify yourself in some way or other. Note what information you or your family members are asked for (e.g., telephone number, birth date, social insurance number). Make a list of all the information that is being collected about you and your family members. Bring your list into class and compare it with lists of your classmates.

Optional: Create a class chart, either on paper or using your favourite word processing program, on which you list the pieces of information that everyone was asked to supply.

WHAT DO YOU THINK?

The growing number of databases and the ability to share information among databases are raising serious ethical questions. Ken Badley in *Worldviews: The Challenge of Choice* asks the following questions about issues of privacy:

• Should a bank in Vancouver sell information about your buying habits to a mail-order retailer in Montreal without your knowledge and permission?

• Should information about your driving record be made available to prospective employers?

• Should insurance companies have access to your health records?

In small groups, discuss these questions. Do you think it is possible to prevent sharing of information from different databases? What steps would you suggest?

Business Applications for Databases

A database is a powerful tool for collecting information for many purposes in business. Information relating to customers, suppliers, product inventory, customer accounts, and purchases are just some of its uses. Integrating all these pieces of information into a relational database can provide business decision makers with valuable information necessary to survive in a competitive environment.

Knowledge Check

1. What is a database? What does it comprise?
2. What are records? What are fields?
3. What is a relational database? What makes it so powerful?
4. When specifying the data type for each field in a record, what are your options? When would you choose each data type?
5. In what two formats can you enter information into a database? Why might one method be preferable over the other?
6. What is a query and how does it work?
7. What is a report and what does it look like?
8. What are some of the common business uses for databases?

How Do I Get My Documents To Look That Good?

Lesley Macaskill

Program Coordinator and Dietician

Lesley Macaskill is a busy person. You may already be familiar with some of her work! Lesley is the coordinator of the Eat Smart! Ontario's Healthy Restaurant Program, an award program that assesses restaurants to see if the restaurants meet certain criteria that would make them a healthy and nutritious choice for customers. Restaurants are evaluated based on the number of nutritious, low-fat choices on their menus, the availability of non-smoking seating, and kitchen practices, including the cleanliness of food preparation areas.

"Once I have gathered information about a restaurant," Lesley explains, "I rely on information technology to get the results out to customers."

First, Lesley inputs all the information about the restaurant into a database. Next, she updates the Eat Smart! Web site with the database information so that people can see the results. "I also have to update the Web site any time information changes, such as when restaurants close or move," she adds.

Finally, as the coordinator of the program, Lesley is responsible for the budget that keeps Eat Smart! going. She uses a spreadsheet to keep track of money coming into the program, expenses, and purchases.

In addition to her work with Eat Smart!, Lesley is also a dietician. She works with people to analyze their diets and provide nutrition counselling. To do this, she uses special computer software to perform a "nutrient analysis" that lets her clients know the amount of calories and nutrients in the food they eat. The software also analyzes recipes and allows Lesley to help clients find alternative ingredients that would allow them to eat the same kinds of food, while improving their level of nutrition.

Though Lesley has a Master of Health Science degree in Community Nutrition from the University of Toronto, she says almost all her computer skills are self-taught. She continues to upgrade her skills as new software becomes available. "I don't think I could live without technology!" Lesley says. "Without it, I certainly could not do the work that I do."

---

1. What is the Eat Smart! program? Describe the service it performs for restaurant owners and customers.

2. Describe the software application programs Lesley uses in administering the Eat Smart! program.

3. How has Lesley's formal education (Master of Health Science degree) helped her in her job? Describe some of the skills she has transferred to her position.

For more information about the Eat Smart! program (and to see Lesley's work) visit the InsighTs Student Page on <www.irwinpublishing.com/students>.

4. What other types of jobs could Lesley pursue with her type of training, background, and obvious aptitude for computers?

CHAPTER SUMMARY

Understanding Information

1. Why is it important for students to know how to create and format business letters and reports? List and describe situations where you can use these skills.

2. What impact has the computer and word processing software had on the creation of business reports?

3. From the information presented in the chapter, list and describe the benefits of using spreadsheet software for business calculations.

4. What does a database allow an organization to do with all of the information it gathers on customers, their suppliers, and the products it sells?

Analyzing

5. Your friend, Faisal, is working on a Geography project assigned by his teacher. He has to prepare a written submission on the climate in a particular region of Canada. Part of the project requires analysis of the temperature and precipitation of that region for two major cities in the region. Describe how Faisal could use different software packages to achieve the best result.

6. Using the Help menu in your spreadsheet software, investigate the proper syntax/format for entering formulas and functions. Prepare a chart showing how to add, subtract, multiply, and divide two cells. Add to this chart the proper syntax for the SUM, MIN, MAX, and AVERAGE/AVG functions for a range of cells.

Applying

7. Over the course of the next week, keep track of the number of hours you spend doing homework each day and the number of hours you spend watching television each day. Enter this information into a spreadsheet entitled "Time Well Spent?" Be sure to clearly label both the days of the week and the two categories of Homework and Television. Use a formula to calculate the total hours spent on each activity. Use the average function to calculate the average number of hours you spent on each activity. Create a graph to compare the time spent.

8. Create the structure for an address database for all your friends and relatives. Identify what fields will be needed, separating last name from first name for alphabetical sorting. How big should each field be? What extra fields might you want to include? What data format would you use for each?

How Do I Get My Documents To Look That Good?

9. Set up a database that will allow you to track your skills and competencies. Decide which fields should be set up in order for you to keep the best possible records.

Communicating

10. Draft a letter to your local Parks and Recreation Department applying for a summer job as a Recreation Counsellor. Use proper business letter format and key the draft. Have a classmate edit and proofread your letter using proper proofreaders' marks.

11. Describe where you can use a spreadsheet in other courses you are currently taking or have taken before. What advantages would there be to using the spreadsheet over the methods you currently use?

Organize your conclusions in chart form, as follows:

Spreadsheet Uses		
Subject	**Topic**	**Advantages**
Mathematics	First differences	Speeds up calculations
		Reduces errors

12. In teams of three or four, debate the pros and cons of the collection of information about customers, students, or other groups of people by various organizations. Put your list of arguments in your portfolio. You may want to revisit this discussion after you complete your study of chapter 9.

Assessing Your Competencies

13. Using the software competency checklists provided by your teacher, check off the competencies that you have mastered during the course of this chapter. Note the competencies that require more attention and review.

14. Interview a classmate to determine the competencies he or she has acquired during this chapter. Also share some of the new skills you have acquired.

CHAPTER FIVE

PROGRAMS WITH PIZZAZZ

In chapter 3, you learned about frequently used office productivity software programs. There are also a number of more specialized applications that are widely used in business today. In this chapter, you will explore graphic design, desktop publishing, and multimedia presentation software that will help you become even more productive and build your competencies in other ways.

Topics

➤ Graphic Design
➤ Desktop Publishing (DTP)
➤ Multimedia Presentations

This chapter explores these questions:

- What is the difference between graphic image formats?
- What are the elements of good graphic design?
- What is desktop publishing?
- What can a desktop publishing program do that a word processor cannot?
- What is a multimedia presentation?
- How can I make my presentations with pizzazz?

In this chapter, you will have the opportunity to

- draw and analyze a bitmap image and a vector-based image
- design a flyer or advertisement using the principles of balance in design
- create a design that illustrates design contrast
- examine Web sites, advertisements, and graphics for consistency in design
- explore graphic formats compatible with your word processor
- explore career opportunities in graphic design
- explore the drawing tools in your word processor
- convert a document to a two-column format
- create your own personal letterhead
- explore what templates and wizards are available to you
- create short, punchy headlines
- determine what combinations of colour work well together
- practise presenting a one-minute speech
- explore options in your presentation software
- design your own customized presentation template

Graphic Design

Everywhere you look, you see the results of efforts by graphic designers—from the logo of your favourite sportswear on the company's Web site, to the advertising you are bombarded with every day. Graphic artists work in all types of businesses, including wholesale/retail sales, manufacturing, printing, and publishing. Today's graphic artists love art, but they also love their computers. This section will examine what can be done in *image editing and graphics programs*, the difference between the various graphic file formats, and the applications for graphic designs.

What Is the Difference Between Graphic Image Formats?

There are two types of computer graphics programs. One is based on creating bitmap images. The other is based on creating vector images. The difference between the two programs lies in the way the images are created.

Bitmap Images

Bitmap images are also known as raster (screen) or *paint images*. A *bitmap image* is made of rows and columns of individual dots or *pixels* (picture elements). These dots are arranged and coloured individually to form a pattern. In a normal-size bitmap image, the pixels form lines and shapes that appear continuous and smooth (Fig. 5.1(a)). The more dots per inch (dpi) on a screen, the sharper your image will appear—hence the name "raster," or screen image. (A *raster* is the rectangular area of a display screen actually being used to display images.) However, CRT and LCD screens are generally only capable of displaying a maximum resolution of approximately 72 dpi, no matter the chosen dimension.

If you enlarge a bitmap image by zooming in on it, you will see the individual pixels that make up the entire image. The image appears jagged (Fig. 5.1(b)). Reducing a bitmap image too much will also distort the image because some pixels are eliminated to shrink the image.

(a)

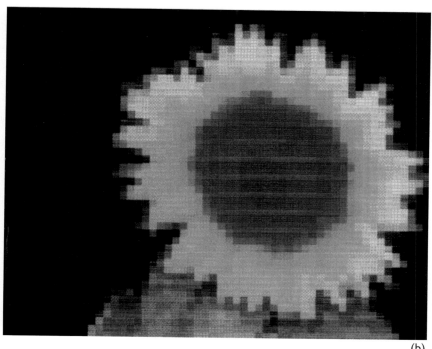
(b)

Fig. 5.1
(a) Normal-size bitmap image (b) Enlarged bitmap image

You can add image enhancements, such as shadows, to your bitmap images by manipulating the colour of individual pixels. To add a shadow, you open the image in a paint program (e.g., Photoshop, Corel PHOTO-PAINT), click on the individual pixel locations, and select the colour you wish to change them to. However, because the image is a collection of pixels, image parts themselves cannot be moved around. For example, you could not change the direction in which the flowers are leaning without redrawing the entire image.

The quality of a bitmap image depends on the *resolution* you choose in the paint program and the resolution that can be displayed on your output device (monitor or printer). The resolution of an image is represented in dots per inch (also known as pixels per inch). If your output device has a lower resolution than the resolution you set in the software, the image will appear more ragged. The reverse is not true. Images will look no better on an output device with a better resolution than they do when you first create them. Images are only as clear as when they are created.

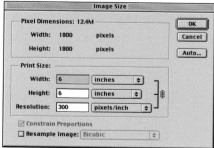

Fig. 5.2
Screen capture showing where you would enter the dpi in Adobe Photoshop

Creating Your Own Bitmap Image

Explore the paint program that is included with your Windows or Mac computer system. Draw a simple image such as a circle or rounded shape. Zoom in on the image. Describe how the enlarged image differs from the normal-size view. On the enlarged image, colour in individual pixels with contrasting colours, then resize to normal. How does the result look? Print out your image and compare it with the screen image. Compare your findings with a classmate.

Graphic designers use bitmap images when the full-colour spectrum is to be used and the image is very detailed. Because each pixel is coloured separately, bitmap images use more memory to store the image file than vector graphics. Bitmap images can be created in a number of programs, including Corel PHOTO-PAINT, Paint Shop Pro, Adobe Photoshop, or Microsoft Paint.

Vector Graphics

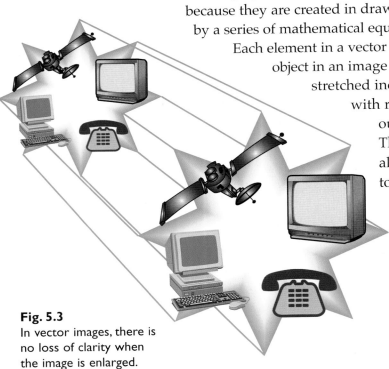

Vector graphics are also known as *object-oriented* or *draw images* because they are created in draw programs. *Vector graphics* are built by a series of mathematical equations each time they are displayed. Each element in a vector graphic is called an *object*. Each object in an image can be manipulated, resized, or stretched independently of the other objects with regard to its size, colour, shape, outline, and position on the screen. These programs are ideal for creating all kinds of illustrations, from clip art to animated characters, CADD (computer-aided design and drafting) drawings, and 3-D graphics. These kinds of images are often resized and changed prior to final output, so being created as vector graphics is ideal. Many fonts are also created using vector graphics so they can be resized without losing their sharp image.

Fig. 5.3
In vector images, there is no loss of clarity when the image is enlarged.

Unlike bitmap images, the output from a vector program will be at the maximum resolution of your printer or monitor. As a result, your final product will be of a higher quality on a 600-dpi printer than on a 300-dpi printer.

Vector-based images can be created in drawing programs such as CorelDRAW and Adobe Illustrator.

 **Activity**

Creating a Vector Image

Explore the basic features of the draw program on your computer. Draw a simple image on the screen and enlarge it (zoom in). Compare the sharpness of this image with the normal-size view. How does this image differ from the bitmap image created earlier?

What Are the Elements of Good Graphic Design?

At one time or another, we have all seen graphic designs (logos, advertisements, Web sites) that we thought were outstanding, and others that we thought were unappealing. This section will examine some common principles of design that will help you to make your graphic designs appear professional and visually appealing.

Balance

When a graphic design is *balanced*, all the graphic elements (text, pictures, shapes, etc.) are visually connected.

An unbalanced object or page causes discomfort in viewers. Unless discomfort is a desired effect, images must be balanced.

You can achieve balance and create visual interest in two different ways—symmetrical or asymmetrical.

Symmetrical balance refers to a layout in which the two sides of a design are mirror images of each other, for example McDonald's "Golden Arches." For this reason, this type of balance is the easiest to achieve. Viewers' eyes are generally drawn to the element placed at the centre of the design and comfortably flow to either side. This type of balance can be used to reflect stability, permanence, and calmness, but has the disadvantage of not being very exciting.

Fig. 5.4

An excellent example of an asymmetrical design.© 2000 Procter & Gamble

Courtesy Procter & Gamble

Asymmetrical balance is more common and often more interesting. It is also more difficult to achieve. Asymmetrical balance is achieved by using elements with different visual interests (such as colour, size, or texture) to draw viewers' eyes to a particular area of the design. For example, the Swiffer™ Wet logo shown in Fig. 5.4 uses design elements to draw your eye to follow the swish of colours behind the words.

 **Activity**

Creating a Balanced Flyer or Advertisement

Create a balanced flyer or advertisement, using up to three graphic images and up to three sentences of text. Draw these images yourself, or cut them out of existing newspapers or magazines. Explain which of the two types of balance you employed in your flyer or advertisement, and why you chose that type of balance.

Contrast

Fig. 5.5

This advertisement for Telus Mobility shows an effective use of contrasting objects.

Courtesy Telus Mobility

Contrast creates interest in a graphic design by providing variety. Placing two different objects next to each other creates visual interest. The arrangement provides visual stimulation, which prevents viewer boredom. Contrast can be created by:

- varying the size of objects and having one small object next to a large object
- using two different fonts to represent different types of text. For instance, you might choose the Arial font for facts, Times New Roman italic for quotes from customers, and Times New Roman bold for address and telephone number.
- using contrasting or opposite shapes next to one another
- varying the texture of objects that are next to one another

It is easy to overuse contrast, creating a graphic design that is busy. Be careful: Viewers will not be able to decide what is important if everything is contrasting. To avoid this problem, limit contrast to one or two elements.

InsighTs: Succeeding in the Information Age

What Is a Font?

In most applications, you use the Font menu or command to change the appearance of your text. The use of the word "font" in this way has become generally accepted. However, in this usage we are using the word "font" when we really mean "typeface."

So what is a *typeface*?

A typeface is a specific design for a set of characters. Times New Roman is an example of a typeface. When you add special characteristics such as size change, italics, and bold, you now have a "font." The font that you use in a document title or paragraph is a combination of typeface, size, and other characteristics.

Typefaces fall into two general categories: serif and sans serif. **Serif typefaces** have small decorative marks on the characters than can make text easier to read. Common examples are Times New Roman and Courier. **Sans-serif typefaces** are made with simple lines. Examples include Helvetica and Arial (see Fig. 5.6).

There are very specific rules for successfully combining typefaces in the same document. Do an Internet search using key words such as "typography," "font," "rules," or "guidelines" to find three general rules for combining typefaces.(You may want to read chapter 9, pages 254-6, on key word searches on the Internet.)

Fig. 5.6 (a) This typeface is Times New Roman.

(b) This typeface is Courier New.

(c) This typeface is Helvetica.

(d) This typeface is Arial.

(e) **This typeface is Thickhead.**

(f) This typeface is ArgosANouveau.

 *Activity*

Creating a Design Using Contrast

1. Using only basic design colours and shapes—lines, circles, ellipses, squares, and rectangles—create a design to illustrate the concept of contrast. Work with a partner to discuss and critique the resulting designs.

2. Locate a graphic design (advertisement, brochure, flier, or Web site) that uses contrast. Explain what elements were contrasted. Do you feel the contrast is effective? Why or why not?

Consistency

While there is value in using some surprise and variation in design, these elements must be balanced against the need for *consistency* and a uniform appearance.

Roger C. Parker in *Ten Rules of Good Design, Part II* writes the following about graphic design for business:

"Design creates unity by using space, type and colors in a consistent way throughout every document your firm produces, and within every page of a single document, presentation or web site."

Mr. Parker is describing the importance of having recognizable graphic images for a company or brand. Think about the advertisements you see for a large company, such as Canadian Tire. Most Canadians will recognize a Canadian Tire commercial, packaging, flier, coupon, or Web site in an instant. They do so because Canadian Tire uses consistent elements of design for all of its publications and packaging.

Fig. 5.7
Examples of consistent elements
Courtesy Canadian Tire Corporation

Creating Consistency in Your Designs

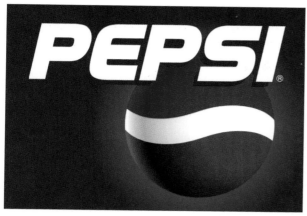

Fig. 5.8
The Pepsi-Cola trademark.

Courtesy of the
Pepsi-Cola Company

- **margins and page layout**—Use the same margins throughout a document and for all related items for a particular company.

- **fonts**—Graphic designers have thousands of fonts to choose from. That does not mean they should use every font in every design. Two fonts are generally enough for most designs.

- **navigation (for Web sites)**—Visitors to a Web site might become confused if navigation buttons are on the left on one page, on the right on another, and at the bottom on another.

- **colour**—If a logo contains two or four colours (such as Pepsi), a graphic designer probably would not dream of switching those colours around. Viewers will feel more comfortable with Web sites and printed designs if a recognizable colour scheme appears throughout. The design palette should be limited to two or three colours, and those should be used consistently and be easy to understand and apply.

Consistency does not mean that everything must be an exact clone. Viewers can feel at home by consistent use of fonts, colours, design elements, and layout.

 *Activity*

Exploring Design

1. Look up the Web site for your favourite television show. How does the Web site use consistency? Does it have the same "feel" as the television show itself? Support your answer with specific examples.

2. If you could design a Web site for that show yourself, what would you do to make it consistent with the show? What elements of design would you use and how?

3. Look through several newspapers and magazines to collect examples of graphic designs. Your examples can include advertisements, brochures, or articles.

   a) Identify one example that you think is a good piece of graphic art.

   b) Identify one example that you think needs improvement.

   c) For each example, identify why you selected it, what elements are good, and what elements require improvement.

Saving and Retrieving Your Images

Graphic designers save the images they create in a number of file formats. Each format has specific characteristics and some formats are better suited to different end uses (e.g., print publication, Web) than others. Figure 5.9 provides a brief overview of some of the more popular file formats, their characteristics, and applications.

Before you decide in which file format to save your graphics, check the Help file of your desktop publishing software (see next section) or word processing software to determine what image formats your program supports. You may discover that you cannot insert a graphic image of a particular file format into your document. For example, a CorelDRAW image in .cdr format cannot be inserted directly into a Word document. In this case, you may decide to use Save As to save your image in a format that will work, such as .jpg or .gif. Occasionally, you will need to convert your files from one format to another (it is not always possible to use Save As to change image format). You can often change files from one format to another by using a command such as Export in programs such as Corel PHOTO-PAINT, Paint Shop Pro, and Adobe Photoshop or Illustrator.

Extension	Description
.bmp	Bitmap—A raster or pixel-based image. Individual pixels make up full image. Format used by Microsoft Windows
.tif, .tiff on Mac	Tag Image File Format—A raster or pixel-based image. Used especially for scanned images because it can support any size, resolution, and colour depth. Is popular in print media productions
.tga	Targa bitmap image—A raster or pixel-based image
.pcx	PaintBrush image—A raster or pixel based image. Supported by many graphics programs as well as most scanners and modems
.gif	Graphic Interchange Format—Pronounced "gif" as in giffy, GIF files were developed as a cross-platform standard. They support up to 256 colours, can have transparent backgrounds, and display fairly quickly on screen. Best choice for line drawings and graphics with few colours or sharp edges. Used mostly on Web pages
.png	Portable Network Graphics—Developed as an alternative to GIF files; supports true colour and maintains picture integrity when other file types converted to .png files. Use on Internet Web pages where true colour is important to image integrity
.jpg	Joint Photographic Experts Group—Commonly pronounced jpeg. Excellent option for photographs and scanned images. Compresses high-quality images for faster image display. Used on Web pages for images with many shades and colour tones (i.e., photographs)
.cdr	CorelDRAW image—A vector-based line drawing. Individual objects can be manipulated within the image
.wpg	WordPerfect Graphic—Vector graphics designed for use with WordPerfect software, primarily
.wmf	Windows Metafile—Vector graphics found in many commercially available clip art libraries. Work well with Windows-based programs
.cgm	Computer Graphics Metafile—Vector graphics, found in many commercially available clip-art libraries
.pict	Macintosh Picture File—This is the standard graphic format used on Mac computers. It is used for both bitmap and vector images
.eps	Encapsulated PostScript File. An almost universal vector graphic image that works in most layout programs. If you save an Adobe Photoshop file as an .esp file, however, it saves as a bitmapped graphic.

Fig. 5.9
Overview of some file formats for saving graphic images and where they can be used

InsighTs: Succeeding in the Information Age

Inserting Graphics from Other Programs

In your word processing program, determine how to insert a graphic or picture file. Explore this feature until you find a list of the file formats that your program supports. Make a list of these formats and keep this list in your notebook as a reference for future activities and assignments.

Explore the programs available to you on your school network to determine how many of these picture types you could create for yourself. Create a simple graphic, save it and then bring it into your word processor. Try enlarging the image—is it a bitmap image or vector image? How can you tell?

CAREER PROFILE

Sonny J. Druer Graphic Designer

Have you ever wondered who came up with the really great logos you see on everything you buy... like the Nike "swoosh" or the little person on your BIC pen? They come from the imaginations of skilled graphic designers like Sonny Druer.

Sonny has worked for Artech Promotional Wear in Orillia, Ontario, for the last 15 years, creating designs for everything from T-shirts to logos for promotional items (give-aways) such as magnets, pens, key chains, or water bottles. He also does an amazing job digitizing images for embroidery on shirts and ball caps.

"I must say, there was a feeling of disappointment with my parents when after four years of architectural and mechanical drafting I chose to design T-shirts." However, Sonny loves his job and that's what counts! Sonny combines his creative imagination with a computer that has a variety of draw programs and Internet access. His position allows him to meet a variety of people from various organizations who perform many different functions. He works with Artech's sales people on current projects, and with customers to ensure that all their requirements are met.

Sonny's "hands-on" experience has allowed him to stay up-to-date with current trends in graphic design. Technological change has had a tremendous impact on this industry. Sonny can now create in hours what used to take a day or more with manual methods of design. Changes in technology have also increased communication and idea sharing between customer and designer. In Sonny's words, "Designing has never been so easy."

Next time you see a logo or design on a pen, shirt or baseball cap, think of Sonny. He just might be the creative mind behind that design!

1. List all the items you have in your possession right now that have some kind of logo or graphic design on them. What is the company represented by the logo and what is the graphic?

2. How do you think Sonny's background and formal training in architectural design and drafting helped him in his position as a graphic designer? What skills has he been able to transfer to this job?

3. Describe some of the other skills Sonny uses in his job.

1. Describe the difference between a bitmap image and a vector-based image. Consider how each is created and edited in your answer.
2. Describe what is meant by balance in graphic design. How is it achieved?
3. What is the difference between symmetrical and asymmetrical balance?
4. What is meant by contrast in design and how can it be achieved?
5. What is consistency in design? What are three suggested methods for achieving consistency in your designs?
6. How can you be sure a graphic image will work in your software application?

Desktop Publishing (DTP)

Learning Link

Word processors generally organize data in paragraphs.

Desktop publishing programs organize data as objects that can be placed anywhere on the page, independent of other data.

What Is Desktop Publishing?

Desktop publishing software consists of special application programs that combine graphics and text to design and prepare pages for publication. Many word processing packages today also include desktop publishing features that allow users to incorporate graphic images into their documents. As well, desktop publishing programs and some word processing programs include templates and wizards. These templates and wizards allow users to create brochures, newsletters, and flyers—virtually any document or publication a business needs to create for internal or external distribution.

Features Common to Desktop Publishing Programs and Word Processors With DTP Capabilities

Regardless of which desktop publishing program you use, you will find certain common features that will simplify your graphic design job. Some word processing programs that contain desktop publishing capabilities also share these features. Some of the most common features are described below.

- **clip art and graphics**—Today's desktop publishing and word processing programs have a built-in library of graphic images in a *clip art gallery* and often a hyperlink to a Web clip art gallery on the Internet. Inserting an image into your work is as simple as point and click.
  - Place your cursor in the position where your graphic is to be inserted.

Fig. 5.10
Examples of text wrapping using Microsoft Word

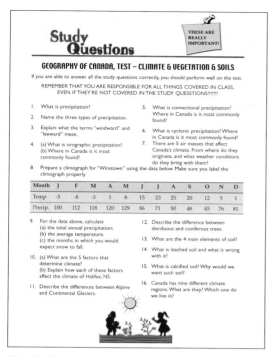

Fig. 5.11
Document created in Word with just a few of the drawing elements that are available

– From the Insert menu, look for an option such as Graphic or Picture and then select the clip art menu.

– Find the image you want and select it.

– The program will insert the image where you left your cursor.

Once you have placed the image in your document, you have a number of formatting options. You can, for example, have the text wrap around the image to the side or above and below it. You can add a border to the image, increase the white space around it so the text and image do not collide, and fade the image to create a watermark (a faded image that appears behind text). Some programs even allow you to rotate and invert the image.

If you do not want to use one of the clip art images that come with the program, you can insert images from another file. For example, your corporate logo may have been created as a vector file and is saved on another disk or shared network folder.

- **WordArt or TextArt**—If you want to insert text that is already shadowed, textured, coloured, or contains other interesting effects, give *WordArt* or *TextArt* a try. Once you have selected the word or group of words you want to change, access the WordArt or TextArt feature. Alternately, the text can be keyed in after you have clicked on the WordArt or TextArt button. Next, choose a shape or design, select the colour or texture with which to fill the design, and manipulate the design to create the desired effect. The text then becomes a graphic object, and can be selected and moved by clicking or dragging it. It can also be resized by dragging one of the handles (small boxes) around the image.

- **text boxes**—If you want text positioned in a specific location on a page you can use a text box.

> Text boxes allow you to key information independent of the main body text.

When you insert a text box, the main body wraps around the box, allowing you to use the text box to highlight information.

- **drawing shapes**—Word processing programs allow you to insert drawing shapes within your document, including lines, arrows, circles, rectangles, stars, banners, and more. These shapes can contain colour, textures, and text. They can be enhanced with 3-D elements or shadows and placed anywhere within your document.

- **columns**—Another feature that adds to the versatility of many word processing programs is the ability to convert text into columns. Being able to convert text into columns is a useful feature when creating newsletters and brochures. You can have multiple columns, with or without lines in between. You can also select uneven column widths, depending on the desired effect.
- **save as HTML**—Once you have created your document with all the graphic images and enhancements, today's desktop and word processing programs allow you to save your work as an HTML document for viewing on the World Wide Web.

 *Activity*

DTP for Beginners

1. Explore the drawing tools contained within your word processing program. Choose three drawing tools and explain how to use them so that a new user will understand. Format your document as a brochure/newsletter. Apply the principles of design studied earlier in the chapter.

2. Convert a document you have already keyed (e.g., a one-page report) into a two-column format. Insert graphics or clip art to correspond with the document text.

3. Using the drawing tools, create your own unique letterhead for your own letters. Business letterhead usually contains the name of the company, the company logo, its mailing address, e-mail address, telephone number, and fax number to allow customers to get in touch with the company.

What Can a Desktop Publishing Program Do that a Word Processor Cannot?

DTP programs use much of the same language as word processors. Margins are set to allow for non-printing areas on publications. Most of the icons on the toolbar are familiar, such as the New, Open, Save, and Print icons. Copy, Cut, and Paste also function in much the same way. However, unlike in word processing programs, when you use a dedicated desktop publishing program, you do not begin a new publication just by starting to key. You first have to tell the program what type of object you want to insert (see Fig. 5.12).

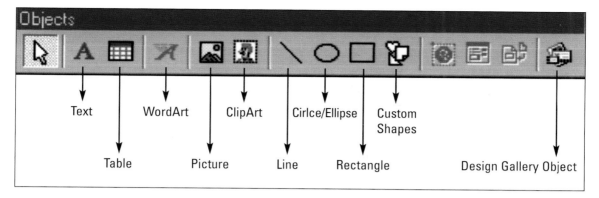

Fig. 5.12

Desktop publishing programs allow you to insert many different object types. For example, Microsoft Publisher has the above object types that can be placed independently on your page to create the desired effect.

If you want to insert text, for example, you create a *text box* on the screen. Text boxes can be enlarged to accommodate more text. They can also be linked to accommodate overflow from one box to another, much like a newspaper.

To insert a picture or graphic, either from a clip art library or file, you need to first create a *picture frame* and then insert the picture or graphic.

WordArt or TextArt is created by clicking the WordArt icon, creating the box on the page and then keying your text.

These objects can be moved around the page independent of the other objects by clicking and dragging. They can also be layered atop one another. For example, if you layer a text box on a drawing shape, you can create eye-catching messages for your audience.

Fig. 5.13
Text box on a starburst

Although you can perform many desktop publishing functions within a word processor, a dedicated piece of desktop publishing software, such as Microsoft Publisher or Adobe Pagemaker, allows for the creation of specialized documents that would be difficult to produce otherwise. Publications requiring special sizes, such as business cards or invitations, are easily set up in a DTP program where those options are pre-set by the software. Colour schemes, professionally chosen, are presented for your consideration. Pre-set designs for business forms such as expense sheets, invoices, purchase orders, and fax cover sheets have been formatted and only require the organization's logo and return address to put them into use.

These programs are of particular interest to the small businessperson, who does not have the money to finance custom-designed documents and business forms.

Activity

Templates and Wizards

Most desktop publishing and word processing programs provide templates and wizards so users can quickly and easily create custom documents. *Templates* are pre-formatted documents (margins, fonts, alignments, etc.) that you can customize to meet your requirements by adding personal or company information. A *wizard* is a software application or part of an application that presents you with a sequence of questions or choices to help you customize your documents. Wizards are most commonly found in Windows-based application programs.

Explore your word processing and desktop publishing programs to determine what options are available to you. Make a list of each of the templates and wizards you would use as a student and as a businessperson. Keep the list in your portfolio for future reference.

Whether you use a word processor or a dedicated desktop publishing program, you can create publications that will dazzle your viewing audience.

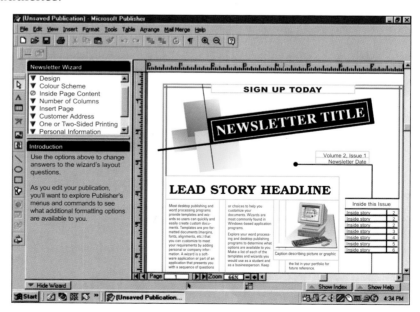

Fig. 5.14
Desktop publishing can bring life to an otherwise dull document.

Knowledge Check

1. Describe three features in a word processing program that can be used to create
desktop published documents.

2. What advantage would there be to using
a dedicated desktop publishing program
over a word processor for creating
publications?

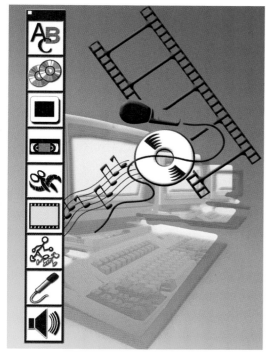

Fig. 5.15

Multimedia Presentations

What Is a Multimedia Presentation?

A *multimedia presentation* can incorporate elements from all communications media—text, speech,
graphics, sound, animation, videos, and film. The
presentation can be output in colour or in black
and white in such media as 35-mm slides, transparencies, projections on a screen, or hard copy.

Making an effective multimedia presentation is a
skill that, not unlike other skills, requires considerable
effort. There are three main components that make
up an effective presentation—the content, the design,
and the delivery. This section will examine how to
prepare and deliver an effective presentation and
will look at the software that can be used to prepare
the audiovisual component.

Content—The Most Important Part!

Before you "put pen to paper" (or key one word), you must first
determine the purpose of the presentation and who the audience
is. Is the purpose to inform, to persuade, or to entertain? Are you
presenting to your classmates, school administration, or people
outside your organization? The purpose and audience will determine
what you say and how you say it. You need to tell the people in
your audience how your presentation is relevant to them. What
action do you want your audience to take after the presentation is
complete? The content and delivery of your presentation should be
focused on reaching your goal.

Once you have determined the purpose of the presentation, the research begins. The audience expects the presenter to be as knowledgeable in as many aspects of the topic as possible. You do not have to be an expert, but you should know what you are talking about. Get information from a variety of sources—books, magazine articles, personal interviews with experts in the field or people who have a background in the topic, company reports and brochures, and the World Wide Web. (For information on research and the World Wide Web, see chapter 9.)

After you have gathered all the information, you have to organize it so that it is meaningful for your audience and helps to meet your goal. Organizing information for a presentation is no different than writing a report in that you should develop a clear outline of the presentation's purpose before you create even one slide. Group points you want to make into categories. Check all your information to ensure that it helps to meet the goal of the presentation. If a point is not relevant, do not include it!

Designing the Presentation

An effective presentation is a well-thought-out combination of text, colour, sights, and sounds.

- **text**—The text the audience sees projected on the screen should list the key points of each topic and subtopic within your presentation. The best-designed screens are the kind of point-form notes people in the audience would write down if they understood the topic well. Use lively words, not clichés; clichés become overused and lose their effect. Adhere to the principle that "less is usually more" in developing your points. Use key words, not full sentences. For example,

Global temperatures rising
instead of
Recent statistics show increases in global temperatures.

The text points on the screen are supposed to act as a prompt for the presenter and give the audience the key facts. It is the presenter's job to fill in the missing text for the audience. Remember, you are the one making the presentation; if people in the audience are reading, they probably are not listening!

- **text appearance**—Choose fonts that help to convey your message, but keep to one or two fonts throughout the presentation. Reserve bold, italics, and capitalization for emphasis. Overuse of any font enhancement loses its emphasis.

Activity

Headlines with Substance

Read three current newspaper articles. Design a short headline for each article that, very briefly, reflects the substance of the article. Use short, "punchy" words that have impact.

Can You See The Difference?

Create test pages in your presentation program using different sizes of fonts. If possible, project your test pages on the screen you may use later in a presentation. With a partner, test to see how far back you can stand before the words become too small to read.

Fig. 5.16
A colour wheel

Balance text on the slides without overloading. Remember to provide enough white space to help frame the images on the slide.

- **font**—Body text should be at least 20-point type, with headings larger still. Remember, the audience needs to be able to read the words on the screen.

- **bullet points and numbering**—Use numbered lists to indicate an order for information or steps in a process. Bullet points do not imply an order, and therefore give equal importance to each point.

- **colour**—The choice of colours for a presentation will be determined largely by the message and the audience. Determine the "feel" you want for the presentation. Colours are either warm or cool. Warm colours are in the orange and red range. Cool colours include greens and blues. Select either a warm or cool hue as the base, adding only one or two other, more vivid hues. A standard rule of thumb is to keep your colour choices simple. Margo Halverson, an associate professor at the Maine College of Art, makes the following suggestion:

    "**Keep it simple**—More is not always better. It is the colour relationships that make or break visual effects. Try to choose only one or two vivid hues and use their tints (mixed with white) and shades (mixed with black) to broaden your palette. Following these guidelines will help keep presentation slides clear, elegant, and to the point."

- **sights**—Select visual images that will complement the message of your presentation. In choosing graphic images, be sensitive to cultural and gender issues, and stereotypes that could offend members of the audience. Place images to enhance the message, not clutter it up! You can use charts from a spreadsheet to help depict information clearly and effectively as well. Sometimes, placing points inside of shapes can more effectively get the message across than simple bullets. Using graphic images to represent thoughts and ideas helps the reader to understand and remember key messages. You can also add slide transitions and animation effects (see page 165) to enhance points on the screen, allowing you to build the points one by one on the screen. Remember the rules you used in graphic design and apply them here, too.

Creativity with Colour

Using paint chips from a paint store, colour wheel from Art class, construction paper, or coloured pencil crayons or markers on a piece of white paper, develop combinations of colours that could be used in a presentation. Make a note of the colours that "work well" together and those that do not. Share your combinations with your classmates.

- **sounds**—Today's multimedia software programs allow you to insert sound bytes into your presentation to enhance the message. You can have the text appear letter by letter and sound like a typewriter on the screen or have points appear like a camera shutter with accompanying sound effects. You can also include recordings of your own voice or add background music from a CD. However, it is best to use restraint when adding audiovisual effects so that the audience does not become overwhelmed. Remember, the message is still the most important component of the presentation.

Delivering an Effective Presentation

For many people, delivering a presentation in front of a group of people can be a nerve-wracking experience. Being nervous is an indication that you want to please your audience. Channel that nervous tension into excitement that makes you appear more confident. Here are some strategies you can employ to channel your nervousness and deliver an effective presentation.

Fig. 5.17
How not to be prepared!

- **be prepared**—Prepare notes to refer to during your presentation, if necessary. Good presenters rarely have to refer to their notes, but it is reassuring to have them. Presentation notes, sometimes called "cue cards," should be in point form in a large font (e.g., 18 point or more) so they can be easily read by simply glancing down at the page. Use a highlighter to indicate points you MUST convey during the presentation.

- **practise, practise, practise**—To develop a skill, you must practise. Remember that making a presentation is a skill. Say your presentation out loud. Try different emphases and phrasing to determine what you are most comfortable with. Practise with a partner for feedback. If you expect audience involvement, prepare to speak for less than the time allotted for your presentation.

- **avoid distracting behaviour**—There are a number of common pitfalls that can hamper people's efforts to make an effective presentation. Watch out for annoying or distracting movements (playing with jewellery, clicking a pen, leaning on anything for support), using too many hand gestures, wearing clothes that "scream" for attention, and the audio fillers like, "ah," "um," and "and." Whatever you do, do not turn your back to the audience. If you have to refer to a visual, make sure you turn no more than 45°.
- **be early**
- **have all your materials organized and quickly available**
- **make eye contact**

Activity

Look at Me!

Prepare a short one-minute speech on any topic related to this course. Practise saying your speech in front of a partner or small group. Better yet, if possible, videotape your speech. View your speech and make note of the things you can improve on in the future.

Multimedia Presentation Software

Check out the *InsighTs* Student Page on <www.irwinpublishing.com/students> for information on "Presenters ONLINE," and its Web site created by Epson America, Inc., makers of presentation equipment. Follow the links in the Training section to a wide selection of articles about all aspects of making and delivering presentations.

There are a number of software programs available to help you create multimedia presentations. Most often, they come bundled with other office productivity software. Examples are Microsoft PowerPoint, Corel Presentations, and Macromedia Director. These programs operate in basically the same manner and have common elements.

The Anatomy of a Presentation

A multimedia presentation is made up of the following elements: slides, design templates, slide layouts, placeholders, and objects.

- **slides**—Slides are the basic elements in a multimedia presentation. They can contain any combination of text, graphics, and audiovisual effects.
- **design templates**—Design templates are pre-set combinations of colour, textures, and graphic images that can be used as background for slides in the presentation. Colours within the design can be customized to suit the presentation.

- **slide layouts**—Slide layouts are pre-set designs for individual slides within the presentation (see Fig. 5.18). They have place-holders for text, clip art, charts, and other objects positioned on the slide. Some common layouts include the title slide, a bulleted list, or text and charts.

Fig. 5.18
Screen capture showing a variety of slide layouts

- **placeholders**—Placeholders are similar to text boxes in a word processor or desktop publishing program. They allow for the insertion of text, graphics, charts, movie clips, sound bytes, and other objects such as paint drawings or HTML Web pages. They can be resized to accommodate smaller or larger items by clicking and dragging the handles around the outside of the placeholder. In predefined layouts, you can launch the Clip Art Gallery dialog box by double-clicking on a clip art placeholder.

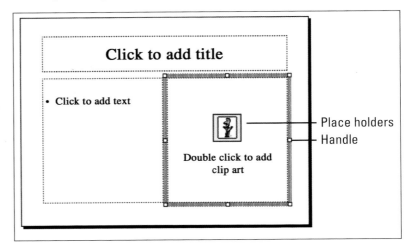

Fig. 5.19
Placeholders accommodate text, clip art, charts, and other objects in your presentation.

InsighTs: Succeeding in the Information Age

- **objects**—A true multimedia presentation is a combination of sights and sounds. You can insert a variety of objects into an electronic presentation. For example, a presentation for a music class could contain a *MIDI (Musical Instrument Digital Interface) file* of your latest composition. *Wave files* containing sound effects could be inserted during a presentation for special effect, for example, thunderous applause at the end. A media clip from a commercial could be inserted into an English presentation examining the effect of television on viewers. The most important factor to ensure is that these elements enhance the content of the presentation and do not leave the audience wondering why they were there.

How Can I Make My Presentations With Pizzazz?

Once you have prepared your presentation, you can add animation to the slides to make them come to life. There are two types of animations—slide transitions and bullet/object animations.

- **slide transitions**—A slide transition is a special effect that adds visual interest to the "movement" from one slide or one screen to the next. Today's programs allow for a visual "turning of the page" within the presentation. You can choose from a wide variety of transitions—everything from vertical blinds to an image that dissolves before your eyes. **But beware!** Too many transitions can distract your audience from the points you are making.

- **bullet/object animations**—Every bullet of text or graphic object can be programmed to appear in the sequence that will build the best effect. They can appear out of nowhere, or bounce across the screen—the options are almost endless. Once again, however, you need to remember that too many animations can distract your audience.

Most presenters animate their presentations after they have inserted all the text and objects. Animating the presentation gives you more control over when points appear on the screen. In this way, you can keep the audience focused on the topic you have on the screen and are discussing, rather than letting them read ahead. Using animation does, however, require more practice on your part to ensure that what you are saying corresponds with the text on the screen.

Printing Your Presentation

One very useful feature of presentation programs is the ability to print out your presentation in a variety of formats. You can print full size 8½" x 11" slides that can be converted into overhead transparencies. You can print speaker notes that show the slide and notes you have keyed for your reference during the presentation. Another option is to print audience notes pages. These pages show thumbnail (smaller than normal) images of each slide and contain lines for audience members' handwritten notes (Fig. 5.20).

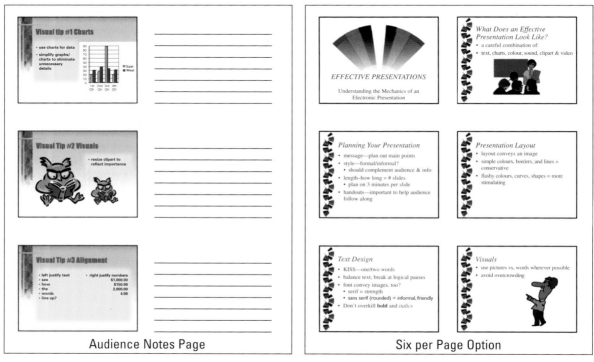

Audience Notes Page

Six per Page Option

Fig. 5.20
A variety of possible print images

 **Activity**

Options, Options, Options

Presentation programs are very powerful and the variety of options is extensive. Explore your presentation software package to find out how to input speaker notes, create your own customized template, set animations for a number of slides at a time, and customize your printout. Once you have explored your software, use what you have learned to design your own customized template.

Multimedia presentation programs are fun to learn and use. With practice, you can develop competency in delivering this kind of presentation.

Knowledge Check

1. What are the three aspects to be considered in the content of a presentation?
2. What are the four design components? Describe each one.
3. What are three tips for delivering effective presentations?
4. What is a slide in a multimedia presentation?
5. What is meant by the design template? The slide layout?
6. What are placeholders? What type of objects can you insert in a presentation to make it "come to life?"
7. What is the difference between a slide transition and a bullet/object animation?
8. What are some of the options you have for printing your presentation?

CHAPTER SUMMARY

Understanding Information

1. Where and when could you use graphics in your work?

2. List and describe the main differences between bitmap images and vector graphics.

3. Describe briefly the three elements of good graphic design—balance, contrast, and consistency.

4. What advantage is there to using a desktop publishing program over a word processing program to create documents?

5. What is the most important element of a multimedia presentation? Why?

Analyzing

6. Think about the presentations that you have seen in various classes. Make a list outlining the features of a good presentation and those of a poor presentation. Suggest strategies that poor presenters could use to improve their presentations.

7. Contact a local company that employs people with graphic design or desktop publishing skills such as a newspaper, printing company, or graphic design firm. Discuss career opportunities in that field and summarize your findings. Be sure to investigate the skills needed in the field and how you could acquire them.

Applying

8. Based on the information presented in this chapter, prepare a 10-slide presentation on the "Fundamentals of Graphic Design" or "How to Make a Good Presentation." Include a title slide, eight information slides, and one concluding slide. Incorporate slide transitions, bullet animations, and appropriate graphic images.

9. Use the information from this chapter and either your word processor or desktop publishing program to prepare a brochure on making effective presentations.

Communicating

10. On the *InsighTs* Student Page on <www.irwinpublishing.com/students> go to the Epson America Inc. Web site for presenters and follow the link to Articles. Read one of the articles relating to the delivery, message, or visuals of a presentation and write a one-page report summarizing the points contained within the article.

11. What advice would you give to a person designing his or her first multimedia presentation? Write a brief outline of the pointers you would give the person.

Assessing Your Competencies

12. Using the software competency checklists provided by your teacher, check off the competencies that you have mastered for desktop publishing and preparing multimedia presentations. Note any competencies that require more attention and review.

13. Interview a classmate to determine the competencies he or she has acquired during this chapter. Also share some of the new skills you have acquired.

CHAPTER SIX:

ELECTRONIC COMMUNICATION TOOLS AND THE INTERNET I

The next three chapters will introduce you to a world of electronic communication tools. Some will be familiar and some will not. Some are familiar tools but used in amazing new ways. In this chapter, you will examine how information travels on the Internet, what you need to connect to the Internet, and how a browser program works with the Internet. Finally, you will explore what e-mail is and how it works.

Topics

➤ How Information Travels on the Internet

➤ Getting Connected to the Internet

➤ Connecting Options

➤ Now You Are Connected: What Next?

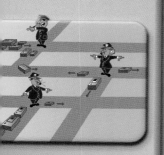

This chapter explores these questions:

- How does it all work?
- What are the essential parts for connecting to the Internet?
- What kinds of connecting options are available to a home user?
- What role does your Web browser program play?
- What is e-mail and how does it work?

MAIL SERVER   MAIL SERVER

In this chapter you have the opportunity to

- consider what computer hardware is needed to enhance productivity by multitasking on an Internet-connected computer
- explore and illustrate how your school computers are connected to the Internet
- explore local alternatives for connecting to the Internet
- research new information about modems and other connection alternatives
- explore features of a Web browser program
- research Internet appliances
- explore and identify the parts of an e-mail message
- explore the features of an e-mail program
- evaluate the school Acceptable Use Policy for e-mail use
- think about issues surrounding e-mail ownership and privacy
- research e-mail practices in the business community

How Information Travels on the Internet

How Does It All Work?

In order to move data such as text, images, or sound from one computer to another computer in a distant location, the computers must have software and *protocols* that transform the data into a form in which it can travel on the Internet (see Learning Link in chapter 1, page 24).

Data for the Internet must be packaged appropriately, much like traditional mail and parcels must be packaged appropriately (according to some pre-set standards or protocols), before they can travel to their intended destinations. Letters and parcels must be properly sealed and addressed before they are handed over to the traditional mail system. In the same way, all data that is about to travel on the Internet must be properly prepared. This is the job of *TCP/IP (Transmission Control Protocol/Internet Protocol)*. TCP/IP is a complex set of rules and procedures that indicate how data should be organized for travel on the Internet. All information on the Internet must travel in small "packets" and it is the job of TCP to divide the data into these packets and make sure they arrive at another computer in the same condition that they left your computer. IP is responsible for addressing the packets so they know where to go. The TCP at the receiving end will piece together the packets to recreate the original data.

The most common use of the Internet is browsing the World Wide Web, so we will use the Web to illustrate how information travels on the Internet. When you key an URL (Uniform Resource Locator) or address of a Web site in the location field (see Fig. 6.2) of a Web browser, several actions take place.

After pressing Enter, you will see the Web page appear, either quickly or slowly. The speed depends on the number of graphics and other complex features on the page and the

Fig. 6.1
TCP/IP at work, preparing data for travel on the Internet

(a)

Fig. 6.2
The Irwin Publishing URL for the main Irwin site is shown in the location field of Internet Explorer. The **location field** is the area on a Web browser screen where a user keys a Web site address. It also displays the address of the currently browsed page. The location field is known as the "address box" in Internet Explorer. For more about browsers, see pages 180-1.

See Fig. 1.18 and page 27 in chapter 1 to review what an URL is and how it works.

speed of your connection to the Internet. Occasionally, error messages will appear because the Web page is not available (is undergoing maintenance) or has had a change in name or location. We will use the Web address <www.irwinpublishing.com/students> as an example. After you key in the Web address, the address must be converted into a form that the Internet can understand. For Web addresses, this form is a sequence of numbers referred to as the IP (Internet Protocol) address. For Irwin Publishing's main site, the IP address is 64.224.192.61.

How is the address converted? The text address <www.irwinpublishing.com> is sent to the **Domain Name System (DNS)** server at your Internet service provider (ISP; see pages 176-7 for more about ISPs). This server attempts to maintain an up-to-date list of URL addresses on the Internet

Visit the Learn The Net Web site on the *InsighTs* Student Page on <www.irwinpublishing.com/students> and do a key word search for DNS. You will see a great explanation and animation to help you understand the Domain Name System (DNS) used on the Internet.

and their IP addresses, much like your local telephone directory maintains an up-to-date list of addresses and telephone numbers. If an address is not found on this DNS server, the server sends a request to another external DNS server until the address is found (if it exists).

When the address is found, the server requests the Web page from its source. After the request is made, the files that make up the page are sent to your computer through a series of networks, routers, and gateways. Remember, all information on the Internet travels in packets. The Web page files are divided up into packets and sent to your computer in small pieces. The packets may travel along different paths depending on the amount of traffic on the Internet at the time you send your files.

Fig. 6.3
"Routers" direct traffic on the Internet.

Routers function like traffic officers. They direct traffic in appropriate directions. If there is too much traffic moving in one direction, they will re-direct some of the traffic (see Fig. 6.3).

Gateways are points where information needs to be translated into some other format for it to pass through a particular network. At these junctions, packets will be pieced together and split up again following some other protocol or set of rules. Barring any unexpected difficulties, the packets will arrive at your computer, be reassembled, and display the Web page for <http://www.irwinpublishing.com/students>.

Knowledge Check

1. What does TCP/IP stand for? What does it do?
2. What is a packet?
3. What is an URL?
4. What is DNS? What does a DNS server do?
5. Describe how Web pages travel through the Internet.

Getting Connected to the Internet

What Are the Essential Parts for Connecting to the Internet?

No matter what method you choose to connect to the Internet, there are several essential parts you will require (and even these can vary considering some of the new and innovative hardware available on the market). The essential parts are:

- a computer
- a connection device that connects your computer to your link out to the Internet (e.g., *modem*)
- telecommunications software and protocols (often available through your *operating system*)
- a link between you and the Internet (e.g, telephone line)
- an account with an Internet service provider (ISP) or online service

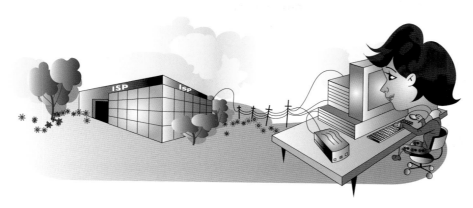

The Computer, the Connecting Device, and the Telecommunications Software

The Computer

Although a high-speed, state-of-the-art computer is not essential to establish your connection to the Internet, it is important that you consider the kinds of tasks you will be performing once you are connected. These tasks will also help you decide if you need additional or upgraded peripherals such as:

- a better video card (to display detailed graphics and animation from multimedia and game sites)
- a larger monitor (for more comfortable viewing)
- a sound card and speakers (for listening to music and voice)
- a microphone (for voice interaction)
- a Webcam (for video captures and conferencing)
- larger hard drives (for downloading and storing multimedia files; for more about downloading, see A Quick Byte on page 179)

You should also consider the extent to which you will be multitasking on the Internet. *Multitasking* is the ability to do more than one task at the same time. Many users expect their computers to run many programs at the same time (and do it quickly and without error). Multitasking requires a fast processor and generous RAM (at least 550 MHz and 128 MB of RAM at the time of this writing). In fact, other than using complex graphic design and video editing programs (which need very fast processors and very generous RAM), multitasking is one of the best reasons for having a computer with a fast processor. Read the Case Study to learn more about multitasking.

Case Study

Multitasking: Pushing the Limits of Your Computer and Your Productivity

Imagine yourself a writer for an exciting new Media and Entertainment magazine. You are researching on the Internet for up-to-date material for your latest article and you need to remain connected to your colleagues who are also researching for similar material at the same time. Since you are writing about one of the most popular music groups to hit the entertainment industry, you have one of the group's music CDs playing on your computer for inspiration. You have the following programs running at the same time:

- your word processor
- your spreadsheet program (for immediate entry and graphing of statistics relevant to your research)
- two Web browsers (because it makes browsing more convenient)
- your e-mail program
- your instant messaging program (for quick contacts with your colleagues)
- your chat program (for discussions with your colleagues)
- your media player (for quick play of video clips)
- your CD player software
- a virus program (to protect your computer when you download files)

Working this way, you find that you are able to complete your research quickly and efficiently, and this enhances your productivity.

1. Find a definition for the word "productivity" and write it down.

2. Find a definition for the word "multitasking" and write it down.

3. How does multitasking enhance productivity?

4. Have you ever done multitasking on a computer? If so, describe how. Did you run into any technical problems? If so, describe them.

5. Think of another occupation that would benefit from multitasking in this way. Describe the occupation and provide examples of the multitasking programs.

The Connecting Device: The Modem

The most commonly used connecting device is an *analog modem*. Once TCP properly prepares the data for travel, the data packets must also be converted into an appropriate format for travelling through the *link* you are using. If you are using a telephone connection, you will likely be using a modem to convert the digital data on your computer to analog signals that can travel along telephone lines. An analog modem will do this for you. It will also convert analog signals returning to your computer into digital data so that your computer can understand them.

When you use an analog modem in your home, your telephone line can only be used for one thing at a time, carrying computer signals or your voice—not both. There are other types of connection devices available that eliminate the need to convert data to analog signals. These devices, although often called modems, are actually able to send your data in its digital format through telephone or cable wires, eliminating the need for analog conversion. When telephone or cable wires are used to carry digital signals in this way, they can be used to carry other signals at the same time—your voice, television images, and other digital signals too!

The Link

Whichever connecting device you use with your computer, you must be able to plug it in somewhere. There are several options, but the most common option for home use is a telephone or cable line. Business users usually use network cables that connect office LANs. These LANs are most likely connected directly to the Internet using high-speed lines that provide constant Internet access to the users, without having to make a connection or dial up. This form of connection is known as a *direct connection*.

Ⓐ Activity

Use the resources available to you (e.g., your teacher, school or board technician, network administrator) to determine how your school computers are connected to the Internet. Draw a diagram to represent your classroom or school LAN, indicating the technology used in your school (modem, routers, gateways, etc.). Where possible, use a graphics program or the drawing tools in your word processing program to draw your diagram.

The Account: Internet Service Provider (ISP)

Using an ISP is similar to using traditional telephone service. Your telephone works because you pay a telecommunications company to provide you with this service (e.g, Bell Canada, Telus, etc.). The most popular way to connect a home computer to the Internet is to pay a monthly fee to an *Internet service provider (ISP)*.

ISPs provide many services, some packaged for home users and some for business users. Some of the popular services for home users are

- access to the Internet (limited or unlimited, usually in hours per month)
- connection to the Internet backbone at a specified speed (the faster the speed, the faster Web pages will download to your computer for viewing; for more about downloading, see A Quick Byte on page 179)
- one or more e-mail accounts
- server space for a personal Web page
- set-up instructions or service

- Web site portal—A *Web site portal* is a Web page that acts as an entry point to the World Wide Web. Some ISPs provide more than just access to the Internet for a fee. They also provide access to Web portals with information and tools such as weather updates, discussion groups, e-mail, chat areas, subject directories, and more. Some popular examples are AOL Canada and MSN (Microsoft Network).

Fig. 6.5
A Web site portal page

Service packages vary. To select the package that is most appropriate for your needs, you must do some homework. Carefully examine what is available in your area. There are some services that are available nationally, while others are only available locally. You can get this information by looking in local newspapers and magazines or ISP Web sites. Decide whether you will be using traditional phone line access, cable, or some other form of access (like a satellite dish).

How you choose to access the Internet will possibly restrict your options. For example, some providers are not capable of offering ADSL (Asymetric Digital Subscriber Line) service or satellite service and some providers are not equipped to handle cable modems.

Many ISPs also provide packages for business users. The list of services is similar to the above except there will likely be more e-mail accounts, more Web space (hard disk space on a Web server—to accommodate a large Web site), and a faster link to the Internet.

 Activity

With a partner, select three Internet service providers in your area. For each provider select a service package. Be sure to select a comparable service package for each provider (e.g., Beginner, Lite User, Business Basics). Use your word processing or spreadsheet program to create a table similar to the one in Fig. 6.6. Research using the Internet and local newspapers to collect the information listed in the first column of the table. Record your findings for each of the ISPs you selected. Be prepared to share your results with the class. Use the Industry Canada Web link to assist you if necessary.

	Service Provider 1	Service Provider 2	Service Provider 3
ISP Name			
Cost per Month			
Limited / Unlimited			
Set-up Fee			
Number of E-Mail Accounts			
Web Page Space? How Much?			
Connection Speed			
Free Software			
Technical Support			

Fig. 6.6
Choosing an Internet Service Provider

Knowledge Check

1. What are the essential parts of a typical Internet-connected home computer?
2. What is the most commonly used device to connect to the Internet? How does it work?
3. What is a portal?
4. What does it mean to have a direct connection?
5. What does ISP stand for?
6. List the most popular services provided by ISPs.

Connecting Options

What Kinds of Connecting Options Are Available to a Home User?

Now that we have summarized the essential parts you need to connect to the Internet and the roles they play, take a look at Fig. 6.7 to see some of the options for connecting to the Internet that are available to you.

Fig. 6.7 Some Popular Connecting Options and Their Features

Connecting Option	Traditional dial-up modem	Cable modem (sometimes referred to as broadband modem)	ADSL modem (Asymmetric Digital Subscriber Line) is most popular for home users; DSL is faster and more expensive so is more likely to be used by business users.
Type of Cabling	Copper telephone wire	Coaxial TV cable (sometimes referred to as broadband cable)	Copper telephone wire
How Does It Work?	Translates digital data to analog data so that the data can travel over telephone lines. Translates analog data to digital data so that it can be understood by your computer.	The cable wire coming into your home is divided (using a splitting device). One part of the wire goes to your television or converter and the other to your cable modem. The cable modem attaches to your computer's Ethernet card (see Learning Link) using a network cable.	Plugs into telephone jack. Modem receives and sends digital data without converting it to any other format.
Speeds Available	Up to 56 kbps (kilobits per second or 1000 bps)	Download (receive) data at up to 1.5 mbps; upload (send) data at rates up to 300 kbps.	640 kbps DSL service speeds are up to 32 mbps.
Service Providers	All	Restricted to cable company	ISP has to support this technology.
Advantages	Inexpensive. A variety of physical configurations are available, for example: Internal, External, Pocket-sized USB (Universal Serial Bus Connections; see Learning Link).	Extremely high speed. Allows simultaneous sharing of cable TV line with television viewers in your home.	Allows simultaneous sharing of phone line with telephone users. Users may operate personal Web servers.
Limitations	Generally slow for full multimedia applications. Does not allow simultaneous sharing of telephone line with telephone users in the same home.	ISP has to support this technology. Users should get a guarantee for the promised speed since speeds can vary considerably. Users may not operate their own personal Web server (see Learning Link).	Service must be available in your area. Your home must be a specified distance from the telephone company's DSL equipment. Speeds are stable only if your home is within a specified distance from the central office (approx. 2.4 km). Charges for services to telephone company *and* to ISP. Noise filters (see Learning Link) may be required if home telephones and fax machines interfere with your Internet connection.

For more information on how DSL modems work, visit the How Stuff Works Web site on the *InsighTs* Student Page on <www.irwinpublishing.com/students>.

InsighTs: Succeeding in the Information Age

Universal Serial Bus (USB) connections are available on most newer computers—they provide a quick, convenient way to connect external devices such as printers, modems, and scanners to your computer.

An **Ethernet card** is a network interface card installed in a computer so that it can connect to a network. Ethernet is the most popular type of card in use today.

A **Web server** is a computer that provides Internet access to a Web site that is stored on the Web server's hard disk. With the right software **and connection** any computer can be a Web server.

Noise filters are devices inserted into telephone handsets or wall jacks to reduce interference from other electronic devices installed on the same connecting lines.

Upload, Download—What's the difference?

To **download** is to copy information from another computer or server to your own. This information may be in the form of a file that is being copied to your hard disk for long-term storage (music, graphics, or text) or simply a Web page that is copied to your computer temporarily for viewing through your browser. Whenever information is travelling *to* your computer, it is downloading.

Uploading is the opposite. To **upload** means to send information or messages from your computer to another computer. Whenever information travels *away* from your computer, it is uploading.

Activity

Researching a Connecting Option

Select one of the connecting options listed in the Fig. 6.7. Research the device (using newspapers, friends and family, the Internet, or phone calls) and identify any new information available for the device you have selected. Create a new table for the device you have chosen and update the information. For the information to be useful to you and the rest of your class, include another column for price!

What Role Does Your Web Browser Program Play?

A browser is not an essential part of your Internet connection, but it provides you with the ability to navigate through the millions of *hyperlinked* pages of text, graphics, video, and sounds. Since browsing the World Wide Web is the most popular use of the Internet, most people would not dream of using the Internet without a Web browser. In fact there are other things you can do on the Internet besides browsing Web pages. Some of these include Telnet, e-mail, and FTP (check out the Quick Byte on the next page to learn more). The most popular Web browser programs are Internet Explorer and Netscape Navigator. These programs have several common features, including:

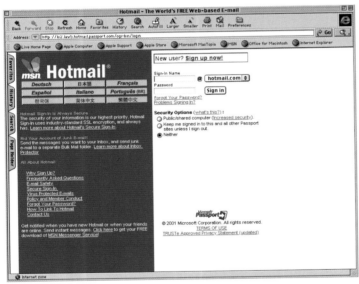

Fig. 6.8
This figure shows Internet Explorer

- navigation buttons that move forward and backward

- a location field or address box where a user keys a Web address (see Fig. 6.2 on page 171)

- a stop button to discontinue downloading

- a way to save and organize links to favourite Web pages (Bookmarks or Favourites). When you Bookmark a Web site (or add it to your Favourites in Explorer), you save the URL of the site so that you can access it again later without having to re-key the URL in the location field.

- a button that reloads or refreshes the Web page that is currently being downloaded. This button will cause the Web page to download again and replace the one that is showing on your screen.

These features are the basics needed to browse—surf—the Internet. Many other features are available and as you become a more experienced Web browser, you will want to learn more about how to use advanced features such as setting preferences or Internet options.

What Else Can You Do on the Internet?

No one will dispute that browsing the World Wide Web is the most exciting way to explore the Internet. The volume of information available on Web sites all over the world is growing faster than technology can keep track of it. However, Internet activity includes more than just browsing the World Wide Web. Here are some of the Internet applications that can work without a browser:

- e-mail—as long as you are not using Web-based e-mail
- Telnet—**Telnet** was one of the original methods for interacting on the Internet. With the right software on your computer, you can dial another computer and interact in its network environment (e.g., connecting with a hospital information system or **electronic BBS** or **bulletin board system**). Electronic BBSs are still in use today. Users post and reply to messages in much the same way that they can with Web-based conferences and forums (see page 201)
- FTP—Using **File Transfer Protocol (FTP)** software (such as CuteFTP or Fetch), you can transfer files from your computer to a distant computer (upload) or from a distant computer to your own (download).

 **Activity**

Using Your Browser

Launch your browser program and do the following:

1. Visit the *InsighTs* Student Page on <www.irwinpublishing.com/students>.

2. Visit each of the links that have been named in the chapter so far.

3. Each time you visit a new link, add the link to your Bookmarks or Favourites.

4. These links will be more useful to you if you organize them into folders. Use the resources available to you (the Help menu, a peer, your teacher) to learn how to organize your links into folders. Create a folder and sub-folders for each of the chapters or units you have studied so far. Save your links in the appropriate folders.

Case Study

Internet Appliances

Internet appliances (also known as ***Web appliances***) are devices that provide access to the Internet without the use of a computer. Many of these devices are designed to provide convenient access to organization and communication tools such as Web browsing, calendars, address books, and e-mail, but they may have other purposes. They sometimes require a physical connection to the Internet, either by connecting to your personal computer or to a connection device (e.g., analog modem, cable modem, ADSL line), but they often have a built-in modem of their own. As ***wireless technology*** develops, many of these devices will be able to work without cables.

Some examples of Internet appliances are

- ***I-Opener from Netpliance***—This is a scaled-down computer with all the necessary parts for browsing and communicating on the Internet.

- ***Interactive television (or iTV)***—With a WebTV box attached to a TV set and a suitable Internet connection, users may browse the Internet, use e-mail, and watch television.

- ***Hand-held and palm-sized PCs***—Often called ***Personal Digital Assistants (PDAs)***, these small devices are designed to work with a limited selection of software such as e-mail, calendars, and scaled-down word processors. They typically sit in a cradle attached to a regular computer. A user may remove the device to take it to a meeting or to access its features when out of the office.

The selection of devices that can be connected to the Internet both directly through a computer and via wireless access is growing rapidly. Some of the more unconventional devices include refrigerators, pop machines, and microwaves. As business communities find new ways to advertise and sell products over the Internet, they will also find and develop new ways to communicate not only with users, but with objects in their homes too!

1. With a partner, visit a computer store to explore hand-held, palm-sized, and PDA computers. Select one device and make a list of all of the communication tasks it can accomplish that are similar to a desktop computer, those that are different, and some important communication tasks that it cannot accomplish. Also comment on the size and weight of the device and whether you would feel comfortable using it on a regular basis. Write a word-processed report on this device, creating sub-headings for each of the topics you

InsighTs: Succeeding in the Information Age

were asked to report on. Where possible, include a digital picture of the device in your report.

2. Explore the Internet for information about Internet appliances or any interesting Internet-connected devices. Using a word processing program, write a short paragraph describing one of the devices, its purpose, who is likely to use it, its usefulness, and what you think about it. If possible, include a digital picture with your paragraph.

Knowledge Check

1. Which connecting device or devices:
   a) offer(s) the fastest speeds for sending and receiving information?
   b) use(s) coaxial cable?
   c) allow(s) for sharing of a telephone line with a telephone user?
   d) require(s) that an Ethernet card be installed in your computer?
   e) translate(s) digital data to analog data?
   f) use(s) traditional copper telephone wire?
2. What is the difference between download and upload?
3. What is an Internet appliance?
4. What else can you do on the Internet besides browsing the World Wide Web?

Now You Are Connected: What Next?

What Is Electronic Mail and How Does It Work?

Ray Tomlinson, a computer engineer who worked on ARPANet, designed a system that allowed colleagues to leave messages for one another. Using his system, known as SNDMSG, the first e-mail message was sent in 1971. It was not long before others recognized this early e-mail as a major milestone in the communications industry!

Electronic mail, or *e-mail*, programs emerged soon after the early Internet (ARPANet) was born. It is now a vital part of our communications in business and in our personal lives.

E-mail is a lot like postal mail. A message is composed, addressed, and sent to a receiver. It is the tools that are different. With regular postal mail, the message may be handwritten or keyed, it must be inserted into an envelope that is properly addressed and stamped, and then it must be delivered to a post office box for pick up, sorting, and delivery. E-mail uses new technology to speed up the communication process, reduce costs, and save trees.

E-Mail or "Snail" Mail?

Brainstorm with a partner and list all the types of postal ("snail") mail that you and your family have received in the last month (e.g., letters from family, birthday cards, telephone bills). For each of the items on your list, indicate whether the item would be better sent by e-mail and why or why not. Be prepared to report your findings to the rest of the class.

E-Mail Basics

Whatever e-mail program or service you use, the basic features are the same. At the very minimum, the main screen will have options to:

- create a new message
- view your inbox (incoming mail)
- view your sent mail

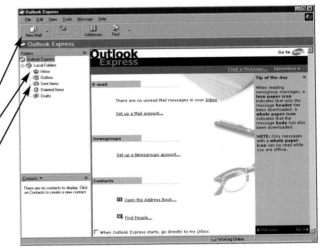

Fig. 6.9
Outlook screen capture, main screen

When creating a new message, you will have options to:

- send the message
- copy (cc)—send a courtesy copy to another e-mail address
- blind copy (bcc)—send a blind courtesy copy to another e-mail address (this user's address will not be visible to the other recipients)
- add an *attachment file* (a separate file that is sent along with an e-mail message)

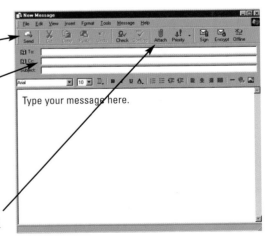

Fig. 6.10
Outlook screen capture, sending

You will have a personal Inbox where you can see a list of messages you have received. When viewing an incoming message, you will be able to:

- reply to the sender
- forward the message to another user (do this only with permission from the originator)
- download an attachment (if there is one)

Fig. 6.11
Outlook screen capture, receiving

 *Activity*

Identifying E-Mail Basics

For the e-mail program or service that you have available in your school, obtain screen captures or use templates provided by your teacher. Label each of the parts listed in the "E-Mail Basics" section above.

E-Mail Advanced Features

In addition to the basic tools, many e-mail programs or services also provide the following features:

- a **signature line**—a custom signature that can be automatically added to the end of each of your e-mail messages, the signature line usually includes your name, your organization, and contact information; use only when you wish to share this information with a receiver
- a **personal address book**—similar to a hard-copy address book, this is a feature in your e-mail program that allows you to save all of your e-mail addresses and their associated names
- a **personal mailing list**—a list of e-mail addresses of a specific group of people—e.g., school friends, project group, cousins—you may send the same message to the whole group by typing the group name in the "To:" field
- **automatic mail forwarding**—allows you to forward your mail to another address you may have

- **return receipt**—choose this option if you want to know if a receiver has opened your message
- **sorting**—you may sort your message lists by name, date received, date sent, etc.

Activity

What Else Can I Do with My E-Mail Program?

Take a closer look at your e-mail program and identify any of the advanced features that you have access to. For each of the advanced features you have identified, list the steps necessary to use the features.

How E-Mail Works

Fig. 6.12
Graphics from Learn the Net. E-mail messages are stored on a mail server until you choose to read them.

To send and receive e-mail messages you must have an e-mail account. If you are accessing the Internet through an ISP you probably have been provided with an account and an e-mail address. If the ISP is called YourISP.com, your e-mail address is probably something like <yourname@YourISP.com>. Your ISP sets up space on its mail server to collect your incoming messages. When you log in to check your e-mail, you will get a list of all the messages that are stored in your inbox on the ISP mail server computer. Your incoming messages do not come directly to your computer. They are stored on the mail server, until you choose to read them. They will continue to be stored on the mail server until you choose to delete them.

Investigate the Web link for Learn the Net on the *InsighTs* Student Page on <www.irwinpublishing.com/students> for some great animations that demonstrate how e-mail works. After viewing this site, describe what happens when you send an e-mail message to a friend.

A Quick Byte

Parts of an E-Mail Address

Let's take a closer look at the e-mail address, <yourname@YourISP.com>:

.ca	**Canada**
.com	**Commercial organization**
.edu	**Educational institution**
.fr	**France**
.gov	**Government agency**
.jp	**Japan**
.mil	**Military organization**
.net	**A network (may be an ISP)**
.org	**Non-profit organization**
.us	**United States**

Fig. 6.13
Examples of e-mail extensions

- "Yourname" is your *online name*.

- @ is a *connector* that links your name to the server name that holds your mail for you.

- "YourISP" is the *domain*, which is either your ISP or the organization name (where you work or go to school) that is giving you access to e-mail services.

- ".com," pronounced "dot com," is an *extension* specifying the type of organization that is identified by the domain name. The extension ".com" identifies a commercial organization. Figure 6.13 shows examples of e-mail extensions and what they represent.

Types of E-Mail Accounts

There are several ways to access and use e-mail services on the Internet: Here are two.

- *Web e-mail*—If you have access to the Internet from home, school, or other institution, you may set up a free e-mail account with a number of free e-mail Web services. These services (e.g., CANOEmail, Hotmail, Yahoomail) do not require you to have e-mail software set up on your computer. This feature makes them very convenient if you wish to check your mail from any Internet-connected computer running any browser program anywhere in the world! Some ISPs also allow you to access your e-mail via the Web (see A Quick Byte on page 188).

If your e-mail service is not available through the Web, try using the services provided by the sites E-Mail Anywhere and Mail Start. You can find their Web sites on the *InsighTs* Student Page on <www.irwinpublishing.com/students>. These services provide a way to check e-mail existing on almost any mail server!

- *E-mail programs*—If you are paying an ISP to provide you with access to the Internet, you will likely have one or several e-mail accounts for you and your family or organization. In this case, your ISP will provide you with e-mail software (sometimes called a client) to install on your computer or instructions on how to set up your existing software (e.g., Outlook Express, Netscape Messenger, First Class, Lotus Notes). The e-mail program actually "lives" on your computer. If it has been set up properly, the program will check the mail server at your ISP and deliver your mail to you at your request! This type of e-mail is usually referred to as "*POP*" or *Post Office Protocol*.

E-mail programs generally have many features that Web e-mail services do not have, but they do not always provide the convenience of Web e-mail. Some providers are also equipped to handle Web access for your e-mail. This feature allows you to check your mail through any browser on any computer (even if it is not running your e-mail program). It would be a "scaled down" and slower version of your e-mail program, but the basic features (sending, reading, attachments) will be there. It is worth asking about!

E-Mail Netiquette

The word *netiquette* refers to the rules of etiquette as applied to Internet communications. As electronic communications such as e-mail become more and more commonplace, many people have written about the proper use of these tools. Some common rules and guidelines are:

- Do not use all capitals in your message. IT GIVES THE IMPRESSION THAT YOU ARE SHOUTING.

- The *subject line* should contain a useful description of the contents of your message.

- E-mail is more casual than memos or letters. Use smileys or emoticons (e.g., :-)) to display emotion and feeling, if it is possible that the reader of your message will misinterpret your tone.

- Keep messages short and to the point.

- When replying to a message, include the important parts of the original message. Doing so helps the reader follow the chain of the conversation, especially if it occurs over several days or weeks.

- Never send chain letters by e-mail.
- For international correspondence, be forgiving of minor grammar and spelling mistakes since English is not everyone's first language and show respect for cultural differences (e.g., do not use local slang expressions or make reference to events and people that would only be recognized by your local community). When confronted with expressions that you are not familiar with, politely ask the sender to clarify or re-phrase the message.
- Do not use e-mail for such messages as personal thank you notes, invitations, or official legal documents.

To get more information about netiquette and cross-cultural communications in business, visit the sites of the following organizations on the *InsighTs* Student Page on <www.irwinpublishing.com/students>:

The Net: User Guidelines and Netiquette, Business Netiquette International, Netiquette Guide for International Communications, and 50 Rules of Business Netiquette.

 Activity

Smileys and Emoticons

Smileys and *emoticons* can be used to add a touch of emotion to your e-mail messages. Use them with care, being sure always to proofread your messages before sending them. The incorrect use of a single character can easily send the wrong message.

Examine the list below. Match the emoticon with the correct emotion or expression from the list provided.

Emoticon	Emotion/Expression
:-)	Screaming
:-(	Surprised
:-o	Mad
:-@	Disappointed
:-I	Wink
:-e	Happy
>:-<	Laughing
:-D	Sad
;-)	Indifferent

Visit the links for NetLingo in the *InsighTs* Student Page on <www.irwinpublishing.com/students> to see more smileys!

Activity

Investigating an Acceptable Use Policy

With a partner, examine the Acceptable Use Policy for your school or organization. Are there any guidelines for the proper use of e-mail in your school? If so, answer the following questions:

- What are these guidelines?

- Provide examples or explanations for each guideline.

- What other guidelines should there be?

If there are no rules of e-mail use, write a list of rules and guidelines that are appropriate for your school. Use your word processor to summarize your responses.

E-Mail Issues

There are a number of issues raised by the growing use of e-mail. Here are two.

- *ownership and privacy*—If you are using e-mail services provided by your school or employer, the school or organization owns your e-mail and the school or employer has the right to look at your correspondence. Do not assume that the messages you send are private. The general rule to follow when using e-mail is, "Don't write anything in an e-mail message that you would not write on a postcard!"

- *e-mail in the workplace*—There is growing concern about the overuse of e-mail in people's lives. It is not unusual for people to receive hundreds of messages per day. Some e-mail programs provide options for sorting messages according to subject lines. This feature helps workers to prioritize and to decide quickly if messages need to be forwarded to another person. The headlines in Fig. 6.14 from *The Globe and Mail* in 2000 reflect some of the concerns about e-mail in the workplace.

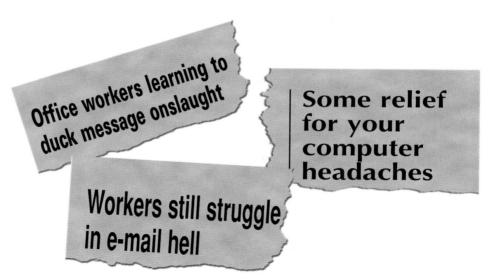

Office workers learning to duck message onslaught

Some relief for your computer headaches

Workers still struggle in e-mail hell

Fig. 6.14
As these headlines from 2000 show, there is a growing concern about too much e-mail in the workplace.

WHAT DO YOU THINK?

The organization that gives you e-mail access (school or employer) officially owns your mail. This means that your e-mail messages (incoming and outgoing) can be read by someone other than yourself. Together with two other students in your class, discuss the following questions and prepare a group response.

1. What advantages does the right to read e-mail provide an organization?

2. How would the fact that your employer or school can read your e-mail influence your use of e-mail?

 **Activity**

With a partner, select an individual from a local business or institution who uses e-mail on a regular basis. Interview the individual to determine his/her e-mail practices. Use the following list of questions as a guideline:

- On average, how many e-mail messages do you receive in a day?

- Do you find it difficult to handle the number of messages you receive? Why or why not?

- Does your organization have rules that you must follow when replying to e-mail messages? What are they?

- Does your e-mail software provide a way for you to sort your messages into separate inboxes?

- What other methods do you use to effectively handle your e-mail?

 For more information on e-mail, select the link for Learn the Net.com on the *InsighTs* Student Page on <www.irwinpublishing.com/students>. Click the link for "Harness E-Mail." Work through each of the lessons to review what you have learned and make notes on any new material.

 Knowledge Check

1. How is e-mail similar to postal mail? How is it different?
2. Who was Ray Tomlinson and what did he do?
3. Describe how a mail server keeps track of e-mail.
4. What is POP e-mail? How is it different from Web e-mail?

5. (a) What is netiquette?
   (b) What are eight rules of e-mail netiquette that all e-mail users should follow?
6. Describe two issues that have arisen with the growing use of e-mail.

Christine Johnston

Communications Manager

How do you get your message heard? When was the last time you tried to get the attention of a busy person? Were you successful? If you were, then maybe you have what it takes to succeed in the field of Communications Management. For Christine Johnston, Communications Manager at Havergal College in Toronto, Ontario, her biggest challenge is deciding how best to reach her selected audience. How can she ensure that her publications will be read?

Christine is responsible for producing a number of publications that are made available to various target groups. The publications might be a glossy brochure for parents, complete with professional photographs, or a student newsletter with all-student content. Her job can include everything from taking pictures at school special events, to writing and editing the articles within the publication. In all of this, Christine uses electronic communication to help her work faster and smarter.

Christine's main tool is a desktop PC. She uses it to send and receive e-mail, to upload content to the school Web site, to exchange files with her publisher, to write and edit content, and to access student and alumnae databases. In addition, she uses a scanner to make quick additions to the school Web site. Not lost in all of this technology, however, is the need for an excellent telephone manner and the ability to work with a team of professionals.

Christine is always learning new things, and exploring new ways to get her message heard. In fact, this is one aspect of the job that she particularly enjoys. In describing a recent project, she says, "Working with a design firm to build our public Web site was very exciting. It took a lot of work to develop a user-friendly content navigation system and that was fun."

Christine obtained a BA (Bachelor of Arts) in Arts Management, and has had a series of occupations, most of them in an educational setting, but always focusing on her skills in public relations and communications management. When asked to offer advice for students who might be interested in this career, Christine advises students to write for different kinds of media, both electronic and print, as the style and content required for each is very different. She also suggests that students speak directly to people who are in the profession to learn about the variety of paths that may lead them into this type of work.

1. What communication tools does Christine use on a regular basis?

2. What kinds of tasks does Christine use her desktop PC for?

3. What do you think Christine means by a "content navigation system" when referring to building a Web site?

4. Why do you think that style and content need to be different for different types of media? Use examples to support your answer.

CHAPTER SUMMARY

Understanding Information

1. In what form does information travel on the Internet?

2. What is the most common use of the Internet?

3. What is an IP address?

4. Identify two reasons why you may see an error message when attempting to visit a Web site.

5. What is the difference between a router and a gateway?

6. What is an ISP? List six popular services provided by ISPs.

7. a) Name and describe the essential parts necessary to connect your computer to the Internet.

   b) What else do you need if you wish to browse the World Wide Web?

8. What is multitasking?

9. What does an analog modem do?

10. What is a PDA? What is it used for?

11. What is the difference between a dial-up connection and a direct connection?

12. What is the purpose of a Web site portal?

13. What is Telnet and who might use it?

14. What is FTP and what is it used for?

15. In an e-mail program how is bcc different from cc?

16. What is an attachment file?

17. What is the difference between a mailing list and a personal address book?

18. What are smileys and emoticons? Why do people use them?

Analyzing

19. Explore the Web browser program available to you (using the Help menu, if necessary) and answer the questions below:

    a) What is the name and version of your browser?

    b) What buttons can you use to navigate the Web?

    c) What menu or button can you use to store a Web site address for a Web site you would like to visit again?

    d) How can you specify your preferred home page?

    e) Make a list of some of the security settings that are possible in your browser.

20. Explore the e-mail program available to you and use the Help menu (if necessary) to answer the questions below:

    a) What is the name of the e-mail program?

    b) Is your e-mail POP or Web e-mail? Explain how you know.

    c) Obtain a printed copy of the main screen and label the parts.

d) What is your e-mail address? Identify the parts.

e) List the steps required to perform each of the following tasks:
- compose a message
- send a message
- reply to a message
- copy a user
- blind copy a user
- add an attachment file
- download an attachment file
- forward a message
- create a signature line
- create a personal mailing list
- automatically forward your e-mail
- get a return receipt
- sort your incoming messages

Applying

21. Consider each of the situations described below. Use the information provided in this chapter to identify the Internet connection device that would be most appropriate for each.

a) I do not plan to spend too much time on the Internet. I need an inexpensive connection option that will allow me to send and receive e-mail and files with colleagues and friends. I have no interest in playing games or spending too much time on the Web.

b) I want a really fast connection because I intend to play games on the Internet. I am too far from my phone company's central office (over 4.8 km) to qualify for its high-speed package.

c) I need a really fast connection to the Internet because I plan to operate my own Web server from home.

d) I already have an Ethernet card in my computer and would like a high-speed option that would make use of this card.

Communicating

22. As part of a community service activity in your neighbourhood, you have decided to provide Internet tutoring to some residents in a senior citizens home. Compose a "user-friendly" definition for each of the terms (or groups of terms) below that you can use when communicating with people with little computer knowledge. Wherever possible, use analogies and pictures. Use your software skills to put this information into a newsletter or brochure for your audience to read.

a) protocol

b) modem

c) Internet service provider

d) Web browser

e) Hyperlink

f) URL

g) IP address

h) Packet, TCP/IP

i) Inbox

j) Download

k) Attachment

23. In your own words, describe how a DNS server is like a telephone book.

24. Imagine you are an employer. Compose an e-mail message to your employees about netiquette. This message should include the following:

a) an introduction including a definition for the word "netiquette"

b) why netiquette is important in general

c) netiquette guidelines as they apply to colleagues within the organization

d) netiquette guidelines as they apply to customers and clients outside of the organization

e) netiquette guidelines as they apply to contacts in other countries

f) a "gentle" request to your employees to follow these netiquette guidelines at all times

25. Where possible, send the e-mail message you created in question 24 to your teacher using your own e-mail account.

Assessing Your Competencies

26. Using the software competency checklists provided by your teacher, check off the competencies that you have mastered during the course of this chapter. Note the competencies that require more attention and review.

27. Interview a classmate to determine the competencies he or she has acquired during the chapter. Also share some of the new skills you have acquired.

CHAPTER SEVEN

ELECTRONIC COMMUNICATION TOOLS AND THE INTERNET II

In this chapter you will continue to explore electronic communication tools and the Internet. The focus is now on electronic communication tools that provide alternatives to e-mail, including mailing lists, online discussion groups, chat, instant messaging, and videoconferencing. You will also examine the netiquette rules that apply to these tools. In addition, you will begin to explore the world of wireless devices and learn about recent efforts to integrate the growing number of electronic communication tools.

Topics

➤ Internet/Web Communication Tools: Alternatives to E-Mail

➤ Wireless Devices

➤ Where Is It All Going?

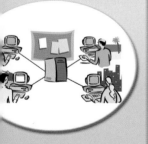

This chapter explores these questions:

- What are standard communication alternatives to e-mail?
- What are wireless devices and how do they work?
- What are possible new uses for wireless technology?

In this chapter you have the opportunity to

- think about the netiquette rules of communicating via mailing lists and online discussion groups and how they compare to the etiquette of face-to-face communications
- share your online chat experiences and discuss privacy guidelines as they relate to these experiences
- compose netiquette rules for videoconferencing
- consider the appropriate use of cell phones in society

Internet/Web Communication Tools: Alternatives to E-Mail

What Are Standard Communication Alternatives to E-Mail?

This section explores some of the Internet communication tools that can be used in addition to or in place of e-mail. Later in the chapter you will look at other tools (not normally associated with the Internet) and how they are evolving. The chart in Fig. 7.1 shows standard Internet communication tools. For each tool, the chart shows the timing restrictions on sending and receiving messages, and the type of data that can be communicated.

Fig. 7.1 Internet/Web Communication Tools

Tool	Timing Restrictions	What Can Be Communicated
Electronic mail	Any time	Text or multimedia (with proper software and hardware)
Mailing lists	Any time	Text or graphics
Discussion groups	Any time	Text or graphics
Chat	Real-time	Text or graphics (with proper software and hardware)
Instant messaging	Real-time	Text or voice (with proper software and hardware)
Videoconferencing	Real-time	Voice and video (with proper software and hardware)

Learning Link

Real-time electronic communication is communication that occurs immediately between users. There is minimal delay between when messages are sent and when they are received. Users respond to one another immediately, just as they would in a face-to-face interaction. Real-time communication is sometimes referred to as **synchronous** (happening at the same time) communication.

In contrast, **asynchronous** communication, often called **any-time communication**, is communication that is delayed several minutes or indefinitely. Sending a message does not depend on the receiver being available to receive the message at a particular time. These messages can be sent or received at any time, as is the case with e-mail and online discussion groups.

Mailing Lists

Mailing lists (also known as *listserv*) are *online* (on the Internet) discussion tools that use e-mail to communicate. When a mailing list, such as <catowners@mailinglist.com>, receives a message from a member of the group, a copy of that message goes to each of the members who subscribe to that mailing list. Anyone in the group can reply to the message. The reply will also be sent to every member of the group. Mailing lists are a great way to keep a conversation going about a topic that is of interest to the whole group!

Subscribing to Mailing Lists

There are thousands of public and private mailing lists on every topic you can imagine. Explore the following Web sites to get more information on the variety of lists that you can subscribe to. Liszt: The Mailing List Directory, Tile.Net/Lists, The Reference to Internet Discussion and Information Lists, and Publicly Accessible Mailing Lists. Follow the links on the *InsighTs* Student Page on <www.irwinpublishing.com/students>.

Business users might use mailing lists to keep a discussion with colleagues and experts going for days, or even weeks. Because messages are conveniently delivered to all members' e-mail inboxes, users can participate in a discussion simply by responding to an e-mail message. This is a great way to share ideas with people all over the country (or even the world) without having to physically meet in one place.

Fig. 7.2
Liszt: The Mailing List Directory, a popular mailing list directory

Using Mailing Lists

When you find a mailing list that you think you would like to join, you should find out more about the list. Look for the e-mail address of the moderator or administrator of the list. Some lists are moderated and some are not. In a moderated list, there is a person who manages the ongoing discussion (screens messages, deletes duplicates and irrelevant messages, and sends messages to members). If unmoderated, each member's message will automatically be sent to every member on the list. Mailing lists are generally free, but they often have rules and regulations for their subscribers, including specific netiquette guidelines. Here are some examples of mailing-list netiquette guidelines:

- "Lurk before you write." Read messages and replies for about a week before sending your first message. This approach is a good way to get a "feel" for the discussion and will prevent you from writing about something that was already discussed.
- Proofread your message before you send it.
- Avoid sarcasm. All members of the list may not easily interpret it.
- Make sure that the subject line of your message clearly represents the contents of your message.
- Do not send attachments. Many mailing list members may not be able to open attachment files that have been saved in a particular format.
- When replying to a message, include only the parts from the original message that are relevant to your reply.

Online Discussion Groups

Step 1: Write your message

Step 3: Members read message

Step 3: Members read message

Step 2: Moderator reviews message

Fig. 7.3
How mailing lists work

Online discussion groups allow people with common interests to communicate with one another. Unlike mailing lists, messages are posted to a common area (much like a public bulletin board), rather than being sent directly to individual members. There are several advantages to this approach over mailing lists:

- reduction in number of e-mail messages (for many business users today, this is a good thing)
- discussion messages remain together and can become quite valuable to new members of the discussion
- applications used to manage these discussions allow for many discussions to take place at the same time

InsighTs: Succeeding in the Information Age

There are a variety of ways that you can participate in these types of discussions. Some require the use of special software, and some do not. In the early days of the Internet, a popular way for participating in online discussions was through *Usenet* (short for *Users' Network*). This collection of thousands of online discussions, also known as *newsgroups*, provided people with ways to carry on discussions about topics of interest. This method is still in use today but requires the use of special newsreader software such as Netscape Collabra, Microsoft Outlook Express, or Newswatcher (for Mac).

New developments in the Web have recently made it possible to participate in online discussions via the Web. Often called *forums* or *conferences*, these online discussions do not usually require special software, but may require users to register and then enter a user name and password.

In most cases, online discussion groups are organized by *thread* or topic. Users may begin a new thread if the topic is relevant and not covered in another thread. When a message is added as a reply to another message or to start a new thread, it is said to be *posted*. Fig. 7.5 on page 202 illustrates a "threaded discussion."

Discussion Group Netiquette

Like e-mail and mailing lists, there are generally accepted guidelines for netiquette when participating in online discussions. In addition to the guidelines listed in the "Mailing List" section, there are also guidelines that apply specifically to online discussions.

- Read the *FAQ (Frequently Asked Questions)* before you ask a question. This is a document that lists the most commonly asked questions and answers that will often appear in an online discussion. The FAQ may answer your question before you ask it.

- Avoid *flaming*. A "flame" is a message with an angry or insulting tone that is directed to one member of the group. It is considered inappropriate to start or participate in this type of discussion (also known as a "flame war").

- Be sure you are posting a message to the appropriate online discussion group.

- Avoid *spamming*. Spamming is posting a message to several online discussion groups, whether the message is appropriate for the group or not. Spam is just like "junk mail" that you receive at your front door.

Companies and educational institutions may set up discussion areas for customers, employees, or students. These discussion areas can be used to provide online technical support, discussion of new products, or can even be restricted areas for groups of students to collaborate on projects together. In business, these tools provide efficient ways to communicate with and support customers. In education, these tools offer new ways to share and collaborate outside of the traditional classroom. See Figs. 7.4 and 7.5 for an example of how students from two high schools in Ontario collaborated on a project together using a Web conferencing tool called WebKF (Web Knowledge Forum).

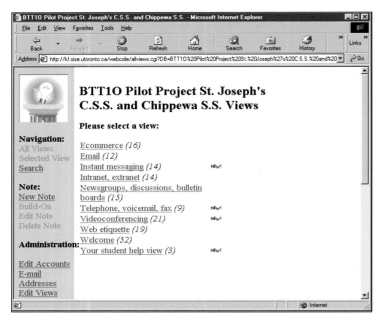

Fig. 7.4

This figure shows a screen capture of the main screen from an Ontario pilot project in which students from St. Joseph's College School in Toronto collaborated with students from Chippewa Secondary School in North Bay using WebKF (Web Knowledge Forum). This conferencing program was used to share files, have group discussions, and collaborate on projects. Numbers in brackets represent numbers of messages in a particular topic.

Courtesy Nancy Smith Lea and Dr. Marlene Scardamalia, Knowledge Forum Project, Ontario Institute for Studies in Education/University of Toronto

Fig. 7.5

This figure shows a threaded discussion by students researching the topic "Instant Messaging." Indented messages (also known as notes) represent responses to previous messages. Messages are colour coded to indicate those messages that have been read and those that are unread.

Courtesy Nancy Smith Lea and Dr. Marlene Scardamalia, Knowledge Forum Project, Ontario Institute for Studies in Education/University of Toronto

Activity

Updating Netiquette Rules

Consider all of the netiquette guidelines you have read about related to online mailing lists and online discussion groups. Now think about the last time you were involved in a "live" face-to-face group discussion. What equivalent etiquette guidelines apply to real-group discussions? What other guidelines should be added when you can see and hear the people in your discussion group? Why?

Knowledge Check

1. What is the difference between a mailing list and an online discussion group?

2. What does a mailing list moderator do?

3. What is the difference between a thread and a posting?

4. Describe four important netiquette rules for online discussions.

Chat

One of the quickest ways to communicate with others on the Internet is through a "live" chat. This does not mean that the participants hear or see each other. Rather, the words that the participants key on their computers are immediately visible to the others in the "chat room." Everyone in the chat room is free to respond at any time. Chats can take place with many people at the same time all over the world!

How Does Chat Work?

The most popular way to "chat" on the Internet is by using **IRC (Internet Relay Chat)**. With this method, every topic of conversation is called a "channel." When a user joins a particular channel, he or she will see what people who have joined this channel are "chatting" about. In addition, he or she will be able to contribute to the conversation or chat with the rest of the group. The chat channels exist on servers that may be anywhere in the world. IRC is based on a client-server model. The user's computer (the client) must have IRC software on it to communicate with the IRC server.

Another way to chat on the Internet is by visiting Web sites that use their own built-in chat software. This method is much like using Web-based e-mail versus POP e-mail that requires software on the user's computer.

 **Activity**

Have you had chat experiences on the Internet? Share your experiences with a partner. What are some useful guidelines for ensuring your privacy when participating in online chats? Using your favourite computer program, make a list of these guidelines to share with the class.

Buddy Lists

If you are interested in chatting on the Internet, but would like to limit your conversations to friends, relatives, and colleagues, you can create **buddy lists**. There are programs available that let you create specific lists of people with whom you would like to chat. A popular program called **ICQ** lets you set up a list so that you can send and receive messages only from those on the list. Other tools available in ICQ include the ability to send files, create personalized greetings, and create a virtual "do not disturb sign" when you do not want your friends to interrupt you. For more information, select the ICQ link on the *InsighTs* Student Page on <www.irwinpublishing.com/students>.

The newest versions of Netscape Communicator and Microsoft Internet Explorer also come with built-in chat client software that allows you to set up buddy lists.

Videoconferencing

To examine features of a program like NetMeeting, visit Microsoft's NetMeeting site on the *InsighTs* Student Page on <www.irwinpublishing.com/students> or check out the features of a new product from Groove Networks on the *InsighTs* Student Page.

Imagine combining the power of e-mail, ICQ, and chat together with the ability to see a real-time video image of the person (or people) with whom you are communicating! This is now possible with the right hardware and software and it is called *online videoconferencing*.

Online Videoconferencing in Business

A number of videoconferencing programs are available that are designed for the business market. They provide added features for collaborating with colleagues on complex projects online. At the very minimum, videoconferencing programs designed for business users are capable of:

Fig. 7.6
With collaboration tools like videoconferencing, workers and students can work on the same project without physically being together.

Courtesy Janet McLeod

1. *document sharing or collaboration*—People from offices in different locations can work on the same file at the same time.

2. *file transfer*—Files can be uploaded from one computer to another while the participants are working on something else.

3. *chat*—A videoconference participant may respond to an urgent message to "chat" about another issue with a colleague, but will not have to interrupt the videoconference to do it. This process is much like the telephone ringing during a meeting. You pause…answer the phone…reply…and then get back to work, except that in online videoconferencing you use your computer keyboard, not your voice.

4. *whiteboard*—This fairly standard feature is much like a classroom blackboard or whiteboard. All participants are able to see a document at the same time. They can make changes, move objects, and more. Imagine working on a school project this way!

 *Activity*

Updating Netiquette Rules

Together with two or three other students in your class, review all of the netiquette rules you have learned so far in this chapter. Use a computer application to make a list of new or revised rules that should apply to people's behaviour when they are videoconferencing.

1. What is a chat room?
2. When using IRC, what does a "channel" represent?
3. Do you need to have chat software on your computer to participate in chat? Explain.
4. What is a buddy list?

5. Describe some of the tools available in the ICQ program.
6. What is online videoconferencing?
7. List four videoconferencing features that make it possible for business users to collaborate on complex projects together.

Wireless Devices

What Are Wireless Devices and How Do They Work?

By now the enormous impact of the Internet on the world of communication should be pretty clear. It will be no surprise then that wireless communication tools like pagers and cell phones are being developed to work with the Internet to bring all of its information and services to people at any time and in any place!

In a cover story, "Five Guys, No Wires," in *Canadian Business* magazine (June 12, 2000), Andrew Wahl wrote,

Welcome to the next communications revolution, already in progress. We're not talking Internet—or at least, not Internet alone. Sure, it's already changed everything. But what comes next? The logical step is to untether the Internet's power—to break the Internet out into the world of wireless. The benefits: more freedom, efficiency and security in the way businesses and consumers communicate. If you're not using some kind of e-mail pager or Internet-enabled cell phone yet, you will be soon. And that's just the beginning. Think of it as the Internet unbound.

– Courtesy *Canadian Business*

Pagers

Pagers are portable, lightweight devices that are carried by individuals who want to know when someone is trying to reach them.

A traditional pager works by receiving radio signals (much like the signals used by our AM/FM radios) that cause the pager to respond either with a tone or a vibration. The user of the pager will then look at the display on the pager and read the message. The message may be simply a telephone number or it can be a short text message, like "Phone home." The owner of the pager will usually respond by using a telephone to dial the number that was sent in the page or by calling the paging company to retrieve a longer message.

E-mail in a paging device?

A device called the BlackBerry behaves much like a pager, but provides wireless access to e-mail, a calendar, an address book, and more. Manufactured by Research In Motion (RIM), a Waterloo, Ontario, company, the BlackBerry runs on a single battery. Business users claim that it provides a single, simple alternative to using a cell phone, a pager, and laptop while on the move. Visit the BlackBerry Web site on the *InsighTs* Student Page on <www.irwinpublishing.com/students> for up-to-date information on this device.

Fig. 7.7
The BlackBerry
Courtesy of Research In Motion

Newer technology has resulted in smaller pagers that contain more and more features. New generations of pagers will contain the ability to immediately respond to text messages without the use of another device. To get full interaction with your callers, read on to uncover some amazing new possibilities with cellular phones.

Cellular Phones

A *cellular phone*, also known as a *cell phone*, is a wireless telephone that uses radio signals to communicate with either another cell phone or a regular telephone. The word "cell" refers to the geographical area that is served by one antenna.

Fig. 7.8
When a cell phone call is made, the antenna or radio base station in that area will accept the call. It then sends the call either to another cell area if it is directed to another cell phone or to the local telephone network if the call is to a regular phone.

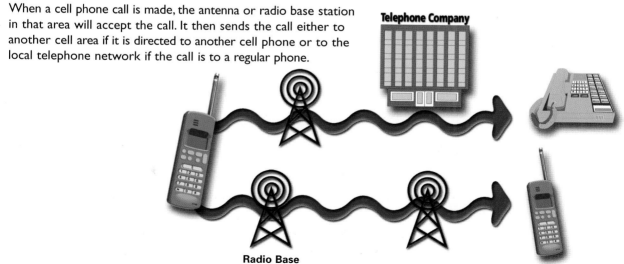

Telephone Company

Radio Base
Station

Learning Link

The true beginning of cell phone technology can be traced back to the development of the first radio wave transmitter by Guglielmo Marconi in 1895. However, it was not until after the Second World War, when portable two-way radios proved useful on the battlefields, that companies started to explore the possibilities of offering this type of portable technology to consumers. The first cellular telephone network was the Nordic Mobile Telephone system in Sweden, which was set up in 1981. In October 1983, Chicago, Illinois, became the first city in North America to offer cell phone technology.

Select the About — Inventor Web link on the *InsighTs* Student Page on <www.irwinpublishing.com/students> to learn more about the history of the cell phone.

The Cell Phone Generations

First-generation cell phones are analog devices that function much like radios. Sound is transmitted by radio waves and, unless there is major interference from other radio devices, they still work quite well.

Second-generation cell phones were introduced in the early 1990s. They use digital technology, which is commonly referred to as *PCS* or *Personal Communication Services*. With this technology, voices are converted to digital codes that can be transmitted through the airwaves. When voice data travels this way it is not as prone to interference. Second generation cell phones work very well in highly congested areas and have an added advantage of being able to carry other digital data such as Internet e-mail and Web files. The only problem is speed. They carry voice data at a suitable speed, but other data is carried at approximately 13 kbps. Not quite up to speed for multimedia on the Internet!

Third-generation cell phones use *3G technology*. With this technology, data is transmitted in much the same way that it is transmitted over the Internet—in packets. Although 3G technology is still developing, it has the potential to cause explosive changes in the way people use cell phones.

Learning Link

Despite research that reports minimal side effects from the regular use of cell phones, there is growing concern about the long-term effects that their use will have. At the beginning of August 2000, the Cellular Telecommunications Industry Association (CTIA) added a new requirement before it will certify new cell phones. Cell phone makers are required to disclose the amount of radiation emitted by the phone on the outer casing. They must also display the address of a Web site that contains information about radiation levels of other phones so that potential customers are fully informed.

First **Third** **Second**

Fig. 7.9

Three generations of cell phones. Anthony Jenkins/ *The Globe and Mail*, May 26, 2000.

Reprinted with permission of The Globe and Mail

 **Activity**

Drawing Up Your Own Cell Phone Etiquette

As increasing numbers of people worldwide own cell phones, *cell phone etiquette*— when to use and, in particular, when not to use cell phones—has become a major international problem. In fact, cell phone etiquette has become such a serious issue that the industry itself is urging people to practise common-sense etiquette when using cell phones. EarthVision Communications Inc. of Las Vegas, for example, has its own commercial Web site dedicated to etiquette. Visit the company's Web site on the *InsighTs* Student Page on <www.irwinpublishing.com/students> and print out its list of etiquette suggestions. In small groups, brainstorm other suggestions you would add to the company's list. Share your additions with the rest of the class.

Case Study

The Canada Safety Council in Ottawa does not advocate the banning of cellular phone use in moving vehicles, as has occurred in several other countries, but it suggests ways to reduce risks.

- Make sure your phone is positioned where it is easy to see and easy to reach. Become knowledgeable about the operation of your phone. Practise using your phone while your vehicle is stationary so you will feel more comfortable using it on the road.

- Use a hands-free microphone (make sure it's installed for optimum sound quality) for a specially installed car phone, or a hands-free kit for the usual type of cell phone. This will allow you to keep both hands on the wheel.

- Use the speed-dialling feature on your phone to program frequently called numbers. Most phones will store up to 99 numbers, and you can access them by touching only two or three buttons. The council also recommends programming the numbers for your local police and fire departments.

- Dial only when stopped. Wait for a traffic light or a stop sign, or safely pull off the road. If you must dial a full phone number while driving, dial the first few digits, then survey traffic before dialling the rest. Better yet, have a passenger do the dialling.

- Never take notes while driving. Carefully pull off the road if you must take notes. Many cellular phones have an electronic scratchpad that lets you key in a new number while having a conversation. You then can press the send button to call the new number after completing your first conversation.

- Let your cellular network's voice mail pick up your calls when you are unable to answer your phone. It's easy to retrieve your messages later. You even can use your voice mail as a notepad by leaving yourself reminders.

- Be a cellular Good Samaritan by reporting crimes in progress, accidents, and other emergencies to the proper authorities. For cellular subscribers, 911 is a free call; however, it should be used only for life-threatening emergencies.

Fig. 7.10
Super Stock/1244/3407

Read the Canada Safety Council's suggestions above and in small groups or as a class, debate the proposition: "The suggestions made by the Canada Safety Council are not enough. Cell phones should be banned in all vehicles." Set up a chart with three columns—one with the heading "Agree," one with the heading "Disagree," and one with the heading "Reasons." In the "Reasons" column, summarize the reasons for each point of view.

Agree	Disagree	Reasons

Knowledge Check

1. What is a pager and how does it work?
2. Describe the features of the BlackBerry device developed by RIM.
3. How does a cellular phone communicate with other phones?
4. How do first-generation cell phones work?
5. How do second-generation cell phones work?
6. What does PCS stand for?
7. Describe how 3G cell phones are like computers and the Internet.

Where Is It All Going?

What Are Possible New Uses for Wireless Technology?

Chances are that by the time you read this text, there will be other new and exciting ways to communicate wirelessly. The most interesting new developments will likely be influenced by 3G technology.

Here are some examples of how you and others might be using wireless devices in the next few years:

- using your hand-held organizer to stay up-to-date on late-breaking news from all over the world, complete with video clips and photos
- immediately transmitting medical X-rays from labs to doctors
- ambulance attendants communicating visually with doctors to get life-saving information for critically ill patients
- security devices in mines and wells monitoring activities and immediately send warnings over the airwaves
- using wireless devices to confirm hotel reservations and being shown the way to your room as soon as you arrive

Integration of Electronic Communication Tools

There is a growing trend towards integrating many of the communication tools that have been described in this chapter. After all, if many of the jobs of the twenty-first century need employees to "stay connected," then it would be helpful to find a way to make these tools "work together."

In a traditional telephone call, a single conversation ties up a circuit for the duration of the call. In Internet telephony, a conversation is broken down into numerous packets of data. Each of these packets may take a separate path through the Internet. The packets are then reassembled at the other end of the line.

You can now use your computer and Internet connection to make a long-distance phone call to a relative in Japan, with no long-distance charges! *Internet Telephony* is also known as *"voice over IP" (VOIP)*. IP, you will recall, stands for Internet Protocol. When making a VOIP phone call, you are sending your voice, using Internet Protocols (IP), over the Internet, to reach a telephone or another computer. To be able to do this, you need a computer with Internet access, a two-way sound card, a microphone, speakers, and Internet telephone software. New technologies and faster Internet travel will eventually turn Internet telephony into something that can compete with our existing telephone systems. Only time will tell.

Fig. 7.11
An Internet Telephony Communications Centre. Using the proper hardware and software, you can turn your computer into a dynamic message centre so you never miss a call, e-mail, or fax. A complete CT set-up will support incoming and outgoing calls, voice messaging and delivery, call forwarding, and more.

Knowledge Check

1. What is meant by "integration of electronic communication tools"?

2. Why is integration increasingly important for the jobs of the twenty-first century?

3. What is VOIP and what is it used for?

CHAPTER SUMMARY

Understanding Information

1. What is the difference between "real-time" and "any time" communication tools?

2. What is a mailing list (also known as listserv)?

3. Identify six important general rules for participating in mailing lists.

4. What is an online discussion group?

5. What is FAQ?

6. What is IRC?

7. What does it mean that IRC is based on a client-server model?

8. Explain why people carry pagers.

9. What is the BlackBerry and why is it used?

10. What does the word "cell" refer to?

11. How does a cell phone work?

12. What is the origin of cell phone technology?

13. When and where was the first cellular telephone network installed?

14. How does an analog cell phone work?

15. When are analog cell phones prone to interference?

16. What makes a digital cell phone different from an analog cell phone?

17. What are some advantages of digital phones over analog phones?

18. What is so special about 3G technology?

19. What does CTIA do?

20. According to the CTIA, what information should be on all cell phones that were purchased after August 2000?

Analyzing

21. Describe three features of Internet chat that make it so appealing to teenagers.

22. Describe three features of Internet chat that could threaten personal security.

23. Reflect on what you have learned and what you know about chat lines on the Internet. Identify three general rules that chat participants should follow at all times.

24. Chat lines are popular because they allow for social interactions among people. Identify three other useful applications of chat lines in business and education.

25. Consider the last time you worked on a project with one or more other students. Describe how you could have used videoconferencing to work more efficiently.

Applying

26. Examine your school's Acceptable Use Policy (AUP) for Technology. Evaluate the netiquette guidelines. Using what you have learned in this chapter, rate the guidelines as follows:

Level 1	Needs some improvement
Level 2	Adequate
Level 3	Satisfactory
Level 4	Excellent

If the guidelines are anything but level 4 (excellent), write exactly what needs to be included to result in an outstanding AUP.

Communicating

27. As part of a community service activity in your neighbourhood, you have decided to provide Internet tutoring to some residents in a senior citizens home who have little computer knowledge. Compose a "user-friendly" definition for each of the terms (or groups of terms) below that you can use when communicating with people who do not know much about computers and the Internet. Wherever possible, use analogies. Use your electronic software to prepare a presentation for your audience on these topics.

    a) mailing list

    b) online discussion group

    c) netiquette

    d) IRC, channel, chat

    e) ICQ

    f) videoconference

    g) VOIP

Assessing Your Competencies

28. Using the software competency checklists provided by your teacher, check off the competencies that you have mastered during the course of this chapter. Note the competencies that require more attention.

29. Interview a classmate to determine the competencies he or she has acquired during the chapter. Also share some of the new skills you have acquired.

InsighTs: Succeeding in the Information Age

CHAPTER EIGHT

ELECTRONIC COMMUNICATION TOOLS IN BUSINESS

Topics

➤ The Telephone and Voice Mail

➤ Fax Machines

➤ The Internet as a Communication Tool in Business and Commerce

Like many of us, business users are finding it impossible to survive without the basic electronic communication tools. In this chapter, we will continue to examine electronic communication tools but will focus on the tools most commonly used by business. In addition, we will explore how the World Wide Web is used to communicate business information.

This chapter explores these questions:

- What is voice mail and how are businesses using it?
- How are fax machines used in business?
- E-commerce and e-business: what is the difference?
- In what ways do businesses use the Internet, Intranets, and Extranets as tools of business?
- How does Web design enhance e-commerce?

In this chapter you have the opportunity to

- explore and evaluate voice-mail systems
- examine the skills necessary to succeed in a career as an information specialist
- identify types of e-business organizations and what category of e-business they are in
- examine how a fictional company called CoolSportz uses its Intranet, Extranet, and the Internet to communicate information
- identify types of information that is best communicated by Intranet, Extranet, or Internet
- explore e-commerce Web sites and evaluate their design and function
- investigate Internet advertising practices
- think about the skills needed for a career as a Web designer

The Telephone and Voice Mail

What Is Voice Mail and How Are Businesses Using It?

The telephone was invented by Alexander Graham Bell in 1876. By 1910, there were seven million telephones in the world! This number grew to 51 million in the 1950s and to 520 million in 1990. The current number of telephones worldwide is estimated at one billion, plus 500 million mobile phones!

Initially, telephone lines were used to exchange voice messages. The modern telephone sends and receives both voice *and* data. Computers are used to manage our complex telephone systems and telephone lines are used to connect computers and other devices. The telephone works by converting information (voice or data) to electric impulses that can be sent over great distances. Although telephones existed before our current computer networks, they work in much the same way as a computer network. Earlier, you learned how computer client-server networks have a central server that (among other functions) manages the flow of information across an electronic network. When networks are attached to other networks (the Internet), we are capable of sending and receiving information worldwide. In the same way, we are able to send and receive information using our telephones because they are all connected to complex switching systems (also called central offices or exchanges)—because they are *networked* with other telephones!

Fig. 8.1(a)
Canada's first telephones for commercial use were leased in 1877 to Prime Minister Alexander Mackenzie for use on a line from his office at the Department of Public Works to the Governor General's residence. Both the Wooden Box and Wooden Hand Telephones were capable of transmitting and receiving conversations.

© Bell Canada

Fig. 8.1(b)
The Vista* 350 telephone set, 1998. Equipped with a display screen, the phone (introduced in 1995) provides users with quick, direct access to a wide range of products and information services.
© Bell Canada
*Trademark of Northern Telecom

Fig. 8.2
Standard answering machine

Although today's telephones can also send data, the primary purpose of telephones remains the exchange of voice messages. A major milestone in the evolution of the business use of the telephone was the development of the *answering machine*. These machines typically connected to a telephone and contained a cassette tape that recorded messages as they came through. Today's answering machines record messages digitally, eliminating the need for a cassette tape. The answering machine made it possible for people to leave messages for other people if they were not available to answer immediately. For business users, interaction with customers and business partners could continue when no one was available to take a call. For home users, important messages were not missed.

Computer advancements in the 1980s made it possible to improve on this technology and voice-mail systems were introduced. *Voice mail* refers to the collection of voice messages that are stored on a computer for playback at a later time. Voice-mail systems use audiotex applications (or programs). *Audiotex applications* are the programs that manage the sending and receiving of voice-mail messages. When callers telephone an organization that uses an audiotex program, they are usually presented with a menu of choices. They will make their selections either by speaking aloud or pressing buttons on their telephone.

The new voice-mail systems have the potential to become very complex and there is growing concern that callers (often potential customers) find them annoying. Here are some approaches that businesses are using to make these systems more user-friendly:

- Provide the caller with an option to speak to a receptionist (right from the start).
- Allow the caller the opportunity to enter a known extension number immediately.
- Provide only four or five options at a time.
- When waiting is necessary, remind the caller that the call is important and estimate the waiting time.

 *Activity*

Assessing Voice-Mail Systems

Select a government organization, an educational institution, and a business organization in your area. Use the telephone to call each organization and listen to the voice-mail system. If you reach a receptionist, tell him/her that you are doing a school survey and ask to listen to the company's voice-mail system. As you listen to the menu choices, make selections according to your interests or at random. When finished, answer the questions below.

1. Were you given an option to speak to a live voice?
2. How many options were you given in the first menu?
3. What features of this system made it user-friendly?
4. What features of this system made it user-unfriendly?
5. What would you advise the organization to change about its voice-mail system?
6. Present your findings in table form as shown in Fig. 8.3.

Fig. 8.3 Assessing Voice-Mail Systems

	Organization 1	Organization 2	Organization 3
Option for Live Voice?			
Number of Options in Menu?			
User-Friendly Features?			
User-Unfriendly Features?			
Advice to Organization?			

As e-mail becomes more and more popular, voice-mail systems have been forced to adapt. Voice-mail systems now provide many of the features of e-mail programs (e.g., saving, forwarding, mailing lists). In addition, e-mail systems in many organizations are set up to integrate both voice mail and e-mail so that users need only check one place for both types of messages! This process is often referred to as "integrated" or "unified messaging." A multimedia computer equipped with speakers and a microphone is necessary for the integration of e-mail and voice-mail messages to work, but this application is quickly becoming standard.

Home users may also use a variety of programs, services, and equipment to manage voice mail. Some of the options include:

- digital answering machines and telephones
- voice-mail services provided by telephone companies
- software provided with multimedia computers or modems

Because of the widespread use of voice-mail systems, it is also helpful to be aware of some of the unwritten etiquette tips for leaving voice-mail messages. Here are some of those tips:

- Speak slowly.
- Clearly state your name, telephone number, and time you are calling.
- Leave a detailed message rather than just your name and telephone number, stating clearly what you are calling about.
- Provide background information if necessary. Examples of background information are describing the issue you are calling about and the last person you spoke to, or giving the date of your last contact and the details of that conversation.
- Indicate in what form you would like a response (telephone call, e-mail, or other) and when you would be available for a follow-up conversation.

Knowledge Check

1. When was the telephone invented and by whom?
2. Why are we able to use telephones to send and receive information worldwide?
3. What major milestone in the evolution of the telephone made it possible for business communication to continue even when no one was available to answer calls?
4. What applications are used to manage voice-mail messages?
5. What services and programs are available to home users to manage voice mail?

Fax Machines

How Are Fax Machines Used in Business?

Fig. 8.4
On March 15, 1962, Bell Canada introduced Phone-Fax, a facsimile transmission service. Bell Canada was the first telephone company in the world to offer this type of service.

©Bell Canada

Digital facsimile (fax) machines made document sharing easy long before the widespread use of e-mail. Fax machines look like a cross between a telephone and a mini-photocopier.

A modern fax machine works much like a photocopier except the copy is sent to another fax machine for printing and the sender keeps the original. A common question often asked by new users in the early days of fax machines was "Why did it come back?" The original copy does not go anywhere! A copy is made and sent electronically to a fax machine at the receiving end where it is printed. The original remains with the sender.

Although there are some variations, all modern fax machines have the following features:

- a scanning mechanism to read a document
- electronic equipment to translate and compress data
- a modem to send data via a telephone line
- a printer to output an incoming document

Learning Link

The origins of the fax machine can be traced back to the work of a Scottish inventor, Alexander Bain, in the 1800s. He invented a machine that could detect black and white parts of an image, transmit this information electrically over telegraph cables, and re-create the image on special paper. An Italian inventor, Giovanni Caselli, used Bain's design to build his "pantelegraph." In 1860, this machine sent the first-ever long-distance fax over 112 km, from Paris to Amiens, in France.

Fig. 8.5
A modern fax machine
Courtesy Xerox Canada

In the same way that telephones and voice-mail systems became integrated with computer equipment, fax machines, too, are capable of interacting with computers. If a computer user needs to send a document to a receiver who prefers a fax transmission, he/she may use faxing software (usually bundled with modem software or available through your operating system) to send text files directly from a computer to a fax machine.

Fax machines are losing popularity as new tools provide more flexibility and more direct access to information. However, they remain a useful tool for transmitting information when

- the document is only available in hard copy format
- the document requires hand-written information or signatures
- using a scanner and computer is inconvenient or cumbersome

Knowledge Check

1. What is another name for a fax machine?
2. What are the four basic features of all modern fax machines?
3. What was the pantelegraph and what was it used for?
4. Many other communication tools are now considered to be more convenient than the fax machine. When is a fax machine still a useful tool?

The Internet as a Communication Tool in Business and Commerce

Business communities are constantly in search of ways to improve how they do business. The electronic communication tools we have discussed so far in this chapter and in chapters 6 and 7 have played a major role in re-shaping the way people work. But what about all the other aspects of business, such as advertising, buying and selling, transferring money? Cell phones and pagers are wonderful for helping people to get on with important day-to-day communication tasks, but they do not contribute much to the more complex tasks of attracting and keeping customers and clients. The Internet has opened a whole new world of opportunities for business owners!

E-Commerce and E-Business: What Is the Difference?

Although the terms "e-commerce" (electronic commerce) and "e-business" (electronic business) are often used interchangeably, there is a difference. Businesses that participate in *e-commerce* use the Internet to sell products and services or to interact with customers and suppliers. Think of e-commerce as everything that you would do if you ran a small store, except you are doing it on the Internet. *E-business* includes all of the industries and organizations that support and develop the Internet. These businesses include companies such as Internet service providers, network hardware manufacturers, and Web designers.

In its publication *Fast Forward: Accelerating Canada's Leadership in the Internet Economy* (January 2000), Industry Canada provides a good summary of the state of e-business and e-commerce in Canada. It also provides supporting statistics and strategies to help both small and big business to participate in this new economy. Figure 8.6 shows how Industry Canada classifies the e-business community.

To see the complete "Fast Forward" document on the Internet economy in Canada, visit Industry Canada's Strategis site on the *InsighTs* Student Page on <www.irwinpublishing.com/students>.

Fig. 8.6
The E-Business Community According to Industry Canada

1. ***electronic commerce (e-commerce) organizations***, which include:
   - organizations that use the Internet to sell products and services to customers and clients
   - organizations that use the Internet to interact with suppliers and customers

   Some examples of e-commerce organizations are Amazon.com, FTD Florists, and Grocery Gateway.

2. ***Internet intermediaries***, which may include:
   - online services such as travel agents, brokerage firms
   - Internet advertisers and advertising brokers
   - ***Web site portals*** (see chapter 6, p. 176) and content providers

   These types of companies facilitate the Internet interactions between buyers, sellers, and other business partners. Some examples are E*Trade, Yahoo!, Ariba, and Doubleclick.

3. ***organizations that supply Internet infrastructure***, such as:
   - Internet backbone providers
   - Internet service providers
   - networking hardware and software companies
   - personal computer and server manufacturers
   - security vendors

   These companies manufacture and sell products that combine to make up the Internet infrastructure. Examples include Cisco, Dell, Nortel, and AOL.

4. **organizations that supply Internet applications**, such as:
   - Internet consultants
   - Internet commerce application developers
   - Web developers
   - search engine software developers

These organizations manufacture and sell products and services that enhance Internet infrastructure by making it possible to complete business transactions **online** (over the Internet). Examples include Netscape, Adobe, Oracle, and Google.

 **Activity**

Investigating E-Business Organizations

Together with a partner, use a variety of resources to find an example of one e-business organization in each of the categories described in Fig. 8.6. Write a short description of what each organization does and how it qualifies as an e-business. Where possible, use your word processing program to summarize your findings in table form.

CAREER PROFILE

Bill Dunn Senior Information Specialist

When you go to the bank and deposit money, a record is created of that transaction. When a record store buys music from a manufacturer, both parties maintain a record. The collection of these transactions forms a **database**. Because this database can be very valuable to the business or institution, the data needs to be "warehoused" in a secure, but readily accessible format. But these days, securely warehousing information is not enough. The data, or some of it, needs to be available to other business partners—instantly, at anytime, from anywhere—to facilitate e-commerce. This access may be achieved through the creation of a Web-Enabled Data Warehouse—a database that is accessible on the World Wide Web.

Bill Dunn has managed the development of such "warehouses" as part of his job as a Senior Information Specialist with EDS Canada in Victoria, BC. His role as a consultant requires him to be up-to-date with the latest technology, so that he is in the best position to make recommendations to his clients, usually large companies or government. Sometimes, his clients are hesitant to accept the new initiatives Bill suggests, because not all companies are yet convinced of the benefits of e-commerce, nor are they satisfied that the data is secure from hackers.

Providing clients with the necessary initiatives can be challenging, since electronic communication is changing so quickly. In fact, it changes so quickly that Bill may recommend several changes during a single project. To carry out his job, he needs to maintain regular contact with his client, and to create a team of professionals who understand the new technology and can use it in project development. If this career sounds demanding, it is, but the rewards are worth it. As Bill describes it, "Not only is it very exciting and interesting to be on the leading edge of technology, but there is also great satisfaction in developing a product that goes beyond the client's expectations. At the completion of the project it is nice to be able to say to your team, 'Well done!'"

When asked to offer advice for high school students who are interested in this type of career, Bill described some of the skills that are necessary in the people who form project teams:

- Team project managers need a solid foundation in the technology of computers and programming as well as having skills in areas like Accounting or Engineering.

- It is always helpful to have a team member with an Accounting designation, for example, Certified General Accountant (CGA) and with a solid technical background when working on e-commerce applications.

- It is equally important to have skilled Graphic Artists to work on Web page development.

Of the IT industry in general, Bill says, "There are so many exciting and new things being developed in this field that as long as you have the educational background, you can go as far as your dreams will take you."

If you are interested in cutting-edge technology, and enjoy working in a constantly changing environment, then a career as an Information Specialist may be for you.

1. What is the purpose of a Web-Enabled Data Warehouse?

2. Bill describes the skills that are necessary to make a successful team in this field. Describe those skills.

In What Ways Do Businesses Use the Internet, Intranets, and Extranets as Tools of Business?

To understand how the Internet, Intranets, and Extranets can be useful to commercial business, we will first summarize some common business activities that take place in a mythical retail store called Cool Sportz.

- Cool Sportz has a head office in a major Canadian city and 1200 retail outlets across the country.

- Cool Sportz also sells its line of CoolWear products to other sporting goods stores around the country.

- Cool Sportz cannot manufacture everything it wants to sell to its customers so it purchases some items such as shoes, ski gear, and camping goods. Sometimes, it deals with suppliers (who get the products from manufacturers) and other times it deals directly with manufacturers.

- Cool Sportz also needs to communicate with designers who may be working on special designs for new products, with advertising agencies working on new campaigns, with accounting firms and banking institutions to keep track of its finances, and with suppliers who provide day-to-day supplies such as paper clips, envelopes, and packaging.

- The company maintains contact with all of its employees (both near and far). It provides its retail store employees with up-to-date information on new products and collects up-to-date information on new orders. It also provides other important information to employees such as benefits (e.g., health care, life insurance) and collects information such as expense reports.

- Cool Sportz also communicates with the public. This group includes consumers and other organizations such as retailers who are interested in buying Cool Sportz's products.

Now, take a look at Fig. 8.7 to see how all of these activities take place using a company Intranet, Extranet, and the Internet.

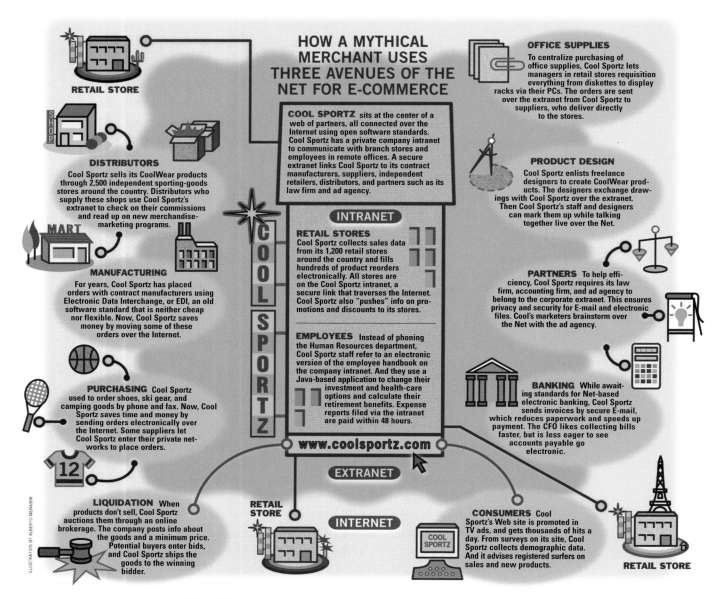

HOW A MYTHICAL MERCHANT USES THREE AVENUES OF THE NET FOR E-COMMERCE

RETAIL STORE

DISTRIBUTORS
Cool Sportz sells its CoolWear products through 2,500 independent sporting-goods stores around the country. Distributors who supply these shops use Cool Sportz's extranet to check on their commissions and read up on new merchandise-marketing programs.

MANUFACTURING
For years, Cool Sportz has placed orders with contract manufacturers using Electronic Data Interchange, or EDI, an old software standard that is neither cheap nor flexible. Now, Cool Sportz saves money by moving some of these orders over the Internet.

PURCHASING Cool Sportz used to order shoes, ski gear, and camping goods by phone and fax. Now, Cool Sportz saves time and money by sending orders electronically over the Internet. Some suppliers let Cool Sportz enter their private networks to place orders.

LIQUIDATION When products don't sell, Cool Sportz auctions them through an online brokerage. The company posts info about the goods and a minimum price. Potential buyers enter bids, and Cool Sportz ships the goods to the winning bidder.

COOL SPORTZ sits at the center of a web of partners, all connected over the Internet using open software standards. Cool Sportz has a private company intranet to communicate with branch stores and employees in remote offices. A secure extranet links Cool Sportz to its contract manufacturers, suppliers, independent retailers, distributors, and partners such as its law firm and ad agency.

INTRANET

RETAIL STORES
Cool Sportz collects sales data from its 1,200 retail stores around the country and fills hundreds of product reorders electronically. All stores are on the Cool Sportz intranet, a secure link that traverses the Internet. Cool Sportz also "pushes" info on promotions and discounts to its stores.

EMPLOYEES Instead of phoning the Human Resources department, Cool Sportz staff refer to an electronic version of the employee handbook on the company intranet. And they use a Java-based application to change their investment and health-care options and calculate their retirement benefits. Expense reports filed via the intranet are paid within 48 hours.

www.coolsportz.com

EXTRANET

RETAIL STORE

INTERNET

OFFICE SUPPLIES
To centralize purchasing of office supplies, Cool Sportz lets managers in retail stores requisition everything from diskettes to display racks via their PCs. The orders are sent over the extranet from Cool Sportz to suppliers, who deliver directly to the stores.

PRODUCT DESIGN
Cool Sportz enlists freelance designers to create CoolWear products. The designers exchange drawings with Cool Sportz over the extranet. Then Cool Sportz's staff and designers can mark them up while talking together live over the Net.

PARTNERS To help efficiency, Cool Sportz requires its law firm, accounting firm, and ad agency to belong to the corporate extranet. This ensures privacy and security for E-mail and electronic files. Cool's marketers brainstorm over the Net with the ad agency.

BANKING While awaiting standards for Net-based electronic banking, Cool Sportz sends invoices by secure E-mail, which reduces paperwork and speeds up payment. The CFO likes collecting bills faster, but is less eager to see accounts payable go electronic.

CONSUMERS Cool Sportz's Web site is promoted in TV ads, and gets thousands of hits a day. From surveys on its site, Cool Sportz collects demographic data. And it advises registered surfers on sales and new products.

RETAIL STORE

ILLUSTRATION BY ALBERTO MENA/BW

Fig. 8.7

How a mythical merchant uses the Intranet, Extranet, and Internet.

Courtesy *Business Week Online*, illustration by Alberto Mena/BW

On the company Intranet, Cool Sportz management and employees share information that is only available inside the organization. An *Intranet* is a network of Web pages and electronic tools that are restricted to users inside an organization. Users need an authorized password to participate. For the most part, Intranets are designed to behave like Web sites on the World Wide Web, but they are not accessible to the general public.

The company Extranet is designed so that Cool Sportz can communicate with its partners such as suppliers, manufacturers, designers, and distributors. These businesses or organizations are given access to some parts of the company's Intranet—also known as an "extra" Intranet. *Extranets* provide limited access, with a password, to a company's Intranet to users outside of an organization for the purpose of streamlining business activities. Cool Sportz may access a supplier's Extranet to place orders instead of faxing or sending them in the mail, and a product designer may access Cool Sportz's Extranet to have a videoconference with the marketing staff about a new design.

 *Activity*

Understanding Cool Sportz

Examine Fig. 8.7, and answer the following questions.

1. What three avenues of electronic communication does Cool Sportz use to communicate with employees and business partners?

2. For each avenue of communication named above:
   a) List the groups of people and/or business partners with whom Cool Sportz is communicating.
   b) Describe a minimum of three typical business activities or communications that take place.

3. How are unauthorized users prevented from accessing secure Intranet and Extranet sites?

4. Consider a typical school or school board setting.
   a) Identify the groups of people that would be communicated with via Intranet, Extranet, and Internet.
   b) Now identify the type of information that would be communicated to each group (e.g., school renovations, employee purchase plans).

Use your word processing program to present your ideas in table form as shown in Fig. 8.8.

Fig. 8.8

Communication Avenue	Group of People	Type of Information
Intranet		
Extranet		
Internet		

The Internet and E-Commerce

The potential to do business over the Internet has caused explosive changes in the Internet over the last few years. These changes are likely to continue well into the new century. Like anything in the world of business and economics, new innovations and inventions are often driven by the demands of industries that sell products and services. For online buying and selling to work well, the technology that facilitates it must be easy to use, fast, reliable (it works properly every time), and secure (personal customer information, such as a credit card number, must be kept confidential).

As you saw in Fig. 8.6, these four important demands have sparked the creation and development of other e-business industries that have become partners to e-commerce: "Internet Intermediaries," "Internet Infrastructure Suppliers," and "Internet Applications Suppliers."

The world of e-commerce is evolving daily. Chances are that by the time you read this book, you will have new information that was not available to the authors at the time of writing. In a report released in January 2000, Industry Canada stated that to compete in the global economy, Canada must develop and support its e-business activities. Companies are increasingly convinced that to remain competitive—and therefore, in business—they must develop their "Internet presence" (Web site).

As companies move towards this goal, they are faced with enormous issues that need to be resolved. Some of the issues that have been identified as potential problems are:

Fig. 8.9
Electronic commerce sites provide a wide range of products and services.

- **shortage and high turnover of technology workers**—People with information technology skills are in high demand and in short supply. They change jobs often because they are continually faced with new opportunities.
- **privacy and security**—Consumers need to feel secure when they are making online purchases. E-commerce sites must convince prospective buyers that their privacy and security will be ensured.
- **push technology**—*Push technology* describes the ability of an e-commerce Web site to deliver custom information to a user (information that this specific user is interested in). For this technology to work, the company must know something about the user's interests and how to contact the user "gently" without being too "pushy." Privacy is also a major concern here.
- **Web design that works**—Competition on the Web is growing! Designing a Web site that consumers will not only visit, but interact with, is a major task. You will read more about this in the next section.
- **e-signatures**—Many industries are concerned that agreements and communications that require personal signatures cannot be easily transferred to the world of electronic commerce. Laws are needed to clarify this issue.

To date there are two main types of electronic signatures—digital signatures and electronic pen signatures. *Digital signatures* are strings of computer code that act as unique online identifiers that can be used indefinitely. These signatures are encrypted. As a result, it is virtually impossible to counterfeit them. Digital signatures are the most common type of electronic signature.

Electronic pen signatures closely resemble traditional written signatures. The electronic pen method is different from the traditional signature, however, in that it offers more precise security. That is because it is designed to measure things such as the way a person moves a pen and the pressure applied while moving it. Electronic pen signatures are not yet common. (Adapted from *The Globe and Mail*, November 9, 2000)

Knowledge Check

1. What is the difference between e-commerce and e-business?
2. List the four major groups in the e-business community according to Industry Canada.
3. Define Intranet and Extranet. What is the difference between the two?
4. Summarize the issues facing business owners when they enter the world of e-commerce.

Activity

Exploring Career Opportunities

Review the discussion about issues in e-commerce and what you have learned so far about careers in technology. Identify two careers that would address an issue identified in the figure. Research on the Internet or use other tools available to you in your school Guidance office to get information about each career and the education needed to achieve it. For each career, write a report that includes

- a career description
- what area of e-business it involves
- the education needed

Activity

Exploring E-Commerce Web Design

When companies decide to venture into the world of e-commerce (online buying and selling), they must plan to make the experience easy, fast, reliable, and secure.

Find a company in your area that has recently launched a Web site. With a partner, interview the owner to learn about the stages in the process and about difficulties along the way. Use your word processing program to compose the questions you will use during the interview. Your questions should help you determine:

- why the company decided to set up a Web site
- the features of the Web site that make it easy to use
- how the company hopes to convince people to buy through its Web site
- what the company is doing to make sure that customer information (e.g., credit card numbers) is kept confidential
- what the company would do differently if it were starting again

1. Submit your list of questions to your teacher for approval.
2. Set up an interview appointment by telephone or by e-mail.
3. Complete the interview. Be sure to take notes during your discussion.
4. Prepare a report to summarize your findings.

Case Study

What is truly amazing about the Internet is that one individual's Web site can be just as accessible to the world as the Web site of a multinational corporation. Talented and innovative individuals have the potential to compete on a global scale. Think of the possibilities! The excerpt below from the "Money and Business Section," page 2, Sunday, December 10, 2000, edition of the *New York Times* shows one of these possibilities.

MY FIRST JOB

Kate Cheney

E-Commerce, After School

Kate Cheney, 13, is a Webmaster for Fandom.com, an entertainment Web site based in Santa Monica, Calif. You can find her site, The Wonderful World of Harry Potter, on the InsighTs Student Page on <www.irwinpublishing. com/students>.

In the summer of 1999 I read *Harry Potter and the Sorcerer's Stone* and *Harry Potter and the Chamber of Secrets* by J.K. Rowling and decided to create a Harry Potter Web site. I bought a book and taught myself HTML, the coding system for the World Wide Web.

A few months after the start-up, I got an e-mail message from Fandom.com, which owns Web sites devoted to characters like Buffy the Vampire Slayer and Batman. They were looking to acquire the best Harry Potter site on the Web and found mine. They didn't know I was 13, and were pretty surprised when they found out. My mom looked into it to see if it was legit, and it was, so I sold it to them. I can't say how much they paid me, but let's say I made a lot more money than I did baby-sitting for my brother and sister, and I won't have to worry about college. I also get stock options and a fee.

The job is pretty easy. I get about 45,000 hits a day, so I update the site every day. I also hold chat rooms and review message boards.

I work alone, in my room at home in Pennsylvania, but over the summer Fandom flew all the Webmasters to California to meet one another. There are 21 of us from all over the world, but I'm the youngest.

Typically, I go to school from 8 to 3, do my homework and spend about two hours updating and chatting and e-mailing. I don't know what I want to do in the future, but computer classes are easy.

It's funny. At first, my parents thought I was spending too much time on the computer. We only had one, and my 9-year old brother needed to use it too. So I bought my own computer, scanner and printer with some of my Fandom money. I don't think they mind any more.

Reprinted with permission of *The New York Times*

1. What did Kate teach herself so that she could create her own Web site?

2. What does Kate do every day to maintain her Web site?

3. How do you think that this experience will help Kate in the future?

4. What do you think Kate is doing when she "holds chat rooms" and "reviews message boards"?

Advertising on the Internet—an E-Business Primer

The Internet provides a new frontier for businesses to advertise their products and services. The Internet is a unique advertising medium in that it allows customers to go directly from an advertisement to a purchase using the same channel.

According to *Marketing Magazine* (December 11, 2000), about half of all business Web site traffic is generated through online advertising. The remaining half of traffic on e-commerce Web sites comes from print advertisements, television commercials, and packaging.

The amount of money companies should spend advertising online varies depending on whom you ask. One rule of thumb is that companies should start small when entering the realm of Internet advertising by spending 3% to 5% of their total advertising budget in the first year. Each year after that, they should increase their spending by doubling it for three consecutive years. This way, companies can experiment with what works and what does not. The important thing to remember is that, in the long run, more money should be made as a result of advertising than is spent on that advertising.

One way of using the Internet to generate business is to use ***e-mail advertising***. This method allows an advertiser to send messages directly to potential customers' e-mail accounts. There are three ways to conduct e-mail advertising:

- purchase space on another company's daily e-mail list

- rent a list of e-mail addresses of companies or people who have asked to receive certain types of information on a daily basis

- distribute your own e-mail messages (which could include coupons, information about products or services, or special promotions) to your own permission-based list (a list of e-mail addresses that are collected from people who express interest in receiving information electronically from a particular company)

Alternatively, ***banner ads*** provide a way to persuade potential customers to click on a link to an advertiser's Web site from another site they are visiting. This type of advertising is popular, but it can be costly. Several pricing structures exist for banner ads. They are

- **CPM (cost per thousand impressions) model**—CPM refers to the total paid for 1000 banner impressions on pages to be seen by customers. For example, if the cost of an ad is $50 CPM, the advertiser pays $50 to ensure that potential customers see the ad on another Web site 1000 times.

- **CPC (cost per click) model**—The advertiser pays a certain amount each time a user clicks on the banner, bringing the user to the advertiser's site.

- **CPA (cost per action) model**—An action can be defined as anything from a sale to a download or a user who registers at a site. The advertiser only pays the Web site hosting the banner if the defined action takes place, so a higher fee is paid. For example, the advertiser may pay the Web site hosting the banner 10% of the purchase price of every sale made from the referral.

Advertisers need to think carefully about where to put their Internet advertising to make sure that the right people—those who would purchase the service or product—see their ad. Measurement companies like AC Neilsen and the Print Measurement Bureau can provide information about the online and offline habits of Internet users that can help advertisers select the right sites for their banners. Software can also be purchased that will measure the habits of certain groups of Web users. Also, looking at success stories of other businesses can assist in selecting the best Internet advertising practices.

• •

1. Why is the Internet unique as an advertising medium?

2. What kinds of activities generate business Web traffic? Which activities generate the most traffic?

3. What proportion of a company's advertising budget should be spent on online advertising in the first year?

4. What are three ways to conduct e-mail advertising?

5. What is a banner ad?

6. What kind of information would be useful to advertisers before deciding where to place their Internet advertising?

How Does Web Design Enhance E-Commerce?

E-commerce and Web design are the subject of a growing number of books and Web sites. It is impossible to simplify in several paragraphs everything that marketing professionals do to raise company profiles and to attract consumers to interact with e-commerce Web sites. Creating and posting (putting on the Internet) Web sites is a very easy thing to do these days. You may have your own Web site or know someone who does.

The rules for Web design are not carved in stone. Different industries will have different requirements. Regardless of a particular company's requirements, users need to feel like they are in familiar territory when they visit the company's Web site. A Web site for a company that has a chain of stores with a particular look should provide the same "look" on the Internet. Potential customers should feel like they are walking into the store when they visit the Web site. Consider the implications for music and video stores. Following this logic, Web site visitors should have access to the same kind of multimedia samples that they experience when they visit the stores (e.g., music playing, monitors showing latest movies and music videos).

Another important issue facing companies these days is Web designing for their mobile consumers. If a company decides that it wishes to do business with the growing number of consumers using mobile devices, it needs to design Web sites that are compatible with this technology. A language called *WML (Wireless Markup Language)*, which is similar to HTML, is now used to develop Web content that is accessible to mobile users. Wireless devices are generally not (at least not yet) capable of multimedia and have limitations on speed, so highly graphic Web content would only cause problems.

Fig. 8.10
With wireless devices, like the BlackBerry from Canada's Research In Motion, users can interact with Web sites anywhere and any time.

Courtesy of Research In Motion

For more information on WML and WAP (Wireless Application Protocol), check out the WAP guide and The WAP.NET sites on the *InsighTs* Student Page on <www.irwinpublishing.com/students>.

September Weir

Senior Web Programmer

CAREER PROFILE

The next time you look at a Web page, take a moment to consider the people who created that page. The designer created the look and structure of the page, but it was someone like September Weir, a Senior Web Programmer in Vancouver BC, who made the design a reality.

Web Programmers are in high demand because they are able to troubleshoot problems on existing Web pages, and they are able to use software tools to create new Web pages according to a client's specifications. As well, during the design process, September must collaborate with other programmers, the designer, and the client. To do this, she relies on her excellent communication skills.

September did not start out planning to be a Web programmer, but she always liked science and solving problems. After she earned a university degree in Chemistry and Physics, she began taking more specialized computer programming courses, the most recent of

which will designate her as a Microsoft Certified Professional (MCP). This is a well-recognized credential.

September is in such high demand due to her excellent communication skills, her specialized programming knowledge (Visual Basic, Cobol, and JavaScript, among others) and, perhaps most important, her willingness to see a problem through to a solution. Seeing a problem through to a solution might involve learning new software from a manual, or using the Internet to collaborate with other programmers. Sometimes, the software tool is so new, manuals have yet to be written. When this happens, September sometimes relies on trial and error to solve problems.

Of all the aspects of her job, however, September finds the design process the most exciting. Creating a Web site that accurately reflects the client's wishes can be an immensely rewarding project.

Does Web programming sound like a profession that you might enjoy?

1. Do some research about Web designers and Web programmers. Check the career ads in the newspaper or on an Internet job site to find out what formal education and experience is required.

2. Read through this Career Profile again and make a list of all the skills that September has that are not specifically computer skills. Now make a list of all the things that you do in school that give you opportunities to develop each of these skills.

Communication Tools are Everywhere

Learning Link

Bandwidth

Webopedia defines **bandwidth** as the amount of data that can be transmitted in a fixed amount of time. For digital data and wireless devices, it is usually expressed in kilobits per second (kbps).

SITE SEEING

To learn more about Cal-(IT)^2 visit the Web site for the California Institute of Telecommunications and Information Technology on the *InsighTs* Student Page on <www.irwinpublishing.com/students>.

As accessibility to high-speed bandwidth increases (especially wireless), many predict amazing new possibilities. Dr. Larry Smarr is a renowned American researcher who was instrumental in persuading the American government to provide Internet access for non-military research (through NCSA, the National Center for Supercomputer Applications). He also set up the conditions for the invention of the first widely used Web browser (NCSA Mosaic in 1993). Dr. Smarr predicts that cyberspace will grow to "mirror the physical world." Essentially, he predicts that microsensors, installed into our roads and bridges and even our walls and doors, will communicate with us as we walk or drive by. They may even help to manage traffic flow patterns and identify potential disasters. In 1997, Dr. Smarr was appointed to the President's Information Technology Advisory Committee. He is now in charge of the California Institute of Telecommunications and Information Technology (also known as Cal-(IT)^2). His institute has received funding from companies such as IBM, Sun Microsystems, Microsoft, and more. The goal of Dr. Smarr's institute is to envision the future…and make it happen! It would be worth paying close attention to the developments of Cal-(IT)^2.

1. What is Cal-(IT)^2 and what is its purpose?

2. Imagine what a typical day would be like if you could communicate with roads, walls, and doors. Do you think that such communication would improve your life? Why or why not?

CHAPTER SUMMARY

Understanding Information

1. List the general rules for leaving good voice-mail messages.

2. What is an audiotex application? List four features of a user-friendly audiotex application.

3. What are four reasons business people use e-mail to send digital information?

4. Use a chart similar to Fig. 8.11 to summarize the types of organizations in the e-business community. Use family, friends, and the Internet to identify local examples of each.

5. Why do companies feel the need to create Web sites?

6. What is an e-signature? Describe two types of e-signatures.

7. What is WML and when is it used?

Fig. 8.11

E-Business Community		
Type of E-Business	Type of Organization	Example of Organization
E-Commerce	Organization that sells over the Internet	
	Organization that uses the Internet to interact with suppliers and customers	

Analyzing

8. Reflect on your experiences (as a caller) with voice-mail systems, both personal and business. Identify three positive and three negative features of the voice-mail systems you have used.

9. Identify the communication tool (voice mail, e-mail, fax, regular mail) that would be best suited to deliver the following information. Explain why.

(a) a signed, legally binding contract

(b) the first draft of a WordPerfect document that your assistant will be formatting for you electronically

(c) a short message that you will be late for a lunch appointment

(d) a short message to request a price quotation and model number for a new piece of equipment

(e) a thank you card to your boss for nominating you for a prestigious award

(f) a hand-drawn sketch

(g) a job application form (completed by hand)

(h) an invitation to a restaurant opening

Electronic Communication Tools in Business

Applying

Communicating

For this section of questions and assignments, you will be asked to imagine yourself in the role of an independent businessperson running a home office. To have a context for the questions that follow, you need to establish a (fictional) setting for your business. Answer question 11 and use this information wherever it is appropriate in the questions that follow.

10. Your business profile:

(a) What is your business name? address? phone number? cell phone number?

(b) What type of business is it?

(c) What is your job title?

(d) Who is your ISP?

(e) What is your URL?

(f) What is your e-mail address?

(g) What are the names, titles, and telephone extensions of your hired staff (at least two)?

11. You depend on voice mail to run your business, but are frustrated because your clients and consumers in general are not using voice-mail communication efficiently. Write a "letter to the editor" to your local newspaper that will convince readers that if they remember a few key rules (that you will describe), voice mail will be more effective.

12. Use what you learned about voice mail in this chapter to compose the voice-mail message that callers would hear when they telephone you. Be sure to provide options to speak to other staff members.

13. What kinds of changes would you make to your message if you knew that clients would be calling you from other countries? What are some of the issues you would have to consider because of cultural differences? (Refer back to the discussion on netiquette in chapter 6.)

14. As part of your business plan you are now ready to plan for the development of your Intranet, Extranet, and Internet sites. Use a chart similar to Fig. 8.7 to identify the groups that you will be communicating with and the types of information to be communicated. Add an extra column to include issues you will have to consider because of cross-cultural communications. Call this column "Cultural Issues."

Assessing Your Competencies

15. Using the software competency checklists provided by your teacher, check off the competencies that you have mastered during the course of this chapter. Note the competencies that require more attention and review.

16. Interview a classmate to determine the competencies he or she has acquired during the chapter. Also share some of the new skills you have acquired.

CHAPTER NINE

HOW CAN I GATHER INFORMATION?

"When I was your age, I looked up information in books—with real pages and covers!" How many times have you heard that as you work on projects for school? Well, books still exist and are still very important in the overall research process, alongside a wide variety of other information sources. In the first part of this chapter, you will briefly explore how gathering and accessing information has changed over time. You will then learn how to develop a research strategy, and about CD-ROMs and search engines and how to use them to access information. You will explore how to evaluate the information you find and make sure your research is the best it can be. Finally, you will learn how to cite your research sources.

Topics

➤ The Changing World of Gathering and Storing Information
➤ Accessing Information from Electronic Sources
➤ Researching on the Internet and the World Wide Web
➤ Evaluating Electronic Information
➤ Good Citations

This chapter explores these questions:

- How has gathering and storing information changed?
- What sources of information are "out there"?
- The Internet and the World Wide Web: How do you find order within chaos?
- How do you research on the Internet and World Wide Web?
- How do you assess the information you have gathered?
- How do you cite your research sources?

In this chapter you have the opportunity to

- consider what you do that requires you to read and to understand what you read
- find out what types of information sources are available in your school library
- use the various search facilities in CD-ROM programs
- use Internet search engines
- use Internet search directories
- evaluate search engine bias
- perform Boolean searches
- perform natural language queries
- evaluate Web sites
- investigate careers that utilize research skills
- research and apply proper citations

239

The Changing World of Gathering and Storing Information

How Has Gathering and Storing Information Changed?

You will be required to complete many research assignments during the course of your academic and professional careers. Learning about new things can be fascinating. Just think about all the new advances in technology you have learned about so far in this book. Research can be very rewarding—when you find what you are looking for, that is!

Activity

The Printed Word in Your World

Imagine a world without the printed word. For many of us the idea seems totally unreal. For one minute, think of all the things that you have done or seen today that required you to be able to read and to understand what you have read. List as many items as you can in that minute. Share your thoughts and list with the class.

Fig. 9.1

Reading and writing are essential skills in this age of information. Every day, we are bombarded with printed messages and instructions, and are required to interpret these messages. But such was not always the case. Prior to the fifteenth century, learning for most people was by word of mouth. Until that time, only the nobility, scholars, and the educated priesthood were taught to read and write. It was not until 1450 CE that the first printing press produced Europe's first typeset book—the Gutenberg Bible. Gradually, the literacy rate rose as the printing process spread throughout Europe, making literary, scientific, and religious texts available to more and more people. As more people demanded printed works, printing technology and distribution and storage methods improved to keep up with the demand. With these improvements came dramatic reductions in the cost of producing printed works, making them even more affordable.

Today, we have the opposite problem to people in earlier centuries—we have too much information! There are books, of course, but they are only the beginning. Encyclopedias, newspapers, television, magazines, microfilm, e-mail, the Internet—how can we sort it all out? Think about the last time you were given a research assignment and were told to go to the library to gather information. Modern libraries are faced with the enormous task of sorting and organizing an increasingly unmanageable quantity of information so that you can find what you need.

Today, in most libraries this information has been compiled into computerized databases, indexes, and catalogues. Users locate sources within the library by keying subjects, authors, or titles of works into the library's database to search for the works' availability. Many libraries share their database with other facilities to increase the number of works that users can sign out. When you locate a book you want on another library database, that library will send the book to your local library for you to sign out.

Fig. 9.2
Researchers use readers such as this to read documents on microfiche.

A growing problem today is how to store all the information we have. Books, encyclopedias, newspapers, and magazines require massive storage facilities. Many sources are irreplaceable and over time, they can become damaged. Many works are no longer in print. To combat these problems, many documents are being put on microfilm and microfiche. Document storage companies photograph the pages in books, files, or newspapers (to name a few sources) and reduce them to tiny images on a sheet or roll. These images can then be viewed in fiche readers (see Fig. 9.2). One microfiche card, usually the same size as an index card, can hold between 100 and 300 pages of a book.

Saving Precious Historical Documents

In the United States, a National Digital Library has been created to preserve many American classics online. Supported by government and business contributions of over $60 million, the Library of Congress in Washington, DC, has begun the massive process of digitizing rare historical photographs, manuscripts, books, maps, sound recordings, and moving pictures held in that institution's collection to save them for future generations to view. To explore the American Memory collection of digitized materials, go to the *InsighTs* Student Page on <www.irwinpublishing.com/students>.

Fig. 9.3
The Declaration of Independence is only one of the important documents being saved through the National Digital Library.

The CD-ROM has revolutionized the way information is stored, accessed, and retrieved. One CD-ROM can hold an entire encyclopedia, plus other reference sources. It has the capacity to store 250 000 pages of text, 7000 pictures, and 72 minutes of video. Multimedia CD-ROMs allow users not only to read about things, but also to watch video clips, listen to voices, and see animated images that help explain topics in non-text ways. For example, to read about the historic 1973 Canada versus Russia hockey series victory is one thing, but to see Paul Henderson scoring the winning goal and hear the commentator describing it adds another dimension.

As you have already learned, the Internet allows users to access millions of Web pages located on Web servers around the world. Unlike the school library, however, the World Wide Web is not an organized collection of information. Clifford Lynch, director of library automation at the University of California's Office of the President, reporting for *Scientific American* said that, "It [the Internet and the World Wide Web] has evolved into what might be thought of as a chaotic repository for the collective output of the world's digital 'printing presses'." In other words, the World Wide Web is not a digital library.

Knowledge Check

1. Why was the invention of the Gutenberg Press so important?
2. How is information catalogued in a library? What essential information is contained in a library's database to help users find books and other sources?
3. What two inventions have helped with the storage of massive quantities of information? Describe them.
4. What do you think Clifford Lynch meant when he said that the Internet is "a chaotic repository for the collective output of the world's digital 'printing presses'?"

Accessing Information from Electronic Sources

What Sources of Information Are "Out There"?

Assume you have a research project for your math class on famous mathematicians over the course of history and the contributions they have made. Where would you start? You must first develop your research strategy. Figure 9.4 suggests steps to follow to get your research project under way.

Fig. 9.4 Steps in Creating a Research Strategy

1. Identify your research topic and how much information you will need at the end of your research.
2. Discuss your topic with other students, teachers, and librarians to get ideas.
3. Write the topic as a question.
4. Create a list of key words or phrases to help you research. A thesaurus can help you get ideas.
5. Identify sources you will use to find information.
6. Let the research begin…

Drafting a Search Strategy

There are many online dictionaries and thesauri available to help you with your searches. Check out the Merriam-Webster OnLine Dictionary or xrefer, a site that cross-references encyclopedias, dictionaries, thesauri, and books of quotations from the world's leading publishers, on the *InsighTs* Student Page on <www.irwinpublishing.com/students>.

The first thing you must do is determine the type of information you need, as this need will dictate where you look for information. Locating information already in print in the library should be your first step. **Not everything is on the Internet**. Many general reference sources are available in the library in both hard copy format and on CD-ROMs in digital format.

 Activity

Investigating Information Sources in Your School Library

Go to the library in your school and find out what types of information sources are available there. Key and format a list of the available resources with descriptions of their contents that you can use for this and other classes.

One of the best places to start your research is with an encyclopedia, which will give you a look at the big picture. Many encyclopedias are available on CD-ROM, so let's start there.

Fig. 9.5
Screen capture of the results of a search for "Boole" on Microsoft's Encarta Encyclopedia

Searching on CD-ROMs

When you launch a CD-ROM encyclopedia, for example, Microsoft Encarta, you have a number of options for finding information. Many CD-ROM encyclopedias include a feature that allows you to search by category, for example, "maps," "images," or "articles," if you are not sure what you are looking for. Using categories will allow you to get a general idea of the topic and may give you some key words to help you in a search of the database.

Use the Find or Search feature of the CD-ROM program. Key in a word or phrase for the CD-ROM to look for in its database of articles and multimedia files. If the CD-ROM finds the word or phrase, it will list the article(s) for you to look in. You still need to read the articles to see if the information will help you in your research. Do not limit yourself to one or two of the articles. **Always look for the best information—not just the first thing you find**.

 **Activity**

Searching in a CD-ROM Encyclopedia

On your school network, or in the library, access an encyclopedia on CD-ROM. Do a search for information on Sir John A. Macdonald for your history class. In what category do you think you will find information on him? How many different categories did you have to look in to find a reference to Sir John A. Macdonald? Record your findings.

Next, try a key word search in the same encyclopedia for Nunavut. Could you find it? Why might you not find references to Nunavut? Again, record your findings to share with the class.

Many of the new CD-ROM encyclopedias also have links to online sources for updated information. The Microsoft Encarta Encyclopedia 2000 edition, for example, has a Yearbook to search for new and updated articles and Web links to explore other Web sites that are linked to Encarta articles.

Knowledge Check

1. What general reference information can you access in the library to assist your research? Create a table in your notes that lists and describes each.
2. What are two ways of finding information on a CD-ROM encyclopedia? Describe each.

3. What other features are CD-ROM manufacturers building into their products to help people find information?

The Internet and the World Wide Web: How Do You Find Order Within Chaos?

The amount of information on the World Wide Web is growing at a phenomenal rate. It is getting more difficult to find the information you want, especially since the World Wide Web is not organized like a library. Searching for information on the Internet is like going into a huge mall for the first time. You have an idea of what you are looking for, but as you walk in, you need assistance in finding the right store, department, and finally, the colour, size, and style to meet your needs.

You have two basic options for finding information on the World Wide Web:

- surf, clicking on *hyperlinks* until you happen onto a site that has something you need
- search using directories or indexes of organized information

In order to search, you need to access an Internet search engine. Some popular search engines are AltaVista.ca, Canada.com, and ca.yahoo.com. There are dozens of these search engines from which to choose. Therefore, an examination of what they are and how they work is essential.

Fig. 9.6
An Internet key word search using the Sympatico Lycos Internet search engine

Search Engines—Get Yours Running

A *search engine* is a computer program that electronically searches the World Wide Web looking for HTML documents. These programs are referred to as *Web crawlers*, *spiders*, and *indexing robots*. They download and examine Web pages and draw out information to assist in describing those pages. This process can be as simple as finding the words that appear in the title or the first few lines of text, or as sophisticated as analyzing the content to find key words or phrases. The program then saves this cataloguing information in a database, along with the URL of the site from which the information came. When you key a word or phrase in the search engine, it is *only* this database, *not* the entire World Wide Web, that is examined.

The search engine then displays a list of the documents in its database for you to choose from. You may get different results if you use a number of search engines to search for the same information. Search engines catalogue the information they find in different ways. Some index every word, others only the top 100 words. Others only index the size of the document and number of words in it.

Fig. 9.7

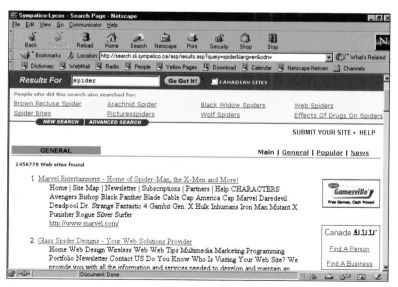

Fig. 9.8
Search engine results for "spider," showing 2 456 770 Web sites found

How Can I Gather Information?

Mouse Quest, Part 1

The mouse on your computer at home needs replacing (the cat chewed the cord off!). In two different search engines (two you might try are AltaVista.ca and ca.yahoo.com), key in the phrase "computer mouse." Use quotation marks to indicate a phrase. See how many "hits"—how many Web pages—are listed and compare the first 10 hits in each search engine. Key a chart comparing the results. You could set up your chart to look like Fig. 9.9.

Fig. 9.9 Comparing Search Engine Results

AltaVista.ca	ca.yahoo.com
http://www.mysteryjigsaw.pe.ca/mousep.html	http://www.howstuffworks.com/mouse.htm
http://www.micropad.com/corporate/	http://www.interlog.com/~artpro/mice.htm

Compare your results with those of a classmate. Make a note of how many of these sites were places to buy mice.

There are two kinds of search engines—single-search engines and meta-search engines.

- *single-search engines*—There are many **single-search engines** available, all of which index their findings in different ways. For example, AltaVista searches the full contents of HTML pages and allows users to search the entire Web or only parts of the Internet such as online discussion groups or images to narrow their search. Google is a relatively new search engine that ranks sites according to popularity, or how often the page is referenced on other pages.

Since each single-search engine indexes in different ways, it can be time consuming if you have to use several search engines before you find what you want. If you want to access more than one search engine at a time, you can try a meta-search engine.

The word "meta" is used to indicate a more comprehensive look at a topic. Hence, using a meta-search engine will provide more comprehensive results than using a single-search engine.

- meta-search engines—**Meta-search engines** take your query and submit it to numerous search engines simultaneously. The results are displayed on one screen. The results indicate which search engine found that particular information. Meta-search engines include Search.com, Dogpile, and MetaCrawler. You can find their Web sites on the *InsighTs* Student Page on <www.irwinpublishing.com/students>.

You access Web site information through a search engine's directory (where available) or by searching its database or index. Once the directory or index provides you with a list of pages, you click on the hyperlink. The hyperlink takes you to that page on the World Wide Web. The meta-search engine does not store the page in its own directory or index.

Directories and Indexes—Is There a Difference?

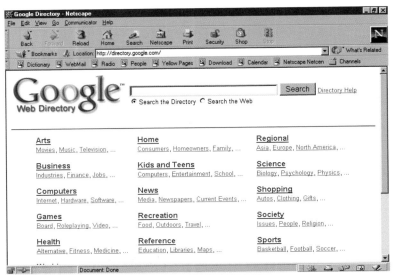

Fig. 9.10
The Google Web Directory page groups Web sites into different categories to help users find information quickly, eliminating the "junk."

Directories

Some search engine companies have classified some of their search results into directories or catalogues for users to access for general information about a topic. *Directories* are somewhat like card catalogue software in a library where you key a subject heading to find the resources available. There are probably many other books and resources on the topic in the world, but not in that library.

Three of the most commonly used directories are Yahoo!, Google, and DMOZ: Open Directory Project. See these directories on the *InsighTs* Student Page on <www.irwinpublishing.com/students>. The Open Directory Project collects the recommendations of Internet-citizens and topic experts for inclusion in its directory. The project is unique in that it is self-regulating, trying to maintain the quality of the directory by limiting the amount of noise (bad or useless sites) and misinformation.

 **Activity**

Mouse Quest, Part 2

Log into the AltaVista site on the *InsighTs* Student Page on <www.irwinpublishing.com/students> and scroll down the page to find the subject categories in the search engine's directory. Find one for "Computers" and click on it. Look for "Hardware" next and click on it. Within the "Hardware" category, you should find a sub-category for "Peripherals," then "Input Devices" to find a category for "Mice." Check out the pages the search engine collected on this topic. Key a description of the type of pages you found using the directory and compare these results to your search results from Mouse Quest, Part 1. Keep both your word processor and Web browser open, and *toggle* between the two while keying your summary.

Web sites tend to change fairly often and these changes may or may not be reflected in a directory. Directories are created when a search engine company first registers its site online and they may not be updated as frequently as an index.

Indexes

As you have just seen, a directory is a quick way to access information about a topic—if it has been catalogued. If you cannot find the information you need in the directory, a full-text key word search of the search engine index is necessary. The *index* is the database the search engine's spider or indexing robot has compiled for users to examine.

 *Activity*

Career Searching

Review the Career Profiles you have read throughout *InsighTs*. Based on these profiles, and your own knowledge, think about the types of organizations that require employees with IT knowledge and skills. List three of these types of organizations.

Next, access the online version of the Yellow Pages on the *InsighTs* Student Page on <www.irwinpublishing.com/students>. Locate two examples of each type of organization in your community and surrounding area.

Add to this information the reasons why you chose that particular organization. Why would the organization need people with the IT skills you are learning about?

Record this information in a chart similar to the one below:

Organization Type	Organization Name	Reasons for Choosing

Limitations of Search Engines

Fig. 9.11
Having to sift through irrelevant information can be very frustrating.

There are some common complaints heard when people look for information on the Internet. These complaints include:

- *too much irrelevant information*—When an indexing robot explores the World Wide Web searching for HTML pages, it categorizes the information differently than people might. As a result, when you do a search, the search engine may list sites that are irrelevant to your quest, and it may leave out others that contain important information. You may have to change the words you use in your search to find what you need.

- *built-in bias*—Another problem is that some search engines have a built-in bias. In other words, they will add a site to their database if it contains numerous instances of a frequently sought-after word, for example "sex." Web developers know that some search engines work this way, so they "hide" popular words within their site so that their site will appear more frequently in a search. The spider cannot see these hidden words or information for what they really are—a trick to get a company's Web page to appear more often in a search.

- *too much commercial information*—Web crawlers cannot make judgments about the content of an HTML page. They do not know the difference between a newspaper article, a play by Shakespeare, or an advertisement for a new product. You have to make those judgment calls.

- *not all Web pages are created equally*—There are no accepted standards for the creation of a Web page. As a result, some of the information you need to judge the validity of a site (author, date of publication, subject, and length of the text) may not be available.

- *search engines only recognize text*—Even though the Web can display multimedia images and sounds, many search engines catalogue text only. Some search engines have developed the ability to find colours and patterns within images. However, to date, no search engine can understand the meaning or cultural significance of an image.

- *the information is old*—The World Wide Web is one of the most up-to-date sources for information. However, some search engines do not update their indexes frequently. The frequency of updates varies from weekly to several months. It is up to the researcher to keep up-to-date on information by searching frequently.

 **Activity**

Surveying Information Technology Careers

Using the Internet, visit several job or career Web sites. Locate advertisements for five information technology jobs. Record the following information about each job advertisement:

- name of company and Web site (if listed)
- job title
- responsibilities of the job
- salary range (if listed)

Create a chart similar to the one below to summarize the competencies required for the positions that you found. In the chart, assess your level of achievement for all competencies listed, as well as steps you can take to improve them. You can use your own portfolio and competencies checklists to help you in your self-assessment.

Competency Required	Frequency with which the Competency Appears on Job Ads (check once for each time it appears)	Do You Possess the Competency?	What Steps Can You Take to Obtain or Improve the Competency?

 # Knowledge Check

1. What is an Internet search engine and how does it work? Draw a diagram to explain the process. Label each step.
2. What is the difference between a directory and an index in a search engine?
3. Explain the difference between a single-search engine and a meta-search engine.
4. What does "bias" mean in terms of Internet searching? How can businesses improve their site rankings when people perform searches?
5. What kind of standards should be put in place for Web pages to assist in the research process?

How Can I Gather Information?

Researching on the Internet and the World Wide Web

How Do You Research on the Internet and World Wide Web?

Now that you know what a search engine is and what some of its limitations are, you are ready to discover how to get the best results from a search query. The word "query" means "to seek information," in this case from a search engine index. Well, unfortunately, there is no magic—only a few suggested techniques.

Search Queries—Quality not Quantity

There are some general strategies that most experts suggest to reduce the number of irrelevant and inaccurate hits a search engine produces. If you get in the habit of using these strategies, you will get better results from many of your searches.

- Only search the part of the Internet you need to search.
- Check your spelling.
- Always key the most important search term first.
- Use singular words, not plural.
- Key in lower case not CAPS (upper case).
- Use nouns, wherever possible.
- Limit your search to three or four words at most.
- If you want to find a particular phrase, contain the phrase within "quotation marks."
- Truncate (cut off to the root) your words, and follow with an *. If you key colour*, the search engine will find pages that contain colouring, colours, colourized, etc. Without the *, the search will only find the word "colour."
- Vary your spelling. Many sites on the WWW use American spelling, for example, color versus colour.
- Use Boolean operators to help your search engine do its job.
- Investigate the Advanced Search section of the search engine.
- **Check your spelling (again!).**

The British mathematician George Boole devised a system of logic that is used by most search engines. Boolean logic uses words called *operators* to look at Web sites to see if they fit the search. The most common *operators* are AND, OR, and NOT. The example below illustrates what happens when these operators are used in a search.

You can also use math to simulate Boole's logic in a search engine. Use a + immediately in front of a word that MUST be contained in the document. Use a – in front of words that you do not want to appear. For example, a search of +metal –heavy will not return Web sites for heavy metal rock bands.

In order to determine which operators to use in a particular search engine, explore the Help or Advanced Search Strategies or Search Tips within the search engine. Using the strategies outlines will help you get better results from your searches.

Using Boolean Operators

Search	Results
mouse AND ergonomic	Lists all sites containing both the words "mouse" and "ergonomic."
mouse OR ergonomic	Lists all sites containing the word "mouse" and all sites containing the word "ergonomic." Many more sites found this way.
mouse NOT ergonomic	Lists all sites containing the word "mouse" but not the word "ergonomic." Limits the search to eliminate sites you definitely do not want.

 *Activity*

Fig. 9.12 Search String

Search String (keyed in the Search box)	No. of Hits
KEYBOARD	
Keyboard	
Keyboards	
Keyboard*	
Keyboard AND ergonomic	
Ergonomic keyboard	
"ergonomic keyboard"	

Performing a Search for Information

Using one of the search engines discussed in this chapter, perform a search for information on ergonomic keyboards. Use the search strategies listed in Fig. 9.12 to refine your search. Record the number of hits for each search result in your notebook.

Natural Language Queries

Some search engines now allow users to key their search query in the form of a question. Such a search is called a ***natural language query*** because the search engine interprets the way we naturally ask a question. No special words are required. For example, "Where can I buy an ergonomic mouse?" These search engines pick out key words such as "buy," "ergonomic," and "mouse" and return a list of Web sites that have those key words in them. One example of such a search engine is Ask Jeeves. See its Web site on the *InsighTs* Student Page on <www.irwinpublishing.com/students>.

Activity

Performing a Natural Language Query

Go to the Ask Jeeves site and perform a natural language query for an ergonomic keyboard. How do the results compare to your earlier searches? Write a short comparison of the results. Create a table or chart to summarize your results.

Knowledge Check

1. What is a search query? Key the 12 tips listed for performing quality searches.
2. How can Boolean logic be used in a Web search? Create a chart in your notes to show what words (operators) are used in a Boolean search and what the outcome of using those words would be.
3. What math symbols can be used instead of the Boolean operators in a search?
4. What is a natural language query? How does it differ from a regular search query?

CAREER PROFILE

Jenna Hennebry Sociologist

"72.5¢ to $1: Women trail men on wages"
Toronto Star,
September 15, 2000

"Census maps Ontario's future needs"
Toronto Star,
August 5, 2000

Do you ever wonder who gathers all these statistics and makes sense of the numbers? Sociologists like Jenna Hennebry do. At 28 years of age, Jenna has dedicated her life to examining social issues through statistics. Currently working on her Ph.D. in Sociology, Jenna is examining such issues as race, gender, religion, immigration, social inequality, and multiculturalism.

For four years, Jenna has worked for Canada's Department of Canadian Heritage in Ottawa, Ontario, as a research officer. When the Canadian Heritage Minister speaks in the House of Commons, he or she may be using information prepared by Jenna on issues such as immigration and health care use, population in Canada's cities, or the aging population and its projected impact on Canada's health care system. As an employee of the Department of Canadian Heritage, Jenna gathers statistics to support research or policy recommendations for the government. She organizes conferences examining social issues that affect many Canadians. Also, her expertise is sought by government agencies and other groups who want to design surveys to collect social data.

Jenna also works as a Teaching Assistant for the Department of Sociology of the University of Waterloo in Waterloo, Ontario, lecturing on sociology, research methods, and other related issues.

Jenna is no stranger to computers in her work. She uses networked computers in every aspect of her teaching and researching. She has developed numerous competencies, including standard office productivity software (e.g., Microsoft Office), specialized statistical software to analyze census data, CD-ROM and Internet searching, development of HTML documents for posting on the Internet and, of course, e-mail for the wide array of correspondence needed to do the job.

Technology has certainly changed how statisticians do their job. "We are using more accurate and powerful techniques that are only possible because of the power of today's computers. We have even started administering surveys via the Internet, reducing both cost and time." Jenna believes that the quality of her research has improved because of the ability to connect nationally and internationally with other statistical researchers.

Personally, Jenna has seen a remarkable change in the way she does her work. Because of the power of computing, she works from home a lot more. She can take on more tasks because she can do more than one thing at the same time. For example, she can teach for the University, work for the government, do contract work for non-governmental agencies in Montreal and Spain, research at five different online libraries, and contact researchers in New York.

And you thought sociologists were stuck behind a desk somewhere! Well, think again. Jenna is a true multitasker.

· ·

1. What does a sociologist examine? Give two examples.

2. What are some of the issues Canada's Department of Heritage examines? How does Jenna contribute to these studies?

3. What information technology competencies has Jenna developed in her career?

4. How has technology changed the way statistics are gathered and analyzed?

5. What changes has Jenna seen in the way she does her work using technology?

6. What kind of standards should be put in place for Web pages to assist in the research process?

Evaluating Electronic Information

Fig. 9.13
Assessing information—
Are you ready?

How Do You Assess the Information You Have Gathered?

If you have decided to include the Internet in your research strategy (remember, not everything is on the Web!), you have to learn to separate the immaterial and inaccurate data from the valuable information. By its very nature, the Internet is "free speech" at its finest. It is very easy for anyone to post information on the Internet. All you need is a Web page and a place to host the page. Many ISPs include personal Web space in their packages to customers. Contrast this ability to "publish" at will to traditionally published information—books, encyclopedias, newspapers, magazines, etc. Most publishers go to great lengths to ensure facts are accurate and that their publications do not contain stereotypes or bias. As well, textbook publishers often have books reviewed by experts outside the firm for accuracy and fairness of treatment before going to print.

Whether you read a book, the local newspaper, or a site on the Internet, you need to develop a healthy skepticism about what you are reading. Do not accept everything you read as the truth. You cannot let yourself be misled by cleverly crafted stories that sound realistic. You have to learn to assess the information you are reading. The following guidelines will help you assess the information you are gathering.

Fig. 9.14
A Web page is divided into three main sections—a header, the body, and a footer. A wealth of information is contained in these sections. Be sure you can identify all three sections.

WHAT Are the Essential Elements?

Just as you can with an entry in a card catalogue (computerized or not) in the library, you should be able to locate certain information on a Web page. Web pages are divided into three main sections—a *header*, the *body*, and a *footer* (see Fig. 9.14). These three sections should provide you with the essential information you need to evaluate the page. Figure 9.15 lists the essential elements of a Web page and gives you an idea of where to look on a Web page to find them.

Fig. 9.15 Essential Elements and Where to Find Them

Element	Location on Web Page
Author or contact person	footer
Link to home page	header or footer
Institution or organization sponsoring the page	header or footer
Date of creation or revision	footer (usually)
Intended audience (e.g., students, customers, activists)	Must be determined by reading the body
Purpose of providing information (e.g., to inform, persuade, sell)	Must be determined by reading the body

If any of the information in Fig. 9.15 is not present, you need to ask yourself whether the Web author is trying to hide something. Without this information it is difficult to determine how reliable the information on the Web page is.

WHO Is the Author?

It is vitally important to ensure that the person who has authored the site is qualified to write on the subject. Is the author's name stated? What are his or her qualifications? Is there a biography on the person available (as a link, perhaps)? Is the writer an expert in the field? Can he or she be believed? For example, an announcement about the school holiday schedule from the principal's office would be more believable than an unsigned notice posted on the Internet. Can you contact the person? Does the author work for the organization that sponsored the site? If so, can you trust him or her to be unbiased? Even if the author is not identified, there should be a means of contacting the writer—through an e-mail link, for example.

WHO Published the Article?

Fig. 9.16
The CBC must adhere to strict guidelines when it publishes information about a topic. It must verify its story and the facts; otherwise the corporation could face charges or lawsuits for publishing falsehoods.

Courtesy, CBC

Even if the author's name is not present, you should be able to determine who published the site. Is the publisher a credible source like the *The Globe and Mail* or the CBC? Does the article come in a hard-copy format as well as electronically? You have some reason for concern if the article does not, as it may not have met the rigorous standards that print documents have to meet.

Knowing who posted information on the Internet and World Wide Web, and knowing where that person got the information gives readers an opportunity to verify the story by checking the facts for themselves. With unsigned or unrecognized sources, there is no way to challenge or confirm what you have read.

WHO Sponsored the Site? WHAT is the Site's Purpose?

If you would like to know more about a Web site, you can log into InterNic (see the InterNic Web site on the *InsighTs* Student Page on <www.irwinpublishing.com/students>). InterNic was established in January 1993 as a co-operative venture between AT&T, General Atomics, and Network Solutions, Inc. You are allowed to search its database to find out who launched a site and the name of the host server.

You can sometimes get a clue to a site's origin by the ***domain name***. If it is a commercial site, it is very likely that the site will be promoting the company's products and services. You cannot expect such sites to be impartial or unbiased if they are trying to sell you something. Commercial sites commonly end in ".com," educational sites in ".edu" and government sites in ".ca" (Canada) or ".gov" (U.S.). (You can review the common extensions by looking at Fig. 6.13.) Even domain names, however, are no guarantee of knowing who sponsored the site. Domain names can be registered by anyone for a minimal fee. This ability has led to "cybersquatting" or people registering domain names, then trying to make money by selling the name to the organization that did not register the name but wants to do so.

Some Web sites try to hide the identity of the sponsoring organization because they want the content to appear like a scientific or research article. For example, a document that looks like a realistic journal article on heart problems that is sponsored by a pharmaceutical company is really just a promotion for the pharmaceutical company's products—a very cleverly disguised one, however!

Many search engines allow you to find out who has linked to the site you have found on the Internet. For example, in AltaVista (see *InsighTs* Student Page on <www.irwinpublishing.com/students>), you can key in link:www.(name of site) and it will list all the sites that have links to the site you have entered.

If you are having difficulty evaluating what has been said on a site, ask yourself, "Who posted the information?" "What is not being stated?"

Fig. 9.17

(A) Activity

Cyber Sleuthing

Do a search on the World Wide Web for information relating to the hazards of cigarette smoking. You will have to use a key word search using the Boolean operators discussed earlier in this chapter. Choose two or three of the pages you find. Can you determine the author and sponsoring organization? Who is it? What does this knowledge tell you? Key a summary of your findings.

HOW Is the Article Written?

You can evaluate a site's writing style for more clues as to the site's authenticity. Are there spelling and grammatical errors? Is there more "flash" than substance, that is, are there more graphics and audiovisual effects than meaningful content? Too much flash and not much substance does not make a good Web page. How detailed is the text? The topic should be covered in adequate detail, from different points of view, and at an appropriate level for the intended audience. Are there enough facts, research data, or links to other information to give you the impression that the site and the information the article contains are real? Has the author referenced other works in the study to indicate he or she has researched the topic, not just fabricated what you are reading?

HOW Up to Date Is the Site?

You should be able to locate the date posted or the last date revised on a site in the footer of the Web page. For some research, timeliness is not essential (e.g., a report on Sir John A. Macdonald, Canada's first Prime Minister). For other topics (e.g., new computer processors), it is critical that you find the most up-to-date information.

Knowledge Check

1. What are three main sections of a Web page? What should you be able to find in each section to help you in your research?
2. Why is it so important to determine who wrote information you find on the World Wide Web?
3. Why should you be skeptical of a site sponsored by a company or other commercial organization?

4. How can you find out who has sponsored a Web site?
5. What can the writing style and presentation of the Web page tell you about a site?
6. Does it matter when a Web site was last updated? Why or why not?

Larry MacKinnon

Business Information Officer

Larry MacKinnon is a lifesaver to budding entrepreneurs. As a Business Information Officer at the London Small Business Centre in London, Ontario, Larry spends his days researching business information for small business clients. He provides general business advice, maintains the Centre's client database and corporate Web site, and searches out new business resources from published sources, electronic databases, and World Wide Web sites. But Larry is not just a "bookworm." An important part of his research is personal and telephone contact with libraries, government agencies, and other businesses.

Using information technology (IT) effectively is an important part of Larry's job. "IT allows me to access vast electronic information resources that would not have existed in the past or would have been relatively inaccessible for a small information resource centre." The technology helps him give his clients better information and faster service. Considering that 80% of all new small businesses fail in the first five years, help from people like Larry is extremely valuable!

Larry uses the World Wide Web extensively. He is able to gather information quickly from authoritative Web sites, as well as explore a topic in search of new information or background material. He stays in contact with clients and other researchers by e-mail, using its capabilities to the fullest. He uses the Web as a gateway to a number of fee-based commercial databases that provide accurate and detailed information on a variety of business topics. Fee-based services charge organizations and individuals a fee to have access to their information banks.

Larry gained most of his IT skills through hands-on experience, and he finds that the skills are easily transferred between programs. "It is often necessary to learn a new software program in order to achieve a new goal." The position of Business Information Officer requires that he have a Master's degree in Library and Information Sciences to ensure that he has the necessary skills to locate, evaluate, organize, and analyze information.

Larry's advice for budding entrepreneurs? Research, research, research!

1. What kind of research does Larry perform for his customers? Who are his customers?

2. What does information technology allow Larry to do for his customers?

3. How has Larry acquired his IT skills? What are some other ways to acquire these and other skills?

4. What advantages does the Internet and World Wide Web offer people like Larry?

Good Citations

How Do You Cite Your Research Sources?

When you write a research paper, you have to indicate from which sources you got your facts or information (as you might have seen in bibliographies at the end of books or research papers). Acknowledging the source of your information is called a *citation*. Guides called *style manuals* show the ways in which sources should be presented in research papers.

Print Sources

All style guides for print sources require that citations contain:

- the name of the author(s) (if known)—usually last names first, followed by a comma
- full title of the work, followed by a period
- where (city/country) the information was published, followed by a colon
- by whom the information was published, followed by a comma
- the date the information was published

For *InsighTs*, the citation would read: Ellerby, Janice Lynn, Pinto, Laura Elizabeth, Brady, Victoria Esposito, *InsighTs: Succeeding in the Information Age*. Toronto: Irwin Publishing Ltd., 2001.

Electronic Sources

Below, you will find the proper ways to cite electronic documents according to the *Modern Languages Association (MLA) Style Manual*.

- *Software Programs, Video Games, and CD-ROMs*

Name of company that wrote the software, video game, or CD-ROM. Name of software/game/CD-ROM. City of publication: Name of publisher, year of publication.

For a software program, the citation would read: Rocking Software. *Ultimate Force*. Toronto: GT Interactive Software, 1995.

- *Internet Web Site*

Author's name (last name first). Document title. Date of Internet publication. Date of access <URL>.

For a personal Web page, the citation would read: Auch, Holly. Home page. 16 Dec. 2000. 1 Oct. 2001 <http://www.uleamington.ca /auchh/personal.htm>.

For a business/organization Web site, such as the Ontario Ministry of Education, the citation would read: *Ontario Ministry of Education Home Page*. 29 Sept. 1999. Ministry of Education. 1 Oct. 2001 <http://www.edu.gov.on.ca/english>.

A newspaper article from an electronic source would read: Kaczmaryk, Christopher. "Dogs really are people's best friends." *LP Newsnet* 5 May 1999. 1 Oct. 2001 <http://lpnewsnet.com/search /daily/fastweb?getdoc+site+874+wAAA+%22a%7Edogs%7Efriend>.

- *E-Mail Message*

Author's name (last name first). Subject line, in quotation marks. Description of message that includes recipient (e.g., *e-mail to the author*). Date of sending.

For example, an e-mail message could be cited as: Sandalperkins, Mark. "How to avoid viruses." E-mail to Andrew Smith. 10 Jan. 2002.

- *Web Discussion Forum Posting*

Author's name (last name first). Title of posting, in quotation marks. Phrase online posting. Date of posting. Name of forum. Date of access. <URL>.

As an example, a posting could read: Finnegan. "Squirrel behaviour." Online posting. 20 Mar. 1999. Rodent Forum. 27 May 2002. <http://www.unme.com/forums/ Index.cfm?CFApp=55ID=18596>.

- *Online Discussion Group Message*

Subject line, in quotation marks. Phrase *online posting*. Date of posting. Date of access. Name of group with prefix of group, for example, *news*, in italics, in angle brackets

For example: Badikonis, V. "Online citations" Online posting. 4 May 2000. 2 June 2001. <news:rec.computers>.

Out of cite!

1. Using your favourite search engine, perform an Internet search to locate the names of three other style manuals in addition to the *Modern Languages Association Style Manual*. Write down the Web sites you find.

2. Next, use an electronic source other than the Internet to get more information about style manuals.

3. Create a one- to two-paragraph conclusion about what you discovered through your research.

4. At the end of your paragraph, create citations using proper format to show what sources you used to complete this research task.

Knowledge Check

1. What is a citation?
2. What is a style manual?

CHAPTER SUMMARY

Understanding Information

1. How can Internet searching fit into an overall search strategy for a research project? What other resources are important to include in your research?

2. How has technology revolutionized the research process? What differences has it made for researchers in terms of speed, quantity, and quality of information?

3. Create a chart comparing the type of information available from CD-ROMs in your school library or computer network for future reference in this course and other courses you might take.

4. Name the style manuals.

Analyzing

5. What are the advantages and disadvantages of using an Internet search directory in your quest for information?

6. Investigate the Advanced Search sections of three Internet search engines. Compare the suggested strategies offered by each site to improve your Web searching. Create a chart to record your findings. Your chart might look like Fig. 9.18.

Search Engine	Search Strategies Recommended	Use of Boolean Operators? Natural Language?
AltaVista.ca		

Fig. 9.18
Comparing Search Engine Search Strategies

265

7. Using your favourite search engine, conduct an Internet search for information on computer peripherals. Out of the first 20 hits, how many were commercial sites? How do you know? Prepare a written summary of your findings.

8. How would a student writing a research paper use a style manual?

Applying

9. Eliza is working on a research project for her geography class on the climate of Canada's West Coast. She has to find the data required to create climographs (average monthly rainfall and average monthly temperature graphs) for Vancouver and Prince George, BC. Design an Internet search strategy for Eliza. Include a key word search using Boolean operators and a natural language query. Key your ideas in the form of a numbered list of steps for Eliza to follow.

10. Compare the citation styles recommended by two different style manuals. Which style manuals are you comparing? How are they similar? How are they different?

Communicating

11. Interview an adult (parent, grandparent, friend, neighbour) about the changes in technology they have witnessed throughout their lives. What impact have these changes made on their everyday lives? Prepare your findings in the form of a one-page newsletter. Divide the information into mini-articles.

12. Prepare a presentation to make to the class on the Advanced Search Strategies contained in one Internet search engine. Your presentation should cover the use of Boolean operators, natural language queries (if the search engine supports them), and other tips and tricks offered by the search engine. In your presentation, illustrate how to narrow down a search in that engine.

Assessing Your Compentencies

13. Using the software competency checklists provided by your teacher, check off the competencies that you have mastered during the course of this chapter. Note the competencies that require more attention and review.

14. Interview a classmate to determine the competencies he or she has acquired during the chapter. Also share some of the new skills you have acquired.

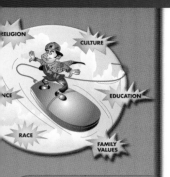

Topics

➤ Ethics, You, and Business

➤ Ethical Implications in the Age of Information

➤ Legal Issues in Information Technology

CHAPTER TEN:

IS IT OKAY IF I DO THAT?

People have always faced ethical choices—choices between right and wrong actions—in their personal, school, and business lives. However, yours is the first generation to grow up with computers as an everyday fact of life. The rapid changes in computers and information technology over the last few years have forced, and continue to force us to make ethical decisions in areas not faced before. In the first part of this chapter, you will explore what ethics are and how you and businesses can make ethical choices. You will then consider the differences between "legal" and "ethical" before you turn to an examination of some of the legal and ethical issues that developments in the Information Age have brought with them.

This chapter explores these questions:

- What are ethics?
- What are the ethical implications of posting, accessing, and transmitting data in an electronic age?
- What are some of the legal issues relating to information technology?

In this chapter you have the opportunity to

- analyze personal decisions and ethical dilemmas
- analyze the actions of business and other organizations within an ethical framework
- find out how to protect your privacy online
- explore Canada's new law protecting the privacy of Canadians while using the Internet
- debate the sharing of digital information
- research intellectual property and copyright issues
- investigate the gap between rich and poor and the role of technology in widening this gap
- develop an Internet Acceptable Use Policy
- research legal issues pertaining to the use of information technology

Ethics, You, and Business

What Are Ethics?

Fig. 10.1
It is not always obvious which way we should head in life.

Webster's Dictionary of the English Language defines **ethics** as "the moral principles which determine the rightness or wrongness of particular acts or activities." "Ethical" has to do with choosing a right action over a wrong action. "Unethical" has to do with intentionally acting in a "bad" or wrong way. But what determines what is right or wrong?

Activity

A Look Back ...

List five things that you were raised to believe were wrong or bad as a young child. For example, it is wrong to lie. Compare your list with those of your classmates. Do you see any patterns in the class? Why might there be similarities?

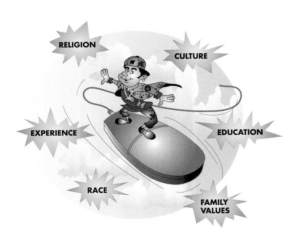

Fig. 10.2
Some of the influences that shape our view of the world and of what is right and wrong

Each person sees the world in a different way. Our individual value systems are the result of many factors—race, religion, cultural background, education, family values, and our own experiences throughout life. These factors all help to shape what we, as individuals, believe is right or wrong.

Sometimes, the choice between right and wrong is straightforward. Most people, for example, agree that it is wrong to commit murder and that it is wrong to hire someone else to commit murder for you. There are many times, however, when choosing to do the right thing is not as easy. For example, you may believe it is wrong to copy a piece of software that you have not purchased.

Then a very good friend tells you that he has the most recent version of a piece of software you desperately want but cannot afford. He tells you he has already made you a copy. You are faced with a dilemma. Your friend is offering you something you really want, yet you believe what he has done is wrong. In business, too, individuals within an organization may feel a form of conflict if they are asked to perform acts on behalf of the company that are not consistent with their own *value system* (a set of personal beliefs about right and wrong).

Conflicts of this sort are called ***ethical dilemmas***. An ethical dilemma involves making a choice where one or more alternatives or solutions provide a benefit but compromise the decision-maker's value system.

 **Activity**

Facing an Ethical Dilemma: What Would You Do?

Suppose you have a 10-page report due for your history class tomorrow (which you should have started working on weeks ago). There are several alternatives to this problem. You could:

- do your best to start the report tonight, admit to your teacher you did not finish, and learn from your mistake
- stay up all night to complete the paper and hand it in on time
- pretend you are ill so that you get an extension to complete the paper another day without a penalty
- copy information from the Internet into a document, and pretend you wrote it yourself

The ethical dilemma you face involves making a choice that does not compromise your value system. The first two alternatives in this example probably do not compromise your value system, while the last two probably do.

1. How or why might the last two alternatives compromise a person's value system?
2. What are the negative consequences you would face for each of these alternatives?
3. Which of the alternatives would you choose? Why?
4. Do you think any of these alternatives break the law? Why or why not?

Fig. 10.3
Ethical dilemmas force us to examine our values and look at our actions critically.

The Business World and Ethics

Fig. 10.4
Formal courses in business ethics are important to ensure that all members of an organization act in an ethical manner.

Courtesy Sidney Harris © 1995

Businesses are made up of people from different backgrounds, holding different moral beliefs. Business managers and executives can be pressured to act in ways that are wrong—such as being deceitful in dealing with customers, labour unions, government officials, or the competition in order to further the goals of the organization or make a profit. Some people believe this "bluffing" is part of a "game," to see who will come out on top of the competitive battle and be the most successful. But sometimes, people can go too far and bluffing leads to more serious consequences.

Today, most Canadians believe that people in business have a *social responsibility*—to act in a manner that is in the best interests of society in general, as well as in the best interest of the company. Many organizations have not always been moral in their behaviour. Consumers, governments, and other stakeholders have spent years pressuring companies to improve their ethical performance. Many individuals besides owners and shareholders have a stake in what businesses do—employees, customers, special interest groups (such as Greenpeace or the People for Ethical Treatment of Animals), and the general public. These *stakeholders* watch to see that businesses uphold their social responsibility. Some areas that stakeholders have particular interest in seeing that businesses act ethically include:

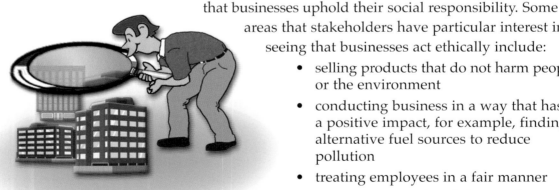

- selling products that do not harm people or the environment
- conducting business in a way that has a positive impact, for example, finding alternative fuel sources to reduce pollution
- treating employees in a fair manner
- not engaging in fraudulent or deceptive practices

Fig. 10.5
Stakeholders, or those individuals and organizations that have an interest in a business, keep an eye on what that business does to ensure it is acting in an ethical manner.

Legal Versus Ethical

According to the *Gage Canadian Dictionary*, **law** is defined as a body of rules recognized by a country, state, province, municipality, or community as binding on its members. **Legal** refers to actions or behaviour that are carried out according to the law. To act according to the "spirit of the law" means to act according to the real meaning or intent of the law. To act according to the "letter of the law" means to act according to the exact wording or actual terms of the law.

You would think that if you do the right thing, your action would be legal and that you would not get into trouble. By the same token, if you do the wrong thing, you are breaking the law. However, the relationship between something that is "legal" and something that is "ethical" is not necessarily that "cut and dried." In other words, there is not always a clear distinction between what is legal and what is ethical. Figure 10.6 depicts four situations to help you understand the difference between legal and ethical.

Fig. 10.6 Legal Versus Ethical

	Legal	Not Legal
Ethical	It is both legal and ethical to protect customer privacy when a customer makes online purchases at your e-commerce site.	It is not legal, but could be considered ethical to leak information that appeared on your employer's Intranet to the media in order to stop illegal activity within the company.
Not Ethical	It is legal but not considered ethical to call in sick to your company message centre when you are not really ill.	It is neither legal nor ethical to sell the e-mail addresses of your customers without their permission.

Learning Link

The 1999 KPMG Canadian Business Ethics Survey reported that 85% of Canadian companies surveyed had written statements of ethical values and principles, while 38% have policies to protect employees who report legal or ethical violations.

A recent national Wall Street Journal survey in the United States found that the following unethical practices were reported as occurring most frequently in business:
- managers lying to employees
- business expense accounts being used for personal use
- nepotism (relatives of managers or business owners receiving special treatment)
- taking credit for other people's work

 Activity

Examine Your School's Internet Acceptable Use Policy.

Using the Internet, find examples of other institutions' policies. Are there any changes you would like to recommend to your school's policy to ensure that your school's system is safe for all to use? Prepare a revised Internet Acceptable Use Policy to present to the principal of your school.

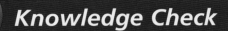

1. What are stakeholders? What is their role in business?
2. Define "ethics." What is an ethical dilemma?
3. Are all legal actions ethical? Why or why not?

4. What are two common unethical practices found in business?
5. What percentage of Canadian companies surveyed have written statements of ethical values?

Ethical Implications in the Age of Information

What Are the Ethical Implications of Posting, Accessing, and Transmitting Data in an Electronic Age?

As we have discussed throughout this text, the Internet and the World Wide Web have led to an "information explosion" in our society. Millions of bits of information are created and distributed daily over millions of kilometres of fibre optical cable, wire, and airwaves. With so much information "out there," a number of ethical issues arise. This section will deal with four of the main areas of concern to individuals and to businesses—privacy, accuracy, ownership, and access to information.

Privacy

Is information about you being collected electronically without you knowing it? When you log onto the Internet, are your movements truly private? What safeguards do you have to protect your privacy? These are some of the concerns that advances in information technology have raised regarding our personal privacy.

We have an increased ability to watch people's movements, communicate with them, perform computations, and store and retrieve massive amounts of information about individuals. It is this information gathering, manipulation, and retrieval that is the biggest concern about information technologies to many people, especially those who believe that people should have a right to personal privacy unless they decide to share information about themselves.

Information about people is valuable—to businesses, to governments, and to individuals with criminal intentions. Why?

- *businesses*—Companies gather demographic data about people (information about age, income, marital status, city or town of residence, etc.) in order to find out who is buying their products. In the past, this information was collected through the use of surveys—by mail, in person, and over the telephone. In all these cases, there was some personal contact. The person knew what information was being gathered, usually by whom, and, generally, why.

Today, information can be gathered about us in many ways and by many companies without us knowing it. If businesses know what we are purchasing online, or which Web sites we are visiting, they can target their messages to us to encourage us to buy their products.

Fig. 10.7
Companies that gather information about our Web surfing habits put the information into massive databases so they can analyze our Web surfing and online shopping habits.

Some companies gather this information and sell it to other companies for a profit. DoubleClick is a company that provides Internet advertising for businesses that want an online presence. It creates profiles of Web surfers. DoubleClick analyzes our browsing habits by writing a small piece of computer code (a *cookie*) on our hard drive if we have allowed our browser to accept cookies. This cookie can track what we buy and where we buy it, and then send us advertisements tailored to our shopping habits.

Many people oppose this use of technology. Others do not mind it. They say being targeted this way saves them time online. Some people are concerned that their name might become attached to this data, eliminating their privacy. Right now, only our IP address is identified (see chapter 6), allowing the advertiser to send messages to our computer.

You can change your Preferences in your browser to not accept cookies or to warn you when one is being requested. Asking your browser to let you know if someone is requesting to put a cookie into your browser can be frustrating, as messages will pop up on your screen all the time.

Some companies use information gathered online to find out more about potential job applicants before they hire them. Again, the people being screened often do not know they are being screened online, nor do they know what information about them is being accessed.

- *government*—One of the largest collectors of information about individuals is government—federal, provincial, and municipal. Each agency that we interact with has data about us, our income, employment history, taxes, and our use of government services (e.g., health care). If all of this information was combined into one super database, it could be a very powerful tool—for finding fraudulent uses of government services and to identify people in genuine need (good thing) or for political power and manipulation by corrupt individuals (bad thing).

- *criminals*—There are a number of people in our society who see the Internet as a means to allow them access to people and computer systems with relative ease and a certain degree of anonymity. Identity thieves collect information about people electronically and impersonate them in real life. Often they will get credit card information and make purchases without us knowing it. Stalkers pursue people with intent to harm or harass them. Pedophiles will try to meet young people online and then in person. Hackers steal passwords and user names in order to gain access to computer databases and systems.

Fig. 10.8

So, are your online movements anonymous? Absolutely not! Think about this story. At least once a year, a student somewhere thinks he or she has found a way to mask his or her online identity and sends a threatening e-mail message to the President of the United States. Using information technology, US Secret Service personnel trace the e-mail and arrive at the student's home, armed and ready to search the student's home—all within 48 hours!

InsighTs: Succeeding in the Information Age

Bill C-6 Affects E-Commerce

On January 1, 2001, Bill C-6, the ***Personal Information Protection and Private Documents Act***, became effective in Canada. The purpose of the act is to provide Canadians with privacy relating to personal information that is collected or used by private sector organizations. Under the act, "personal information" is defined as "information about an identifiable individual" such as ethnic origin, age, marital status, religion, education, medical or financial history, address and telephone number, Social Insurance Number, fingerprints, blood type, and personal opinions. Information that is already publicly available (such as a listing in a telephone book) does NOT apply. The privacy provisions in the act are based on the Canadian Standards Association's *Model Code for the Protection of Personal Information*, recognized as a national standard in 1996. Those standards are:

1. *accountability*—An organization is responsible for personal information under its control.

2. *identifying purposes*—The purposes for which personal information is collected will be identified by the organization at or before the time the information is collected.

3. *consent*—The knowledge and consent of the individual are required for the collection, use, or disclosure of personal information, except when inappropriate.

4. *limiting collection*—The collection of personal information will be limited to that which is necessary for the purposes identified by the organization.

5. *limiting use, disclosure, and retention*—Personal information will not be used or disclosed for purposes other than those for which it was collected, except with the consent of the individual or as required by the law. Personal information will be kept only as long as necessary.

6. *accuracy*—Personal information will be as accurate, complete, and up-to-date as possible for the purposes for which it is to be used.

7. *safeguards*—Personal information will be protected by security safeguards.

8. *openness*—An organization will make its privacy policy available to individuals.

9. *individual access*—Upon request, an individual will be informed of the existence, use, and disclosure of his or her personal information and will have access to that information. An individual may challenge the accuracy and completeness of the information and have it updated.

10. *challenging compliance*—An individual will be able to address a challenge concerning compliance with the above principles.

For more information about Bill C-6, visit the Government of Canada Web sites on the *InsighTs* Student Page on <www.irwinpublishing.com/students> and click on the links for Bill C-6.

Bill C-6 changed the way companies do business and exchange information. Before it was passed, there was little a person could do if personal information was sold by a company to another organization. Now, companies who sell or disclose personal information without a person's permission can be charged, taken to court, and fined.

Jane Dargie, a consultant for the accounting firm of Deloitte & Touche in Toronto, in an article that appeared in the November 2000 *Digital Marketing* supplement of *Marketing Magazine*, explained: "An organization that decides to use existing information for new uses or to link or match them together (as would be common in implementing a customer relationship management tool) must be prepared to return to individuals to gain their consent first."

For example, if you give your e-mail address to a software company for the purpose of a warranty, the company should not use that information to send you electronic advertisements unless it asks your permission to do so.

Organizations and businesses are also required, under the "openness principle" of the act, to make their privacy policies available to the public.

• •

1. Describe the purpose of Bill C-6.

2. As a consumer, what do you see as the benefits of Bill C-6?

3. If you were a business owner, what would your opinion of Bill C-6 be? Why?

4. In what ways might Bill C-6 help businesses? How might it be a disadvantage to them?

5. If you have access to the Internet, visit the Government of Canada Web site identified in Site Seeing above. There are four exceptions to disclosing information in Bill C-6. What are they?

6. Create a privacy policy that could be used in a small business.

Accuracy of Information

The second concern many people have about the gathering and distribution of electronic information relates to its accuracy. The information in a computer database is only as precise as the people who have entered it. If errors are made in the collection, entry, or analysis of the data, or if someone deliberately inputs incorrect and damaging information, then the output and the decisions made based on the data can be faulty, too. What if you were denied graduation because the school's computer system erroneously said you had not completed all your compulsory credits? Organizations must take care to ensure that the information they publish is as accurate as possible.

Fig. 10.9
Look at these two cartoons. What points relating to ethics do you think the cartoonist is trying to raise? How valid do you think these concerns are, given the changes in information technology?

Courtesy Sidney Harris
© 1995

"You must have faith in the confidentiality of this office. Nothing you say here will go beyond the data bank."

© 1995 by Sidney Harris

© 1995 by Sidney Harris

"The data bank is slightly mistaken. I'm not an alcoholic. I never attempted to assassinate the premier. I haven't been married seventeen times. I don't owe $86,000 in gambling debts..."

It is particularly important that information stored electronically be accurate if the decisions made based on that information pertain to people's health or well being. Consider this true story. One day in 1980 Peter Brown, a fisherman, was headed out to his lobster traps near Nova Scotia. He typically monitored the weather conditions using a long-range radio that receives weather forecasts at least 160 km out to sea. The forecast advised him that the region might get showers, but not the hurricane-like storm that was predicted to go far to the east of his course. He soon found himself in the midst of a raging storm with 80-knot winds and waves cresting at 18 m. One crew member, Gary Brown, was thrown overboard in the storm and drowned.

The source of the error was one weather buoy, which was out of service. Without the data from this buoy, the computer model that took information from high atmosphere balloons, satellites, ships, and buoys to develop weather forecasts went astray. The storm's path was miscalculated by several kilometres. This story illustrates the need to ensure that the information collected by our information technology and the systems that use that information are as accurate as possible.

Activity

Predicting Disasters

Brainstorm in small groups other possible "disasters" that might be caused by faulty information gathering or information systems that are not functioning properly. Share your ideas with the class.

Ownership of Information

If you come up with a great idea for a product or a way of doing business, you should be protected from anyone else stealing your idea. Legally, there are a number of ways you can protect yourself, as you will read later in this chapter.

Why do we need laws to protect our ideas? With the technology available today, it has become easier to duplicate digital information, to the point where it is difficult to tell which is the original and which is the copy. Think of the CDs you have purchased with your hard-earned money. Part of the cost of the CD goes to the artist in the form of royalties to pay the artist for his or her hard work. So why should we hesitate to copy that CD? The artist gets nothing when we copy his or her work. Are we acting in an ethical fashion by copying the CD?

Look at various *Personal Digital Assistants (PDAs)* available on the market. The Palm Pilot was the first on the market. Why do you think the other PDAs look so much like the Palm? Are the producers being ethical in making their product look so similar to the Palm Pilot in design and features?

Your personal value system and set of ethics will influence your answers to these questions. Our society feels so strongly about the protection of ideas, products, logos and trademarks that we have created laws that deal with these ownership issues.

Is it Sharing or Stealing?

Years ago, if you wanted to have a copy of a song from a record, you recorded it from your record onto a blank cassette tape. You could then enjoy all of your favourite tunes in your car as well as at home on the record player. That was okay, right? Actually, no. You should have purchased that album on a cassette for use in the car. Otherwise, you were violating copyright and the artist was not paid the royalties for the songs you copied.

In recent years we have seen the development of online sharing of music files between individuals. Companies such as Napster, Inc. have facilitated this sharing. Using the Napster site, users could download a very small program that allowed them to search the Internet for music stored on the computers of other individuals. The music was stored in MP3 format, highly compressed to allow for easy transmission and downloading. No music was actually stored or sent by Napster. This service only gave users the ability to share music electronically. Napster made users agree not to use the software to exchange copyrighted music prior to downloading it, but users were on the honour system.

Critics of Napster and similar services argue that such services make it easy for users to infringe copyrighted material and that artists as a result are not properly compensated for their work. Napster argued in court that increasing access to music would fuel sales of CDs in stores. However, the opposite may be true. Some studies suggest that users only went on to buy 10% of the music they downloaded. Other fans of the program argued that lesser known artists would become more widely known as a result of this type of "sharing." No one, however, is disagreeing with the reality that the Internet has had, and will continue to have, a tremendous impact on the distribution of music—legally or not.

On March 6, 2001, a United States federal judge issued an injunction ordering the song-swap service to eliminate copyrighted materials in its system. Internet law expert Michael Geist of the University of Ottawa felt that Napster might survive if it could come up with a subscription-based system that is more attractive and convenient for users than free Napster clones that are popping up on the Internet.

1. Divide into two groups in the class. Brainstorm arguments on both sides of the Napster issue—to share or not to share, to pay for copyrighted material or not to pay. Create a list and share your arguments with the other group.

2. Research other intellectual copyright issues that have surfaced as a result of the Internet. Prepare a short electronic presentation about your issue for the class.

Access to Information

Fig. 10.10
There are still those in our society who cannot afford to purchase the technology that is available today.

Another serious ethical issue raised by information technology is the degree to which all Canadians have equal access to information. In an information literate society, we have to be able to read and write. We must then have access to the computer hardware and software that will allow us to access the wealth of information that is available. The cost of computer hardware has dropped significantly over the course of time. This reduced cost has made technology accessible to more individuals and organizations. But there are those in our society who still cannot afford to purchase information technology, nor do they have the training to use it wisely and safely. Also, much information has been converted to digital-only formats. Unlike the hard-copy resources that are widely and cheaply available in libraries, digital information requires computers to access it. Often these digital banks of information are available on a pay-per-use basis, another cost that many cannot manage.

A 1999 United Nations report suggested that while advances in technology may be improving life for some people, at the same time, those same advances may be widening the gap between rich and poor. For example, a personal computer would cost the average Canadian one month's wages. The average Bangladeshi would need eight years' income to buy the same computer. Other examples included:

- Eighty percent of all Web sites are written in English, but only one in 10 people worldwide speak English.
- In the area of communications, there were 99 telephone lines per 100 people in the principality of Monaco; in Cambodia there was one telephone line per 100 people.
- People in Switzerland make an average of six hours of international telephone calls per year; in Pakistan, the annual average is one minute!
- Internet users were increasingly young, white, male, and well educated.

The UN report spoke of the need to boost efforts to meet the needs of the poor in areas of medical research, communications, and information technology.

Fig. 10.11

At a conference on environment and development in 1992, the Canadian delegation wanted to include the phrase "We the people of the Earth, being the first generation to have seen our planet from outer space," referring to photographs that had begun to appear in the later 1960s. Delegates from the less developed nations pointed out that most of their populations had not seen the photographs, and that if they had, they would not know what they represented. Ours was the first *wealthy* generation to have seen photographs of the earth from space. Today, new developments in information technology threaten to widen the gap between the developed and less developed nations even further.

Courtesy of NASA

Is It Okay If I Do That?

Within Canada, the problem between well-to-do and poor exists as well. When writing *InsighTs,* the authors had to take into consideration schools that have few computers and limited access to the Internet, as well as those that have generous access to technology.

1. In small groups, brainstorm ideas that will help our society deal with the problem of inequity of technological resources in Canada.

2. Survey your own class to determine the varying levels of technology in your own homes. List all of the types of technology people might have in their homes. Prepare a summary of your findings in a spreadsheet similar to Fig. 10.12.

Fig. 10.12 Comparing Technologies in the Home

Available Technology	No. of Households	Class Size	% of Class
Microwave			
CD Player			
Computer— 286 or earlier			
Computer— 386 or 486			
Computer— Pentium level			
etc.			

Another concern about the access to technology is the policing and restricting of that access. Read the Case Study that follows to see how one government is attempting to restrict what information its citizens have access to.

Bureau to Regulate Internet News

The Chinese government set up the Internet Information Management Bureau in the spring of 2000 to "promote development of the [IT] industry by establishing copyright standards and counter the 'infiltration of harmful information on the Internet'." The government had already barred some Chinese news sites from running foreign news on their sites in an attempt to stamp out "harmful" information. State officials said the bureau was seeking to limit content related to pornography and gambling and to help to develop all Web sites, state or privately owned. Some people are concerned that the bureau is an attempt to reduce the amount of information that Chinese citizens are allowed to read over the Internet.

1. What kind of information would you consider to be "harmful" to citizens?

2. What are the implications of reducing the amount of information available?

3. Investigate the involvement of the Canadian government in the distribution of news in Canada.

 **Activity**

Doing the Right Thing—International Style!

As Canadians do business in our increasingly interconnected world, they interact with people from countries around the globe. Some Canadian companies have been started specifically to introduce businesspeople from other countries to common Canadian business practices. At the same time, Canadian businesspeople need to realize that business practices common in Canada may, in fact, offend people from other cultures. The Canadian practice of making direct eye contact with someone with whom you are doing business, for example, is seen as rude in some cultures.

As students of business, we can use information technology to better prepare ourselves for interactions with people of other cultures.

It is important to understand the meaning of three important terms:

- *customs*—practices common to many people or a particular place
- *etiquette*—conventional rules of social behaviour or professional conduct
- *protocol*—a code prescribing strict adherence to correct etiquette (as in diplomatic exchange and in the military services)

When we do business with people from other cultures, we must find out as much as we can about their customs, etiquette, and protocols so that we can show proper respect for their customs and avoid offending potential customers or partners.

1. In pairs, choose a country that Canadian businesses trade with. Your first step is to find out some basic information about the country. Using the Internet, research that country, gathering information under the following headings:

Continent	Map Title
Capital City	
Land Area	
Population	
Official Language	MAP OF THE COUNTRY
Currency and Exchange Rate	
Major Industries	
Imports	*Capital City noted on map
Exports	

2. Next, continue your research, and gather as much information as you can about the following areas:
   - traditional greetings (business and social settings)
   - business clothing and appearance
   - gift-giving customs
   - the ways people identify themselves (rank, position in the company, status)
   - business negotiations
3. Taking all the information you have gathered, be prepared to participate in a United Nations-style round-table discussion by presenting your research to the rest of the class. Dress in the customary style of the country you represent.

Knowledge Check

1. What are four major ethical areas of concern relating to the Internet?
2. Which groups are interested in collecting information about people from the Internet? List reasons for each group.
3. Are your movements on the Internet anonymous? How can you be tracked?
4. What are some of the legal ways to protect the work of individuals in our age of information?
5. What are the five factors involved when we refer to access to information? Describe each factor.

Legal Issues in Information Technology

What Are Some of the Legal Issues Relating to Information Technology?

The Canadian Internet Law Resource Page (see the site on the *InsighTs* Student Page on <www.irwinpublishing.com/students>) provides a complete look at Internet Law in Canada.

Throughout our discussion of the various ethical issues raised by information technology, some legal concerns—copyright and ownership of information being two—have been discussed. As we suggested at the beginning of this chapter, advances in information technology have raised a number of legal issues.

Anonymity

There is an ongoing debate about whether privacy or anonymity online is good or bad. Figure 10.13 shows some of the arguments on both sides.

Fig. 10.13 To Be Anonymous, or Not To Be Anonymous?

ONLINE ANONYMITY	
Reasons to Abolish Anonymity Online	**Reasons to Maintain Anonymity Online**
• Reduces hate crime because the identity of the person posting the hate mail is known • Reduces incidences of selling and distributing pornographic material • Keeps predatory people from stalking or harassing us	• A person's right to privacy must be maintained regardless of the actions of a few who break the law. • People can send "snail mail" without being identified—e-mail should be no different. • When you post information online (such as in a public forum), your opinions are recorded for all time. It is not like speaking your opinion at school. When you "speak" online, you can and may be reminded for the rest of your life of what you said. • Protects identity of people who let others know of illegal acts or wrong doings (e.g., Crimestoppers)

Is It Okay If I Do That?

Consumer Protection

When consumers buy products online, there are a number of decisions they have to make. For example, do they have enough information about the product and seller to make an informed decision before buying? Is the "store" reputable? What happens if the product has to be returned? Is their personal and financial information secure? There have been many cases of Internet fraud documented. For example, many people have been enticed by investment schemes they found out about online and have lost their life savings in the process. Others thought they were buying expensive watches at a bargain price only to get a product of far less value. Be sure to find out all you can before you buy online.

Cybercrime

The most frequently cited crime on the Internet is hacking or gaining illegal entry into another person's or organization's computer system. This action is a direct violation of the Internet Acceptable Use Policy you agree to when you sign up for Internet service from your local provider. In recent years, incidents of individuals hacking into major

Web sites and virtually shutting down their services have made headlines around the world. A 15-year old Montreal student, known as Mafiaboy, was charged with two counts of "data mischief" after he allegedly attacked CNN.com. These attacks cost the organization millions in lost revenue and in finding where the data breach took place in order to block other unauthorized users from gaining entry.

Fig. 10.14

Gary Brookins,
Richmond Times-Dispatch

RCMP reports suggest that Canadian companies are not well prepared to combat this mounting crime and that police agencies do not have enough trained officers to investigate the rising number of attacks. Some companies left themselves vulnerable to attack in their haste to fix Y2K bugs in their systems. Many organizations gave computer programmers unrestricted access to programs and systems in order to rewrite code, without first conducting security checks on the programmers or putting safeguards in place.

E-commerce providers sometimes fail to protect the data of their customers. A student unintentionally downloaded a file of over 300 names, addresses, and credit card information from one online vendor. After repeated attempts to get the vendor to close the loophole, the student eventually called the police. This information in the wrong hands could have cost the customers involved millions of dollars.

Arni Stinnissen Cybercop

Police recover diary on accused's computer!

More and more, police officers are using information technology to help solve cases. The e-Crime Team of the Ontario Provincial Police (OPP) is no exception. The team is made up of highly trained investigators who use computers to solve a wide variety of cases, including cybercrime. In charge of this e-lite group of officers is Arni Stinnissen, a 22-year veteran on the force. "I always gravitated to computers to help me to do the job," says Arni. He adds that he took every available training course he could to improve his IT skills.

Arni joined the Anti Rackets Branch of the OPP Investigation Bureau in 1994. Anti-Rackets traditionally investigates "white collar" crime such as fraud or municipal corruption. One of the branch's primary functions is to use imaging technology to take hard copy documents, convert them to digital information, and organize the information for investigators to use. The investigators are then able to search the computer database of information to build briefs or reports for the courts, rather than having to search through masses of paper to do the job. Just imagine how much time this use of technology saves the officers.

Arni has been involved in the e-Crime Team since 1998. The team was formed in that year to deal with the increased number of requests for support in investigating technology-related crimes. The unit has four main functions:

- *repository for evidence*—The team pulls information from computers to support charges laid by the police and to assist in investigations. Members of the team once retrieved data that a suspect had deleted from a hard drive a year before! The data they retrieved helped to convict the suspect of murder. The data also confirmed information the police had received from a jailhouse informant in the case. "Forensic acquisition software is the key to retrieving this kind of data," says Arni.

- *investigate computer crimes as defined by the Criminal Code*—There are two types of computer crime in the Criminal Code of Canada—mischief and unauthorized access. *Mischief* deals with people who "hack" into other computers and then distort or destroy data. Planting a virus is one example of mischief. *Unauthorized access* covers other "hacking" incidents up to and including using the services without permission or stealing passwords, credit card information, etc. When e-commerce sites ask you for your credit card number, you should be sure they ensure that unauthorized parties cannot retrieve the information. Look for sites that encrypt the data you send them.

- *economic deprivation*—This function falls into the fraud category of the Criminal Code. A person "hacks" into another computer, steals data and/or programs, then sells the stolen data or programs for profit. In doing so, the hacker deprives the original owner of the data or program from making his or her own living.

- *consultation services*—With the increase of cybercrime, the e-Crime Team's services and expertise are in great demand, both within the OPP and by other police services.

Arni's advice for people using the Internet? "Don't wander into unknown territory or talk to people you don't know, or have reason to trust. You wouldn't do it in real life, so why do it online? In fact, this is even more important in cyberspace."

1. What are some of the skills a police officer needs to investigate cybercrimes?

2. Is data you delete from your hard drive really gone? What evidence do you have from this profile to lead you to believe one way or another?

3. What is the difference between mischief and unauthorized access in the Criminal Code of Canada? Give examples to support your answer.

4. Over the next two weeks, collect newspaper articles that deal with police investigations involving cybercrime. Key a summary of these articles, categorizing each case into the type of crime it involves.

Ownership of Domain Names

When you set up a Web site, you have to register your domain name or Web site address. When some organizations have gone to register their names, they have been shocked to find that some unscrupulous individual has beaten them to it, registering the name first. These individuals, known as "cybersquatters," then demand millions of dollars for the sale of that name to the organization. Such was the case with <www.juliaroberts.com>, which was registered by Russell Boyd of Princeton, NJ. Ms Roberts complained to the World Intellectual Property Organization. The organization found in her favour, saying that she had "common-law trademark rights in her name," and that Boyd had "no rights or legitimate interest in the domain name." Boyd tried to argue that his site was merely a tribute to the actress, even though he put the name up for sale on the e-Bay auction site, refusing over $2500 US for it at one point.

Fig. 10.15

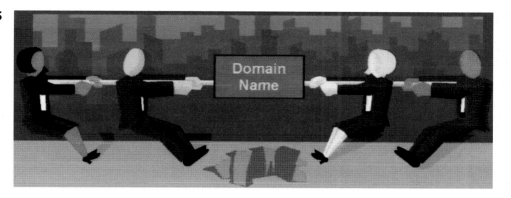

Encryption

In an effort to promote privacy on the Internet, the Ontario government's privacy commission produced a pamphlet called "E-Mail Encryption Made Simple."

 *Activity*

Contacting Your Local Member of Provincial Parliament (MPP)

Using the Internet, locate the name and mailing address of your local MPP. Compose and key a properly formatted letter requesting a copy of the pamphlet "E-Mail Encryption Made Simple." See chapter 4 for a refresher on letter preparation.

Many provinces have also drafted legislation regarding the use of encrypted data for e-commerce transactions through establishing standards for the safe transmission of financial data over the Internet. This legislation is designed to ease some of the worries that online financial transactions cause consumers.

Intellectual Property

We have already examined some of the copyright issues that can occur with respect to domain names and recorded music. *Intellectual property* is a term that refers to any form of creative work that can be protected through copyrights, trademarks, or patents.

Copyrights (©) protect an author of work (such as literary, artistic, dramatic or musical works, computer programs, and sound recordings) from having that work reproduced by others

Bell logo is a trademark of Bell Canada. Reprinted courtesy of Bell Canada

The Coca-Cola trademark appears courtesy of Coca-Cola Ltd.

The Sears trademark is reprinted with permission of Sears Canada Inc.

Fig. 10.16
These trademarks are all legally protected from unauthorized use.

without permission. In Canada, the law that governs this protection is called the Copyright Act. Several important things to note are

- In Canada, you acquire copyright automatically when you create an original work. That means that if someone reproduces an essay you wrote for school without your permission, he or she has violated your copyright.
- If a person (such as an employer) pays someone to produce something for him or her, the employer holds the copyright, not the author.

You can register your copyright with the government. Registration gives you a certificate that states you are the copyright owner. This certification is helpful in a situation that leads to a court of law.

A *trademark* is a word or phrase, symbol, or design (or combination of these) used to distinguish the product or service of one person or organization from those of others. A trademark recognizes the owner's exclusive right to use that mark. Trademarks can be either registered or unregistered. However, it is wise to register a trademark as registration is proof of ownership. If a company is considering exporting products or services, the company should register its trademark in each country in which it intends to do business. Your *trade name* (the name under which you operate your business) can also be registered as a trademark IF it is used to identify your product or service, for example Coca-Cola. Many companies, including Michelin, Levi Strauss, and computer chip giant Intel, consider their trademarks to be their most valuable assets. Trademarks are more than just symbols and slogans. Consider Pizza Pizza Limited's phone number which everywhere in Ontario ends in "1111," or the three stripes used on all ADIDAS AG's sportswear, or the orange colour used in HARVEY'S advertisements. These are all trademarks!

According to the Canadian Intellectual Property Office, *patents* are rights granted for new inventions or new/useful improvements of existing inventions—a reward for being ingenious! The first inventor to file an idea with the government is granted the patent, giving that person or company exclusive rights for 20 years from the date of filing. The patent allows for information sharing, as the inventor must describe in detail how the idea works. This information is available for anyone to read. Patents can also be applied to the ways in which companies do business. For example, patents

Intellectual property legislation is extremely complex. For more information, visit the Canadian Intellectual Property Office site on the *InsighTs* Student Page on <www.irwinpublishing.com/students> and read the Frequently Asked Questions (FAQs) for each type of intellectual property.

in the United States have protected awarding frequent flyer points for online purchases, and name-your-own price reverse auctions.

3-D integrated circuit topographies are now protected in Canada under separate legislation. This legislation includes the designs for innovative "microchips," which are at the heart of everything from home appliances to space technologies. Earlier designs were covered by patent laws—in fact, the first integrated circuit was patented in 1961 in the United States.

Privacy

Fig. 10.17
Maintaining your privacy while using the Internet and the World Wide Web is very important.

As discussed in the section "Ethical Implications in the Age of Information" and in the Case Study "Bill C-6 Affects E-Commerce," privacy is the number one concern of most Internet users. Some people believe that the new law does not go far enough to protect consumers. A 1998 Angus Reid survey reported that:

- Eighty percent of Canadians think personal data should be kept strictly confidential.
- Sixty-five percent of Canadians think it is "not at all acceptable" for companies to sell, trade, or share detailed lists of personal information with other organizations.
- Nine in ten Canadians strongly disapprove of companies trafficking in information about their private lives without their consent.
- Ninety-four percent of Canadians feel it is important to have safeguards to protect personal information on the Internet.

Unsolicited E-Mail or "Spam"

Named after the Hormel Foods Corp. processed meat product, *spam* is unsolicited e-mail, sent to thousands of recipients, often promoting an electronic sex site, pyramid-type marketing scheme, or the spam industry itself. Spamming is popular because it provides an efficient and relatively inexpensive way to advertise online. For the cost of an Internet account, spammers can send thousands or even millions of e-mails with the click of a mouse. While most people delete these e-mails, if even one percent of those reached by the advertising respond, a company can make big sales, with few expenses.

Theft of Company Resources

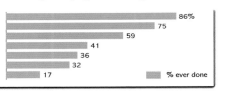

Fig. 10.18
Are you a cyberthief?

Theft can take many forms. Employees who bring home company pens, pencils, computer paper, or other such physical items for personal use are stealing. At the job site, employees are supposed to use company equipment for company business. Personal photocopying without paying for it is stealing resources—paper, toner, etc. While on the job, individuals are supposed to carry out the duties of the job, leaving personal business for personal time. However, in a survey of Internet use while at work, it was found that Canadian workers waste nearly 800 million hours a year surfing the Web for personal reasons—not related to their jobs at all. Many of the individuals surveyed stated that their companies had no policy governing use of the Internet at work. The use of company equipment for faxing, e-mailing, and accessing the Internet is an issue that requires many companies to take action or suffer losses in productivity.

There are many more legal issues that can be explored and discussed as this age of information and technology develops further. The law and the Internet is a fascinating area that can only become more exciting to watch as it develops.

Personal Web Surfing at Work

Sending personal e-mails — 86%
Checking out news or sports headlines — 75
Comparison shopping — 59
Checking stock markets/online investments — 41
Making purchases online — 36
Doing personal online banking — 32
Viewing adult sites — 17

% ever done

Business Web Surfing at Work

Sending business e-mails — 93%
Conducting research about their industry — 84
Searching public information about their company — 56
Researching the competition — 53
Shopping around for company-related purchases — 45
Conducting business-related transactions — 26
Doing business-related online banking — 13

% ever done

Fig. 10.19
An Angus Reid Group Inc. survey of Web surfing in the office, July 2000. Douglas Coull and Carrie Cockburn/*The Globe and Mail*

Reprinted with permission from The Globe and Mail

Ⓐ Activity

Pick one of the topics discussed in this section or visit one of the many sites on the Internet that explore legal issues related to technology. Prepare a research paper or presentation to make to the class on the issue you choose. Three sites to get you started on your research for legal issues related to information technology are

- Canadian Internet Law Resource Page
- Consumer Information at Industry Canada's Strategis Web site
- FindLaw.com, one of the best Internet sites for legal information

You can find these sites on the *InsighTs* Student Page on <www.irwinpublishing.com/students>.

Or, develop your own research strategy to find information using the techniques learned in chapter 9.

1. What are some questions consumers should ask before they buy online merchandise or services?
2. What is the most frequently cited cybercrime? What policy are you violating when you commit this crime? What are the costs to organizations that have been attacked in this manner?
3. Who owns a domain name? What are "cybersquatters"?
4. What is encryption and how can it help to prevent cybercrime?
5. a) What is a registered trademark?
   b) What is a patent?
6. What did a 1998 Angus Reid survey determine about Canadians and online privacy? List the four findings.
7. What is spam and how does it work?
8. How is the personal use of the Internet at work stealing?

CHAPTER SUMMARY

Understanding Information

1. What are ethics?

2. What is an ethical dilemma?

3. What are some benefits to businesses of incorporating ethics into their business practices?

4. Name two ethical dilemmas that are unique to information technology.

5. What is a cookie?

6. What are the ways in which work you produce is legally protected from being stolen or copied in Canada?

7. What is intellectual property?

Analyzing

8. Describe two similarities and two differences between ethical and legal issues.

9. How are legal dilemmas and ethical dilemmas different?

10. Describe ways in which the role of a cybercop is the same as that of a regular police officer, and ways in which their roles differ.

11. What implications does the patenting of e-commerce methods have for small businesses trying to make inroads in e-commerce?

Applying

12. Design a checklist of three to five things to ask yourself when faced with an ethical dilemma.

13. In what ways is privacy in information technology important to you?

14. What steps can businesses take to address privacy issues among customers?

15. What steps can governments take to address privacy issues among citizens?

16. How does Bill C-6 affect you? Discuss which parts of the bill make you feel secure.

17. What advice would you give a friend who is investigating registering a domain name on the Internet? Why?

18. Describe the intellectual property you own so far. Have you ever had to protect your intellectual property?

Communicating

19. Describe an ethical dilemma you have faced in the past six months. What was the problem? What were the alternatives? What decision did you make and why?

20. Discuss your personal reasons for either (a) abolishing online anonymity, or (b) maintaining online anonymity.

Assessing Your Competencies

21. Using the software competency checklists provided by your teacher, check off the competencies that you have mastered during the course of this chapter. Note the competencies that require more attention and review.

22. Interview a classmate to determine the competencies he or she has acquired during the chapter. Also share some of the new skills you have acquired.

GLOSSARY

3G technology—technology used by third-generation cell phones; offers faster and more dependable data transmission; provides one set of standards that users all over the world can understand

Address box—in Internet Explorer, the area on a Web browser screen where a user keys a Web site address or where the address of the currently browsed page is displayed

Analog modem—a connection device that converts digital data on a computer to analog signals for travel on the Internet along telephone lines; also converts analog signals sent to a computer into digital data so the computer can understand them; see also *Digital data*

Answering machine—a device connected to a telephone that records messages as they come through the telephone line

Any-time communication—in electronic communication, communication that is delayed several minutes or indefinitely; also called *asynchronous communication*

Application—software designed to allow users to perform / apply a specific task (calculate numbers, enter text, play a game) or function (word process, produce graphics, and so on); also called *application; program; software*

Application software—software designed to allow users to perform / apply a specific task (calculate numbers, enter text, play a game) or function (word process, produce graphics, and so on); also called *application; program; software*

Application suites—all-in-one business software that usually contain a word processor, spreadsheet, and database and sometimes include presentation software (Corel WordPerfect Suite, Claris Works, Microsoft Works, Microsoft Office)

ARPANet—an early version of the Internet by the Advanced Research Projects Agency (ARPA) of the US Department of Defense that linked together mainframe computers to form a communications network

Artificial intelligence—the ability of special computer programs that allows machines to imitate the thinking, learning, emotions, and decision-making processes of people

Asymmetrical balance—a term used in a graphic design to describe a design in which the two sides of the visual are not equally balanced

Asynchronous—in electronic communication, communication that is delayed several minutes or indefinitely; also called *any-time communication*

Attachment file—attached to an e-mail message, a separate file for sending over the Internet to be opened or saved by the receiver

Audiotex applications—programs that manage the sending and receiving of voice-mail messages; see also *Voice mail*

Backbone—a term used to describe a structure that handles the major traffic in a networked system. The backbone is like a highway; a message travels along a "secondary road" to the highway, then along the highway, then along another "secondary road" to its final destination.

Balanced—in a graphic design, when all the graphic elements (text, pictures, shapes) are integrated in a way that comes together seamlessly to the viewer's eye

Bandwidth—the amount of data that can be transmitted over a network in a certain amount of time; usually expressed in bits per second (bps)

Banner ads—advertisements that aim to persuade potential customers to click on a link to the advertiser's Web site from another site they are visiting

Bar charts—charts that show horizontal bars ideal for side-by-side comparisons of data; show the contribution of each value to a total across categories; see also *Column charts*

BBS—see **Electronic bulletin board system**

BCC (Blind courtesy copy)—a notation on a letter that does not let the person to whom the letter is written know that a copy has been sent to another recipient; the notation includes the other recipient's name at the bottom of only the sender's and other recipient's copies of the letter

Bill C-6—see **Personal Information Protection and Private Documents Act**

Binary code—the fundamental language code that computers understand, represented by a series of 0s and 1s

Biometric—a physical characteristic or personal trait that can be analyzed and recognized through automated means

Biometric authentication—method of determining the identity of a person using biological characteristics of that individual (such as fingerprints, facial features, or voice recognition); see also *Biometric identification*

Biometric identification—a measure of the unique biological characteristics of an individual (fingerprints, facial features, or voice recognition); see also *Biometric authentication*

Bit—the smallest unit of data a computer can use; a bit can be either a 0 or a 1

Bitmap image—an image made of rows and columns of individual dots or pixels; see also *Pixels*

Blind courtesy copy—see **BCC**

Block letter style—a style of letter wherein the return address, date line, complimentary closing, and writer's identification start at the centre of the line

Body—in a business letter, the content part of the message; use full sentences and use clear, concise words; an element of a Web page that refers to the core content

Boolean operators—words or signs used in an Internet search engine to refine a search

Boot sector—the area on a computer disk containing the

program that loads the operating system; see also *Operating systems*

Browser—see **Web browser**

Buddy lists—programs that allow users to create specific lists of people with whom they wish to chat; see also *Chat*

Bulletin-board systems—see **Electronic bulletin board system**

Bullets—large printed dots, shapes, or icons used to highlight items in a printed list; in presentation software, bullets are visual elements that appear on the screen in a sequence for effect

Bus—a set of conductor wires that transport data among components inside the computer through an electric path

Bus topology—a computer network arrangement whereby all nodes and peripherals are attached to one main cable; one broken connection will bring down the entire network; see also *Nodes*; *Peripheral devices*

Bus width—the number of bits of information the computer's conductor wires can transport at one time; see also *Bit*

Byte—the unit of memory needed to store one character such as a letter, a number, or a punctuation mark; equivalent to eight bits of binary code; see also *Binary code*

Cache—a fast storage area in the central processing unit of a computer; see also *Central processing unit (CPU)*

Carpal tunnel syndrome (CTS)—a disorder of the hand characterized by pain, weakness, and numbness in the thumb and other fingers; the most common ergonomic-related injury in North America; see also *Ergonomics*

CC (Courtesy copy)—a notation on a letter that indicates to the receiver that a copy has been sent to another party; the notation is keyed with the other recipient's name at the bottom of the letter below the writer's identification

CD Rewritables—compact discs that can be rewritten over and over again

CD-ROMs—compact disc-read-only memory discs

Cell—in a spreadsheet worksheet, a location where values and formulas are stored; cells are identified by the row and column in which they occur

Cell address—the identification of a cell in a spreadsheet by specifying the row and column to which the cell belongs; for example, a cell located in column C and row 2 would be identified as cell C2

Cell phone—see **Cellular phone**

Cell phone etiquette—a series of rules and protocols that outline "good manners" relating to cell phone use

Cellular phone—telephone using radio frequencies to send messages in small areas called cells; also called *cell phone*

Central processing unit (CPU)—the main computer chip that processes instructions, calculates data, and manages the flow of information in the computer; also called a *microprocessor*

Chat—a feature of online conferencing programs that allows users to communicate with other users outside an online conference without interrupting the online conference

Circuit board—in a computer, a plastic board on which a number of circuits are connected and arranged in a specific way; computer circuit boards also contain computer chips that perform specific functions in the computer

Citations—a list of all of the sources of information for a report; also called *references*

Client/server network—a computer network arrangement that designates one computer the leader (server) of all the other computers in the network (clients or nodes); the leader is bigger, faster, and more powerful and can run the network operating system software; in a client/server network, the clients communicate with each other through the server; see also *Clients*; *Network*; *Nodes*; *Operating system*

Clients—a term for all of the computers but the leader in a client/server network; see also *Nodes*

Clip art gallery—a library of graphic images built into many software applications or available through electronic means such as CDs or on the Internet

Clipboard—in a computer, an electronic storage area where data is stored temporarily during some operation (Move, Cut, or Copy)

Column charts—charts that show vertical bars; ideal for side-by-side comparisons of data; see also *Bar charts*

Command-driven interface—an interface in which a user enters commands by keying them in; see also *User interface*

Communication software—software designed to facilitate communication among computer users (First Class, Outlook)

Competencies—skills, knowledge, and behaviours that can be classified into categories

Compiler—see **Utility compiler**

Complimentary closing—in a business letter, the nature of the closing depends on the nature of the letter; use a formal closing (Respectfully yours) for a formal letter; use a more friendly closing (Cordially) for a friendly letter; located below the body of the letter

Compressed—made smaller and more compact

Computer—a programmable machine that responds to specific instructions and can execute a pre-recorded set of instructions

Computer games—software designed to allow users to play games (Solitaire, Duke Nukem, NHL Allstars Hockey, Quake)

Computer viruses—programs that insert themselves into computer program files and boot sectors and create mischief; can be very destructive, preventing use of computer or erasing data on drives; see also *Boot sector*; *Program files*

Conductor wires—wires that transmit electricity

Conferences—meetings, either electronic or in person, at which two or more people discuss matters of common concern

Connector—an element of an e-mail address that links your name to the server that holds your mail for you; "@" in <yourname@YourISP.com>

Consistency—harmony; agreement; accordance

Contrast—in a graphic design, visual interest created by strategically placing objects, fonts, shapes, or textures that are opposites of one another; see also *Font*

Cookie—a message given to a Web browser by a Web server. The browser stores the message in a file called *cookie.txt* that is sent back to the server each time that browser requests a page from the server.

Copyrights (©)—rights that protect the author of work (literary, artistic, dramatic or musical, computer programs, sound recordings) from having that work reproduced by others without permission

CPU—see **Central processing unit**

CTS—see **Carpal tunnel syndrome**

Customs—practices common to many people or a particular place

Data—raw, unprocessed information such as numbers, characters, or symbols

Data encryption—a function performed by special software that protects information transmitted between computers by scrambling the signals so that only the sender and intended receiver can interpret the signals

Data files—files created by information input by users through a software application program (a report keyed using a word processing program, a graph made in a spreadsheet program, an image created in a graphics program)

Data label—in charts or graphs, words that describe the contents of each chart item

Databases—organized collections of records and related files

Database software—software designed to organize a collection of records or related files, such as class lists and report card data (Microsoft Access, PeopleSoft)

Date line—in a business letter, immediately below the return address, this line gives the date the letter is keyed (June 1, 2001 or 1 June 2001)

Decode cache—an area of the central processing unit chip where information is decoded; see also *Central processing unit (CPU)*

Decodes—translates into ordinary language; produces an output when fed by certain inputs

Default alignment—in most word processors, the pre-set document setting which justifies the lines of text at the left-hand margin and leaves the right-hand margin ragged

Default font—the pre-set typestyle and type size in a particular software application

Default settings—pre-programmed settings (fonts, margins, formatting), chosen because they are the most frequently set functions

Defragmenting—a process that rearranges all the files saved on your hard drive in a tightly packed way, eliminating gaps and putting fragments (or pieces) of files closer to other similar fragments in the proper order

Desktop—the primary screen users see as soon as they start their computer (if their computer has a graphic user interface) or when they have turned the computer on but have not opened any software applications

Desktop publishing—creating specialized products such as brochures, newsletters, and newspapers using software similar to word processing that allows users to more easily combine text, graphics, and complicated layouts

Desktop publishing software—software designed to create specialized products such as brochures, newsletters, and newspapers; similar to word processing software but allows users to more easily combine text, graphics, and complicated layouts (Microsoft Publisher, PageMaker, QuarkXPress)

Dialog box—a special window that appears on a computer screen when the user clicks on a menu item and that permits the user to interact with a program

Dial-up—an Internet connection made by dialling an Internet service provider's telephone number

Digital data—information that is presented and processed as digits of some number system (usually binary); see also *Binary code*

Digital facsimile (fax) machines—devices that include a scanning mechanism to read a document, electronic equipment to translate and compress data, a modem to send data via telephone lines, and a printer to output an incoming document

Digital scents—smells that can be programmed into Web sites, video games, or any application software; the user can smell the attachment using the iSmell™ device

Digital signatures—strings of encrypted computer code that act as unique online identifiers that can be used indefinitely; virtually impossible to counterfeit

Digital video/versatile disks—see **DVDs**

Direct connection—a link that provides constant Internet access to the user, without having to make a connection or dial-up; see also *Dial-up*

Directory—an index of computer files in storage; typically contains the file names and file-related information (file sizes, creation dates); search engine catalogue that classifies search results for users to access general information about a topic

Disk drives—slots that receive different disk formats (such as 3 1/2" floppy disks, CD-ROMs)

DNS—see **Domain Name System**

Document—information input by users through a software application program (a report keyed using a word processing program, a graph made in a spreadsheet program, an image created in a graphics program); also called *data files*

Document sharing or collaboration—a feature of online conferencing programs that allows users from different locations to work on the same file at the same time

Domain—an element of an e-mail address that is either your ISP or the organization name that is giving you access to e-mail services; "YourISP" in <yourname@YourISP.com>

Domain name—an element of a Web page that lists who registered the site; a clue to a Web site's origin

Domain Name System (DNS)—the Internet service provider server to which a Universal Resource Locator (URL) address is sent for identification; a DNS server attempts to maintain an up-to-date list of URL addresses; see also *URL*

Download—to copy information/data from one computer or server to another; information travelling to a computer

Draw images—in graphic design and desktop publishing, images created in Draw programs; also called *object-oriented images*; see also *Vector graphics*

Drive bay—slots in the computer case where disk drives are housed; see also *Disk drives*

DVDs (digital video/versatile disks)—a compact disc playable by a DVD-ROM drive and holding digital information (such as text documents, music, or digitally recorded movies)

E-business—a broad term that includes all aspects of business on the Internet

E-commerce—part of e-business; using the Internet to interact with suppliers and customers to sell products and services

Editing—preparing, especially for publication, correcting errors, checking facts, etc.

Electronic bulletin board system (BBS)—an application that allows users to post and reply to electronic messages

Electronic mail—mail delivered electronically; also called *e-mail*

Electronic pen signatures—signatures written with an electronic pen; electronic pen technology is designed to measure not only the shape of the letters but the way the signature is constructed and even the pressure used to write each letter

Electronic presentation—the presentation of information in one or more elements of multimedia (text, graphics, video, audio, Internet hyperlinks)

Electronic tools—devices that help people manage information (computers, communications networks, the Internet)

E-mail—see **Electronic mail**

E-mail advertising—messages sent by advertisers directly to potential customer's e-mail accounts; see also *Banner ads*

E-mail software—a program on a user's computer that checks the mail server at the user's Internet service provider and delivers the user's mail on request

Emoticons—expressive icons created from keyboard characters; also called *smileys*

Ergonomics—the study of workers' interactions with their working environment

Ethernet card—a network interface card installed in a computer that enables it to connect to a network; see also *User interface*

Ethical dilemma—a conflict involving making a choice where one or more alternatives or solutions provide a benefit but compromise the decision-maker's value system

Ethics—the moral principles that determine the rightness or wrongness of particular acts

Etiquette—conventional rules of social behaviour or professional conduct

Expansion cards—components that plug into the motherboard of a computer and contain chips that add new features to a computer; see also *Motherboard*

Expansion slots—sockets on the motherboard into which expansion cards can be added, see also *Motherboard*

Extension—the last few characters of the file name (usually three) after the period that specify the type of file (.doc, .pdf) OR the last characters in a URL that a browser uses to determine how the file is formatted and viewed (HTML)

External cache—memory that is external to the central processing unit and is used for high-speed storage; holds the information most recently used by the processor so that the information can be more quickly accessed; see also *Central processing unit; Secondary cache*

Extranets—networks that provide limited access, with a password, to an organization's Intranet via the World Wide Web to users outside of the organization for the purpose of streamlining business activities; see also *Intranet*

Factory memory—computer memory on which information has been pre-recorded; one or more factory memory chips are attached to the motherboard; also called *ROM (read only memory)*

FAQ (Frequently Asked Question)—a document that often appears in an online discussion group that lists the most commonly asked questions and answers

Fax machine—see **Digital facsimile (fax) machine**

Fields—each piece of information in a record is contained in a field; fields are the columns in the table generated from a database

File—see **Data files**

File transfer—a feature of online conferencing programs that allows users from different locations to upload files from one computer to another while participants are working on something else

File Transfer Protocol (FTP)—software that allows users to transfer files from their computer to another (upload) or from another computer to their own (download)

Find—in an Edit menu, a feature that helps you locate all instances of a word or formatting option in the document

Firewall—software that prevents other computer users or hackers from gaining access to the information on a computer while online

Flaming—sending an electronic message with an angry or insulting tone

Floppy disk—a thin, square, magnetized flexible plate used for storing data

Folder—a user-created electronic compartment in which information or documents can be saved

Font—in printing, a complete set of type in one size and style

Font sizes—settings that determine the size of type in a document; type sizes range from tiny (4 point) to very large (72 point); many business documents are keyed in 12-point type

Font styles—styles of type; two basic varieties—serif (tails) and sans serif (no tails)

Footer—an element of a Web page that lists the Web page author or contact person and might include a link to the home page and a listing of the institution or organization sponsoring the page; also found in many office productivity programs allowing for constant information to be printed at the bottom of a page; see also *Web page*

Form—in a database or spreadsheet, an electronic version of what you might see on a printed document used to collect data

Formatting—any change to the look or organization of a document; features found in the Format menu of a word processing program

Formulas—in a spreadsheet cell, the mathematical functions used to calculate a result from values in other cells or numbers

Forums—online communities where users can communicate about a common topic

FTP—see **File Transfer Protocol**

Full block—a style of letter wherein all of the letter parts are aligned at the left-hand margin

Function keys—special keys on a computer keyboard (usually F1 to F12) that activate different commands depending on the software application currently running

Functions—for microprocessors, the input, storage, processing, and output of computers

Gateways—junctions on the Internet where information/data packets are translated into some other format for transmission through a particular network

Grammar Check—a feature of most word processing software designed to check your document for grammatical errors

Graphics card—a component that gives a computer the ability to digitize video so that the computer can reproduce graphics

Graphics software—software designed to create graphic images or manipulate photographs or pictures (CorelDRAW, Adobe Photoshop)

Graphic user interface—see **GUI**

GUI (graphic user interface)—a visual computer environment that represents programs, files, and options with graphical images, such as icons, menus, and dialog boxes on the screen

Hackers—people who gain unauthorized access to computer systems, usually for the purpose of stealing or corrupting information.

Hand-held and palm-sized PCs—smaller variations of computers; often designed to work with a limited selection of software; also called *Personal Digital Assistants (PDAs)*

Hard copy—the copy of a computer file that has been printed

Hard (disk) drive (HD)—a disk drive that holds, reads from, and writes to a hard disk; see also *Hard disk*

Hard disk—memory storage area in a computer, retaining data when the power is shut off

Hardware—the physical components of a computer system, including any peripheral equipment such as printers, modems, and mice; see also *Peripheral devices*

Header—an element of a Web page that might include a link to the home page and a listing of the institution or organization sponsoring the page; also found in many office productivity programs allowing for constant information to be printed at the top of a page

Help menu—a feature of most software programs designed to help you solve common problems with the software; includes Contents and Index

Highlight—also called "Select"; isolating a selection of text (so that it appears with black background and white lettering) on the monitor by holding down the (left) mouse button and dragging the mouse to the end of the selection; highlighting, or selecting text, must be done before the user can change the format of the item, copy, or cut

Home row—the middle row of alpha keys on a QWERTY keyboard; the ASDF and JKL; keys over which the user's fingers should hover for accurate keying; see also *QWERTY keyboard*

Hot links—term for hyperlinks in documents that have been uploaded to a Web server; see also *Hyperlink; Web server*

HTML (Hypertext Markup Language)—a computer scripting language used to create and display files on the Internet

HTTP (hypertext transfer protocol)—a set of rules that govern how documents written in HTML are interpreted and displayed through a browser; see also *HTML*

Hub—a central device that connects several computers or networks together; allows the computers in a network to share the server's processing power and share information

Hyperlinks—hypertext document links that, when selected, lead Internet users to another World Wide Web page or another place within the same document

Hypertext—in a piece of software, document, Web page, etc., a feature whereby supplementary textual information, linked to a text or image but not displayed on the screen, can be accessed and displayed by selecting a specially marked word or icon on the screen; the text so accessed

Hypertext Markup Language—see HTML

Hypertext transfer protocol—see HTTP

Icons—the little pictures on a computer screen that represent software or functions; users activate icons by clicking them with a mouse

Image editing and graphics programs—computer software that allows the user to edit visual images (Corel PHOTO-PAINT, Paint Shop Pro)

Index—in a Help menu, a list of topic headings in the Help program; in a search engine, the database compiled by a spider, indexing robot, or Web crawler; see also *Indexing robots; Search engine*

Indexing robots—search engine programs; also called Web crawlers, spiders; see also *Search engine*

Indicator—the first sign in a spreadsheet formula (=, @, or other symbol)

Information—data that has been processed so that it can be understood and used for decision making

Information technology (IT)—the collection of technologies (printing, publishing, telephones, radio, television, computers, electronics, telecommunications) to process and distribute information and to manage information among people and machines

Infrared mice—mice that send infrared signals to a receiver attached to the computer's mouse port; these mice are cordless but require a clear line of sight (i.e., no barriers) between the mouse and the receiver

Infrared signals—waves, currents, impulses of long, invisible light waves (just beyond the red end of the colour spectrum) serving to send messages from one electronic device to another

Infrastructure—the basic, underlying framework features of a system

Input—information/data provided to computers by users; include keying using a keyboard, pointing and clicking using a mouse, pointing a stylus, speaking into a microphone

Inside address—in a business letter, the name and address of the recipient of the letter; includes name, title, company name, company's address, city, province, postal code

Instruction cache—temporary memory where a computer's instructions are stored just before they are used

Integrate—to bring in (individuals or groups) as part of a larger group

Integrated software package—software program that performs some or all the functions of word processing, spreadsheet, database, desktop publishing, and electronic presentation programs (Microsoft Office, Corel WordPerfect Suite)

Intellectual property—any form of creative work that can be protected through copyrights, trademarks, or patents

Interactive television (iTV)—an appliance that allows users to browse the Internet using their television sets

InsighTs: Succeeding in the Information Age

Interface—see **User interface**

Internal cache—memory that is inside the central processing unit; the first place the CPU looks for recently used data or instructions; see also *Central processing unit (CPU)*

Internet—a very large Wide Area Network (WAN) connecting computers and networks around the world, making it possible for millions of computer users to connect to one another via telephone lines, cable lines, and satellites; also called the *Net*

Internet appliances—devices that provide access to the Internet without the use of a computer; sometimes require a physical connection to the Internet (analog modem, cable modem, ADSL line); also called *Web appliances*

Internet browser software—software designed to allow users to access and read Web sites (Microsoft Internet Explorer, Netscape Navigator)

Internet Relay Chat—see *IRC*

Internet service providers (ISPs)—local user networks providing access to the Internet's information and communication services

Internet Telephony—technology that allows users to make long-distance phone calls without paying long-distance charges; users need a computer with Internet access, a two-way sound card, a microphone, speakers, and Internet telephone software; also known as Voice over IP (VOIP), Computer Telephony (CT), PC Telephony, and Computer Telephony Integration (CTI)

Internetworking—the process of linking a collection of networks

Intranet—a term used to describe a local area network similar to the Internet but only accessible to people within a specific organization

Introduction—part of a report; should provide the reader with four pieces of information: purpose, scope, sources of information, authorization

I-Opener from Netpliance—a scaled-down computer with all the necessary parts for browsing and communicating on the Internet

IRC (Internet Relay Chat)—the most popular way to chat on the Internet; based on a client-server model whereby every topic is called a channel; chat channels exist on servers that may be anywhere in the world; users (clients) must have IRC software to communicate with the IRC server

ISPs—see **Internet service providers**

iTV—see **Interactive television**

Joysticks—levers that move in all directions and control the movement of a pointer or other display symbol; used mostly for computer or video games

Justified—an even alignment of text at both left and right margins

Keyboards—devices that consist of typewriter-like keys that enable users to enter information into a computer

L2— see **Secondary cache**

Labels—in a spreadsheet cell, the word "label" refers to any text information contained in a cell; see also *Cell*

LAN—see **Local area network**

Landscape orientation—the orientation of a page that is wider than it is long

Law—a body of rules recognized by a country, state, province, or community as binding on its members

Legal—actions or behaviours that are carried out according to the law

Legend—in charts or graphs, indicates which colour or treatment represents which element/category

Level 2 cache—see **Secondary cache**

Line graphs—ideal for showing the trend of data over time

Line spacing—a setting that determines the distance between the lines of type in a document

Link—connection; path

Listserv—online (on the Internet) discussion groups that use e-mail to communicate

Local area network (LAN)—a group of networked computers that are all in one building (school, office building); users can share software, hardware, information/data

Location field—the area on a Web browser screen where a user keys a Web site address or where the address of the currently browsed page is displayed; see also *Web browser*

Machine language—a translation of the source code which the computer can understand; see also *Source code*

Machine-oriented issues—issues that relate to ways in which information technology equipment (computers, modems, communication devices, the Internet) actually work

Mailing lists—online (on the Internet) discussion groups that use e-mail to communicate

Mainframe computers (mainframes)—very large first- and second-generation computers; see also *Supercomputers*

Manage information—plan and oversee the use of information technology

Mechanical software—a special type of software (e.g., CADKey) used to design a three-dimensional model of a mould or an object

Memory—the internal storage areas on a computer located on chips

Menu—in computer programs, a list of topics, operations, etc., from which the user makes a selection

Menu bar—found immediately below the title bar at the top of the screen when the window is maximized (File, Edit, View)

Menu-driven interface—an interface in which a user selects command choices in the form of a list provided by the computer; see also *User interface*

Meta-search engines—search engines that submit users' queries to numerous search engines at the same time and display their findings on one screen (search.com, Dogpile, MetaCrawler); see also *Search engine*

Microprocessor—the main computer chip that processes instructions, calculates data, and manages the flow of information in a computer; also called *central processing unit (CPU)*

MIDI (Musical Instrument Digital Interface) file—computer file containing sound; also called *wave file*

MILNet—In 1983, the ARPANet split into two parts—ARPANet and MILNet; defence agencies and the military used MILNet; see also *ARPANet*

Mischief—a computer crime in the Criminal Code of Canada that includes people who hack into other people's computers to distort or destroy data (e.g., planting a virus)

Modems—devices that enable a computer to receive and send data over telephone lines or cables

Monitors—devices that provide a visual display of a computer's output

Motherboard—the main circuit board of a computer; see also *Circuit board*

Mouse—a hand-held input device for a computer that controls the location of an object or a cursor on a screen and allows commands to be entered; the location of the object or cursor is changed by moving the mouse correspondingly on the desktop; commands are entered by depressing buttons on the mouse; the most common computer pointing device

MSI—see **Musculo-skeletal injuries**

Multimedia presentation—a presentation that can incorporate elements from two or more communications media (text, speech, graphics, sound, animation, videos, film)

Multitasking—the ability to do more than one task at the same time; requires a fast computer processor and generous random access memory; see also *RAM (random access memory)*

Musculo-skeletal injuries (MSIs)—ergonomic-related injury that occurs when a person performs the same task over and over, damaging nerves, muscles, tendons, or other body tissues; also called *repetitive strain injuries (RSIs)*; see also *Carpal tunnel syndrome (CTS)*

Nanobots—machines created by the process of nanotechnology

Nanotechnology—the process of building molecule-sized machines (called assemblers) that can be programmed to produce larger machines (called Nanobots) made up of these molecule-sized pieces, similar to the way human cells multiply to create a whole person

Natural language query—a search engine question keyed the way a user naturally asks a question; no special words or symbols are required

Net—common term for the Internet; see also *Internet*

Netiquette—the rules of etiquette (manners) as applied to Internet communications

Network—the connection of two or more computers so they can communicate or share resources

Network backbone—a "cyberspace highway" made up of high-speed cables and switching stations (interchanges for network traffic)

Network interface card (NIC)—an expansion card that allows a computer to act as a client or node in a network; see also *Nodes; Peripheral devices*

Network topology—the physical layout of the cables that connect the nodes and peripherals of the network; see also *Network; Nodes; Peripheral devices*

Newsgroups—online (on the Internet) discussion groups that allow users with common interests to communicate with one another; users must have newsreader software (Netscape Collabra, Microsoft Outlook, Free Agent)

Nodes—a term for all of the computers except the leader in a client/server network; also called *clients*

Noise filters—devices inserted into telephone handsets or wall jacks to reduce interference from other electronic devices installed on the same connecting lines

NSFNet—a high-speed network created by the National Science Foundation (NSF) in the mid-1980s

Object—in graphic design and desktop publishing, an element in a vector graphic; see also *Vector graphics*

Object-oriented images—in graphic design and desktop publishing, images created in Draw programs; also called *draw images; vector graphics*

Online—on the Internet

Online discussion groups—groups of people who exchange messages about particular topics; often associated with newsgroups, they also take the form of interactive message boards, forums, and e-mailing lists

Online name—an element of an e-mail address; "yourname" in <yourname@YourISP.com>

Online videoconferencing—Internet communication that combines the power of e-mail and chat together with the ability to see a real-time image of the person (or people) with whom the user is communicating; see also *Chat*

Operating system software—software that controls the overall activity of the computer (such as MAC OS, Windows, and DOS); also called *platforms*

Operating systems—computer programs that provide the overall control of a computer system by directing the detailed operation of its hardware and software

Operators—words in the Boolean system of logic used by most search engines (e.g., AND, OR, NOT); see also *Search engine*

Output—in a computer, the results of processing, whether sent to the screen or printer, stored on disk as a file, or sent to another computer in a network; see also *Processes*

Page orientation—the orientation of the page when setting up a document; portrait orientation describes a page that is longer than it is wide and landscape orientation describes a page that is wider than it is long

Pagers—small, portable electronic devices used to page someone; beepers

Paint images—bitmap images; named for one of the first programs (PC Paintbrush) to create graphic images; see also *Bitmap image*

Paper sizes—letter-size paper (8 ½″ x 11″) and legal-size paper (8 ½″ x 14″) are the two most common paper sizes used in business in North America

Patent—a government grant giving the right to exclude others from making, using, or selling an invention

Path—in file management, begins with the name of the drive in which the file is contained followed by the names of folders to follow to find a document; a backslash (\) separates the names of the drive and the folders

PC Telephony—technology that allows users to make long-distance phone calls without paying long-distance charges; users need a computer with Internet access, a two-way sound card, a microphone, speakers, and Internet telephone software; also known as Internet telephony, Voice over IP (VOIP), Computer Telephony (CT), and Computer Telephony Integration (CTI)

PCS (Personal Communication Services)—technology that converts the human voice to digital codes that can be transmitted through the airwaves; digital codes are made up of a sequence

of 0s and 1s and are less complicated than analog patterns

PDA—see **Personal Digital Assistant**

PDF (Portable Document Format)—a popular document format that ensures that the layout of graphics and text can be easily viewed on any computer that has the Acrobat Reader software installed; this type of file can be identified by the .pdf extension that appears on the end of the file name

People-oriented issues—issues that concern people's interaction with information technology

Peripheral devices—devices that are plugged into special sockets at the back or side of a computer (ports) using appropriate cables (modems, speakers, mouse, printer, etc.); also called *peripheral hardware*

Personal Communication Services—see **PCS**

Personal Digital Assistants (PDAs)—appliances that typically sit in a cradle connected to a computer; users remove the PDA from the cradle to take it with them to access its features when away from the computer; common features are e-mail, calendar, and note taking; also called *hand-held* and *palm-sized PCs*

Personal Information Protection and Private Documents Act—an act designed to provide Canadians with privacy relating to personal information that is collected or used by private sector organizations (Bill C-6)

Picture frame—a feature that creates a space to accommodate a picture or graphic in a desktop publishing program

Pie charts—show the contributions of each value to the total in a round chart that resembles a pie

Pixels—picture elements that are represented by coloured dots that make up a printed picture or a picture displayed on a computer monitor

Plain Old Telephone System (POTS)—a link (telephone line) through which computer information/data is sent over the Internet

Platforms—software that controls the overall activity of the computer; also called operating system software

Pointing devices—electronic devices such as a mouse that can be used to move the cursor, select and drag objects, launch software applications by clicking an icon, perform an action on a highlighted object

Point-to-Point Protocol (PPP)—a set of standards that indicate how data packets will be sent over the Internet; packets are double-checked for problems and if they do not arrive intact, they are sent again at no additional cost to the sender; much like traditional registered mail

POP (Post Office Protocol)—a type of e-mail program set up to check the mail server at the user's Internet Service Provider and to deliver the user's mail on request

Portable Document Format—see **PDF**

Portfolio—a collection of work samples created by an individual or group

Portrait orientation—the orientation of a page that is longer than it is wide

Ports—receptacles on a computer to which you can plug a cable to connect another device (such as a printer) to a computer

Posted—a message is posted when it is added as a reply to another message or to start a new thread; see also *Thread*

Post Office Protocol— see **POP**

POTS—see **Plain Old Telephone System**

Power supply—a device that changes normal household electricity from a power cord into electricity a computer can use

PPP—see **Point-to-Point Protocol**

Presentation software—software designed to allow users to produce slide shows with animations, graphics, and sound effects (PowerPoint, Corel PRESENTS)

Printers—devices that print text or illustrations on paper or acetate

Processes—in microprocessors, a function whereby users' inputs are added, multiplied, divided, found, or manipulated to complete a task

Program—software applications designed to allow users to perform/apply a specific task (calculate numbers, enter text, play a game); also called application and application software

Program files—software files containing instructions to execute tasks or launch programs (video games, word processors, antivirus software)

Programmers—people who bring software to life by creating a detailed set of instructions in a programming language

Programming language—a language in which programmers write programs; the programs written in a programming language are changed into machine language for the computer to execute; see also *Utility compiler*

Projection devices—devices, similar to an overhead projector, that project images that appear on a computer monitor on a wall or screen

Proofread—read in order to locate and mark errors to be corrected

Property bar—in some programs (WordPerfect), a toolbar that changes with the tasks the user is currently performing

Protocols—a set of rules or standards designed to enable computers to connect with one another and to exchange information with as little error as possible; a code prescribing strict adherence to correct etiquette (as in diplomatic exchange and in the military services)

Push technology—the ability of an e-commerce Web site to deliver specific and relevant customer information to a user

Quick-reference cards—brief instructions available on the computer screen or on paper about how to use a particular software or feature

QWERTY keyboard—the most common keyboard; has four rows of alpha/numeric keys

Radio mice—electronic mice that are able to communicate with the computer through low-power radio signals, rather than through a mouse cord

RAM (random access memory)—temporary memory that stores information for the length of time a computer is left on or a program is left running; also called *user memory*

Random access memory—see **RAM**

Raster—the rectangular area of a video display screen actually being used to display images

Read only memory—see **ROM**

Real-time—in electronic communication, communication that occurs immediately (or with little delay) between users

Record—all the information relating to an individual item or person in a database

Record number—in a database, the unique identifier assigned to each record

References—a list of all of the sources of information for a report; also called citations

Registered trademark—a word, symbol, or design used to distinguish one product from another

Relational database—a database that stores records in two or more tables, and can co-ordinate information from different tables; sometimes, data only needs to be entered once since the database determines how each piece of data is related to one particular piece of data (e.g., the phone company collects lots of data on its customers but can pull it all together with just the customer's phone number)

Repetitive strain injuries (RSIs)—ergonomic-related injuries that occur when a person performs the same task over and over, damaging nerves, muscles, tendons, or other body tissues; see also *musculo-skeletal injuries (MSIs)*

Reports—documents prepared in business to provide information, analyze information, propose a project, summarize a project, or suggest actions to be taken and predict their outcomes; formatted in a standard manner

Resolution—the quality of a graphic image; measured in dots per inch

Return address—in a business letter, the sender's address; keyed 1"–1.5" from the top of the page

Rich Text Format (RTF)—a file format that can easily be shared with other word processing programs in Windows and MAC environments

Ring topology—a computer network arrangement whereby all nodes and peripherals are connected in a circular chain; one broken connection will bring down the entire network; see also *Network; Nodes; Peripheral devices*

ROM (read only memory)—computer memory on which information has been pre-recorded; one or more ROM chips are attached to the motherboard; also called *factory memory*

Routers—functions of the Internet that direct information/data traffic in appropriate directions

RSI—see **Repetitive strain injuries**

RTF—see **Rich Text Format**

Salutation—in a business letter, the greeting; specific if the recipient's name is known (Dear Mr. Jonsmagh), generic if the recipient's name is not known (Dear Sir or Madam)

Sans-serif fonts—typestyles that have no tails on the letters (Arial, Futura); less formal typestyles

Sans-serif typefaces—see **Sans-serif fonts**

Screensaver—the pattern or animated screen that appears on the monitor when the computer is left idle; varies the colours and patterns on the screen

Search engine—a computer program that electronically searches the World Wide Web looking for HTML documents; see also *HTML*

Secondary cache—additional memory available for information storage; see also *External cache*

Semi-block format—a style of letter that is like the block letter style, but with the paragraphs indented as well; see also *Block letter style*

Semi-block letter—see **Semi-block format**

Serial Line Internet Protocol (SLIP)—a set of standards that indicate how data packets will be sent over the Internet; much like traditional first-class mail

Serif fonts—typestyles that have tails on the letters (Times New Roman, Courier); more formal typestyles

Serif typefaces—see **Serif fonts**

Server—the computer that is designated the leader in a client/server network; see also *Client/server network*

Single-engine searches—search engines that submit users' queries to one search engine at a time and index their findings in different ways (Alta Vista, Google, HotBot)

SLIP—see **Serial Line Internet Protocol**

Smileys—see **Emoticons**

Social responsibility—acting in a manner that is in the best interests of society in general

Software—a set of electronic instructions that tell a computer what to do; the two types are operating system software and application software

Software designer—a person who develops a plan for what software will do, how it will accomplish its tasks, and what users will have to do to communicate with the software

Sound card—a component that gives a computer the ability to digitize sound so that the computer can reproduce sound

Source code—the basic building block of all software programs; the program instructions in their original form in a programming language (C, Java)

Spam—unsolicited e-mail, sent to thousands of recipients, often promoting an electronic sex site, pyramid-type marketing scheme, or the spam industry itself

Spamming—e-mailing a message to a large number of people without their consent; also known as unsolicited commercial e-mail (UCE), or junk e-mail, it is usually sent to promote a product or service

Speakers—peripheral devices attached to the sound card that allow sound to be heard by the user; see also *Peripheral devices*

Spectrum—range; scope; compass; scale or continuum

Speech recognition software—software that works with a word processing program, a sound card, and a microphone to convert speech into text on the computer screen

Spell Check—a feature of most word processing software designed to check a document for spelling errors

Spiders—search engine programs; also called Web crawlers, indexing robots; see also *Search engine*

Spreadsheet—an electronic worksheet that allows the user to make calculations in rows and columns

Spreadsheet pages—elements of a spreadsheet workbook consisting of a grid of vertical columns and horizontal rows; a letter identifies each column and a number identifies each row

Spreadsheet program—software application designed to allow users to enter numbers and perform mathematical functions (Microsoft Excel, Lotus, Quattro Pro)

Spreadsheet software—software designed to allow users to enter numbers and perform mathematical functions (Microsoft Excel, Lotus, Quattro Pro)

Spreadsheet workbook or **notebook**—the file in which you create and work on your spreadsheet data

Stacked bar chart—a chart that shows the contribution of each value to a total across categories; also called *stacked column chart*

Stacked column chart—charts that show the contribution of each value to a total across categories; also called *stacked bar chart*

Stakeholders—individuals who have an interest in what businesses do—employees, customers, special interest groups, the general public

Star topology—a network arrangement whereby all nodes and peripherals are connected to one hub at the centre of the network with separate cables; one broken connection will not affect the rest of the network; see also *Hub; Network; Nodes; Peripheral devices*

Storage—memory located on disks and tapes

Storage devices—devices that allow information to be stored electronically such as disks, CD-ROMs, DVDs

Store—a function of computers whereby data are saved in its memory

Subject line—an element of an e-mail message or letter that should contain a useful description of the contents of the message

Supercomputers—mainframe computers that are capable of very fast processing; used for tasks such as worldwide weather forecasting, oil exploration, weapons research

Symmetrical balance—in a graphic design, when the two sides of the design are mirror images of each other

Synchronous—in electronic communication, communication that is happening at the same time

Syntax—in spreadsheets, the order of the elements in a spreadsheet formula; follows the order of operations of mathematics (brackets, exponents, division, multiplication, addition, subtraction)

Table of Contents—part of a formal business report listing each heading contained within the report and the page on which the heading appears; typically used only when the report is five or more pages long

Taskbar—the line that appears across the bottom or along the side of the screen (Start button, the time); the MAC operating system has no taskbar

TCP/IP (Transmission Control Protocol/Internet Protocol)—standard network protocol for communication across networks; all communication across the Internet uses the TCP/IP protocol

Telnet—one of the original methods of interacting on the Internet; an application that allows the user, without a browser, to dial another computer and to interact in its network environment

Templates—pre-formatted documents (margins, fonts, alignments, etc.) that a user can customize

TextArt—in a desktop publishing program, created by clicking the WordArt icon, creating a box on the page, and then keying text; also called *WordArt*

Text box—a feature that creates a space to accommodate text in graphics or desktop publishing software, and in some spreadsheets and word processors

Thesaurus—a feature of most word processing software programs that allows the user to replace a selected word with an alternate word with the same or similar meaning

Thread—the topics by which online discussion groups are organized; see also *Online discussion groups*

Title—in charts or graphs, describes the content

Title bar—the bar at the very top of the screen when the window is maximized; displays the program and the file the user has open on the screen

Title page—part of a formal business report listing the title of the report, the author's name, the person or organization for whom the report was prepared, the date the report was submitted, and the organization to which the report was given

Toggle—rapidly switch between two open software applications by clicking on ALT/TAB or clicking on the buttons on the taskbar (if you can see them)

Toolbars—a series of icons that activate the most commonly used features of software programs (New, Open, Save, Print)

Touch pad—a tracking device that looks like a small square located near the keyboard; users slide their fingers across the square to move the cursor, and use nearby buttons to activate commands

Trackball—a pointing device that looks like a ball that has been lodged into the computer; users roll the exposed part of the ball to move the cursor, and use buttons located next to the ball to click or drag

Transmission Control Protocol/Internet Protocol—see **TCP/IP**

Tutorials—instructions in software application programs describing how to use a particular feature

Typeface—the design or style of type

Unauthorized access—a computer crime in the Criminal Code of Canada that refers to people who hack into other computers to use the services without permission or steal passwords, credit card information, etc.

Uniform Resource Locators—see **URLs**

Universal Resource Locators—see **URLs**

Universal Serial Bus (USB)—a connection that provides a quick, convenient way to connect external devices such as printers, modems, and scanners to a computer

Unjustified—a ragged alignment of text at the margin

Upload—to send information/data from one computer to another; information travelling away from a computer

URLs (Universal Resource Locators)—addresses that identify Web pages; also called *Uniform Resource Locator*; see also **Web page**

USB—see **Universal Serial Bus**

Usenet (User's Network)—the official name for the worldwide collection of thousands of online discussion groups (or forums)

User interface—the part of any software application that determines how the user will make the program work; see also **Menu-driven interface**

User memory—temporary memory that stores information for the length of time a computer is left on or a program is left running; also called *RAM (random access memory)*

User's Network—see **Usenet**

Utility compiler—a program that translates source code into machine language, the language that a computer can understand

Utility software—software used to maintain your computer and make sure it runs efficiently (McAfee VirusScan, Norton Utilities, WinZip, Acrobat Reader)

Value—in a spreadsheet, the value refers to any numerical data in a cell

Value system—a set of personal beliefs about right and wrong

Vector graphics—images that contain a series of mathematical equations that join a series of points by lines; see also *Draw images; Object-oriented images*

Version number—the number given to new software when it is released; allows users to determine which is the most recent software

Virtual—data storage or memory that is temporary, consisting only in the use of disk space to store information while a large program, occupying the regular memory, is being run

Voice mail—an automated answering system for telephone networks having touch tone, using a series of pre-recorded prompts to which callers may respond by pressing the appropriate button to transfer them to the line they need

Voice over IP (VOIP)—technology that allows users to make long-distance telephone calls without paying long-distance charges; users need a computer with Internet access, a two-way sound card, a microphone, speakers, and Internet telephone software; see also *Internet Telephony; PC Telephony*

Wallpaper—the background image on a computer desktop

Wave files—computer files containing sounds; see also *MIDI (Musical Instrument Digital Interface) file*

Web (W3)—common term for the World Wide Web

Web appliances—devices that provide access to the Internet without the use of a computer; sometimes require a physical connection to the Internet (analog modem, cable modem, ADSL line); also known as *Internet appliances*

Web authoring language—the most common language of hypertext documents (Hypertext Markup Language or HTML); see also *Hypertext; HTML*

Web browser—a program that interprets hypertext documents on the Web and displays them on screen; see also *Hypertext*

Web crawlers—search engine programs; also called spiders, indexing robots; see also *Search engine*

Web e-mail—a service that allows users to set up a free e-mail account without having e-mail software set up on their computers; users may check their e-mail from any Internet-connected computer running any browser program anywhere in the world; see also *Web browser*

Web page—a document on the World Wide Web identified by a unique URL (Uniform Resource Locator); see also **URLs; Web site**

Web server—a computer that provides Internet access to a Web site that is stored on its hard drive

Web site—a location on the World Wide Web, containing a home page (the first page seen upon entering the site) and, often, other pages

Web site portal—a Web page that acts as an entry point to the World Wide Web

Webphones—an appliance that combines several tools into one device; for example, the iphone from InfoGear plugs into a telephone jack, can be used with most Internet service providers, and serves as a telephone, Web browser, e-mail tool, speaker-phone, and digital answering machine

Whiteboard—a feature of online conferencing programs that allows many users to see a document at the same time; participants can make changes, move objects, and more

Wide area network (WAN)—a group of networked computers located in a variety of locations in a large geographic area (all the schools in a city); can be set up to transmit information between computers by telephone line, microwave, satellite; see also *Network*

Window—a rectangular area on the screen that displays the contents of a disk, folder, directory, or document; appears when the user opens documents or clicks on icons

Wireless Markup Language—see **WML**

Wireless technology—a developing technology that will allow many Internet appliances to work independently

Wizards—pre-designed page layouts or tasks with instructions to guide users in how to use certain aspects of a program (Chart Wizard, AutoContent Wizard)

WML (Wireless Markup Language)—a language used to develop Web content that is accessible to mobile users

WordArt—in a desktop publishing program, created by clicking the WordArt icon to open a box on the page, and then keying text; also called *TextArt*

Word processing—the creation of written documents (letters, reports)

Word processing software—software designed to make the creation of written documents (letters, reports) easier; provides tools to change the size and appearance of words, edit the text, check spelling, and other features (Microsoft Word, WordPerfect)

World Wide Web(WWW)—a collection of millions of hypertext documents; see also *Hypertext*

Wrap around—the feature of word processing software that moves the cursor to the beginning of the next line following each keyed line of continuous type

WWW—see *World Wide Web*

X-axis—the horizontal axis of a chart

Y-axis—the vertical axis of a chart

Index